D1289217

WITHDRAWN
No longer the property of the
Boston Public Library.
Sale of this material benefits the Library.

Energy, the Modern State, and the American World System

Energy, the Modern State, and the American World System

George A. Gonzalez

Published by State University of New York Press, Albany

© 2018 State University of New York

All rights reserved

Printed in the United States of America

No part of this book may be used or reproduced in any manner whatsoever
without written permission. No part of this book may be stored in a retrieval
system or transmitted in any form or by any means including electronic,
electrostatic, magnetic tape, mechanical, photocopying, recording, or otherwise
without the prior permission in writing of the publisher.

For information, contact State University of New York Press, Albany, NY
www.sunypress.edu

Library of Congress Cataloging-in-Publication Data

Names: Gonzalez, George A., 1969– author.
Title: Energy, the modern state, and the American world system / George A.
  Gonzalez.
Description: Albany : State University of New York Press, [2018] | Includes
  bibliographical references and index.
Identifiers: LCCN 2017030301| ISBN 9781438469812 (hardcover : alk. paper) |
  ISBN 9781438469829 (ebook)
Subjects: LCSH: Energy policy—United States—History. | Energy policy—
  History. | Energy development—Political aspects—United States—History. |
  Energy development—Political aspects—History. | United States—Foreign
  relations. | United States—Politics and government.
Classification: LCC HD9502.A2 G656 2018 | DDC 333.790973—dc23
LC record available at https://lccn.loc.gov/2017030301

10   9   8   7   6   5   4   3   2   1

For Ileana and Alana

Contents

Theoretical Overview

In the most abstract, minimalist sense, the modern state is a result of energy (wind, coal, oil) because energy allows for the relatively inexpensive projection of political power. This creates the collaborative and affirmative union of capitalism and political authority (in the sixteenth century)—which is the substance of the modern, contemporary state (chapter 1). More broadly, energy serves as the basis of the modern economy. Hence, a prime function of the modern state is garnering access to energy to reliably power and grow the economy. Historically, energy is more of a zero-sum resource than capital, markets, labor, technology, therefore, a greater cause of geopolitical tension and even violence (war).

The most theoretically salient point of this volume, however, is that we cannot meaningfully understand the state as a theoretical abstraction, but only as a function of specific (energy) politics. Hence, for instance, the Nazi state can only and exclusively be understood as a response to the American turn inward in the 1920s and 1930s—a policy, politics directly predicated on the U.S.'s copious amounts of domestic fossil fuels (i.e., urban sprawl) (chapters 3 and 4). Similarly, virtually any state in the nineteenth century can only be understood in relation to the British Empire. Thus, we can only understand German politics and state in the late nineteenth century by reference to this empire—based on the naval mastery of energy (coal, by this period of time) (chapter 1). Today, we can only comprehend the American state in relation to its hegemony over the world's oil system. In the absence of this hegemony, the U.S. state would be completely, decisively different. Conversely, all other states must cope with this hegemony (chapters 5 and 6).

This explains the U.S.'s historic and current hostility toward alternative sources of energy—solar power (including wind), plutonium (chapters 5 and 7). The successful development of either source of energy would necessitate or bring about a radical reorganization of state power at the global level—with plutonium requiring the formation of world governmental institutions and solar/wind power bringing about a substantial diffusion of political authority.

Preface

This is my fifth book on the relationship between politics and energy.[1] This volume was inspired by my 2016 visit to the Hanseatic League Museum (opened in 2015) in Lübeck, Germany. As I indicate later, this museum outlines how a robust capitalist economy existed in Europe prior to the rise of the modern nation-state. This realization prompted me to extend my analysis of energy politics back to the advent of the modern state. I conclude that the state is not the result of capitalism or war (as often thought), but of energy.

Energy has profoundly shaped the state and international politics since the sixteenth century. Energy politics caused both world wars, was a central factor in the Cold War, and (unsurprisingly) accounts for the global warming crisis.[2] Over time the relationship between energy and the state, as well as global politics, became more and more intimately intertwined—coming to something of a crescendo in the twentieth and twenty-first centuries. In the U.S. the uniting of energy and the state was overseen by economic elites (chapter 2). Apart from discussing the causes of the world wars, I specifically delve deeply into the American state's decision to turn against plutonium in the 1970s. (This hostility was reaffirmed in 2012.) Plutonium held the promise of overcoming the key liabilities of the nation-state system. Internationalizing the global energy system (via plutonium power) could have worked to move humanity toward a world regulatory system to manage such momentous issues as conflict, weapons proliferation, and the environment (e.g., global warming).

In chapter 1, I outline modern history by tracing the history of energy politics. Utilizing this approach allows me to account for the creation of the modern (capitalist) state, the cause of World War I, and the current global warming crisis. Chapters 3 and 4 focus on the causes of World War II. This war was caused in significant part by the U.S. turning inward and seeking to capture for itself the economic benefits of energy-intense urban sprawl. With the Cold War, the U.S. took a leadership role in the world—relying on oil-dependent urban sprawl to propel the global capitalist economy (chapter 6). During the Cold War, the U.S. adopted a new international relations strategy—the global dominance of energy to establish global hegemony. Nuclear power in the 1950s and 1960s served this end, whereas solar/wind energy did not (chapter 5). Precisely because energy serves as an imperial instrument for the U.S., in the 1970s the American government turned against plutonium—because as already noted it potentially served as a basis to supplant the nation-state system through the internationalization of energy (chapter 7).

Chapter One

Energy and the Modern State

To fully grasp the development of the modern state, we must distinguish between capitalism with a small "c" and Capitalism. The former describes an economy that is predicated on free market relations, credit, liquidity, advanced accounting techniques, international firms, and so on. Capitalism with a capital "C" is the unity of capitalism with the state. It is this unity that serves as the basis of the modern state (both historically and in the contemporary era). Why did this transition from *capitalism* to *Capitalism* occur?

The answer to this question lies in energy—the shift from muscle power first to wind (in shipping) and later to fossil fuels (coal, natural gas, petroleum). The early revolutions in energy use resulted in the British Empire. Contemporary global politics is characterized by an American fossil fuel (especially oil) empire.[1]

Early Capitalism

I recently had the privilege of visiting the Hanseatic League Museum in Lübeck, Germany. The museum effectively shows that European premodern history is not so premodern. The European economy of the late Middle Ages (1200 to 1500) had all of the accoutrements of a modern trade regime.[2] The importance of the museum is that it educates us to the fact that prior to the rise of nation-states there was an economic, political regime that achieved a very broad scope and high level of sophistication. Thus, neither modern history nor capitalism begin with the rise of the nation-states. Quite the contrary (and this may be why

European history prior to the sixteenth and seventeenth centuries is obscured to many of us), European capitalism began with cities and in some opposition to the aristocratic classes that would be the precursor to the modern Western state. Exactly what was premodern about Europe in the centuries leading up to the modern era was precisely that there was a bifurcation between economic and political power. European economic vibrancy was centered in cities like Lübeck, Venice, among others, but political power was invested in a landed gentry, aristocracy.

Leading cities in Europe were key centers of trade, industry, banking, and so forth. Through such devices as the Hanseatic League, urban elites regulated trade and economic activity—with the aristocracy almost entirely outside of the trade, economic, regulatory processes that dominated the continent.

In this way capitalism developed outside of the state—with the military, political apparatuses serving as something of a parasitic role (taxing an industrial, finance, and trade regime it arguably contributed nothing to). Worse still, monarchical governments in the late Middle Ages were something of a liability to the Eurasian trade regime—in that a lot of the risk associated with long-distance trading came from political authorities that could arbitrarily, unduly interfere with even established trade routes. Most deleterious of all, aristocracies would go to war with one another and this could shut down trade and, by implication, economic activity. The great irony was that monarchical regimes were growing richer from increasing trade and they used that wealth to engage in conflicts that disrupted profitable activities. Moreover, war and conflict created greater need to tax wealth-creating urban zones. Hence, contrary to Charles Tilly's thesis that war forwarded the creation of the state, in premodern Europe war subverted key political regimes—those of urban elites and the aristocracies that were maintained by them.[3]

Unsurprisingly, thriving cities manifested a hostility to the pretense of government outside of the urban-based trading, manufacturing network. This hostility was ostensibly most clearly manifest in the Republic of the Netherlands. Established in the sixteenth century by freeing itself from the Spanish crown, early Netherlands was a confederacy—with authority vested in provinces (Holland being most important) that tended to be dominated by urban zones (the most significant being the major entrepot of Amsterdam).[4] Rather ironically, this republic of free trade played something of a key role in the rise of Capitalism (the unity of the state and capitalism).

Wind Power and the Early Modern State

The key to the founding of the modern state was wind power—particularly because it served to propel navies. Both the Dutch and the British pioneered in shifting their navies to wholly operating via wind sail. Venice and other Mediterranean naval powers still relied on oars (muscle power) for their military ships. According to historian Carlo M. Cipolla, Spain was slower in the sixteenth century to shift its naval vessels to wind power than the Netherlands and Great Britain. These latter countries combined wind power and cannons into an effective and devastating naval strategy, while others stayed with the ram and board approach.[5]

Where Great Britain and the Dutch diverged on the question of the prowess of their respective navies was each country's political institutions. The Dutch polity was highly fragmented on the question of military policy. Most glaring, the country's admiralty was divided among its provinces.[6] Additionally, the Netherlands was threatened in its interior (by France) and this created internal divisions over whether to emphasize naval or (land-based) military challenges. In contrast, the British polity (and its military policies) was centered in London[7] and able to focus research and development on naval matters. Thus, when geopolitical tensions came to head in the seventeenth century with the Anglo-Dutch Wars, British naval ships outclassed those of the Netherlands. Maarten Prak, in his history of the Netherlands' golden age (when it was a world power), highlights that once England settled its civil war in 1648 it set upon a sustained effort in developing and deploying a new advanced navy: "The English immediately launched an ambitious program of fleet construction, producing a whole series of specialized warships that were larger than the Dutch ships and could carry more and heavier artillery." Prak goes on to explain that "the consequences were harsh indeed. The Dutch, suffering one defeat after another, were forced to accept the humiliating terms of the Treaty of Westminister."[8]

Hence, beginning in the fifteenth and sixteenth centuries military technologies (such as naval ships) required an ever-greater concentration of resources to develop, and this favored political establishments that could absorb the substantial and sustained costs associated with developing such technologies. Individual cities didn't have the resources to successfully engage in such long-term endeavors. Nevertheless, it bears noting that if the provinces of the Netherlands could have agreed to focus sufficient resources on advancing their navy, the modern era could have been ushered in under the banner of republicanism, as opposed to monarchy.

This conclusion would seemingly confirm Tilly's supposition that war and at least the modern state are coterminous. I would respectfully submit that Tilly's formulation obscures more than elucidates. What in fact spurs the development and expansion of state power in the modern era is that the interests of capitalism and national political power merge with the advent of wind-powered ships. It is this merging that serves as the political foundation of Capitalism (the unity of state and economy). What the capturing of wind power by ship did was revolutionize Eurasian trade. Portugal was the first to establish direct shipping links to Central Asia in the fifteenth century by circumnavigating Africa. This effectively ended the millennia-long centrality of Eurasian land routes (as well as of the Mediterranean)[9] and shifted power to the Atlantic states of Europe—even before the colonization of the Americas.[10] When the Dutch and the British aggressively entered the oceangoing Eurasian trade, Portugal was displaced. Subsequently, the Anglo-Dutch Wars established British hegemony on the high seas[11]—which it maintained into the twentieth century.[12] Now political power in the form of navies was key to trade since governments were the institutions that patrolled the shipping lanes that made long-distance trade possible—again, this relationship was most pronounced, salient in the case of Great Britain. To take it one step further, now states were making affirmative and necessary contributions to economic activity.

Wind power prompted, however, an even more fundamental change in global politics. By accessing wind power (later coal—railroads[13]) political authorities could rather inexpensively project power. This, along with advancing armaments, meant relatively small armies could be used to expand a polity's sphere of influence/control.[14] This was clearly evident in the carve-up of Africa, where the various European powers with rather limited financial outlays were able to rapidly overrun a massive, well-populated continent.[15]

This is the modern nation-state system: political, military apparatuses able to control territory beyond the principality without the need of large, expensive militaries. Whereas under capitalism merchants and entrepreneurs in essence sought to avoid political authorities in seeking economic and trading opportunities, with Capitalism economic interests became reliant on military power to maintain sovereignty and to secure access to markets and raw materials.[16] This is consistent with Karl

Marx's view that modern capitalism is the product of a distinct political configuration, not the result of new economic processes as suggested by Adam Smith and others.[17]

Coal and the Modern State System in the Nineteenth and Early Twentieth Centuries

The matter of improved armaments deserves attention. Significant for this discussion, the advancement of armaments is centered on energy. The heat needed to melt and mold iron ore is not trivial. Forests in Great Britain and elsewhere were depleted in the process of making cannons. With ships serving as key strategic tools, wood became a prime strategic resource in the sixteenth century and beyond.[18] Thus, another resource was needed to make the cannons that were increasingly central in early Capitalism. This resource was coal. With coal, we start to see happenstance play a key role in global affairs, because not every country has coal—nor iron ore, for that matter.[19] The prime sources of coal on Eurasia are in China and Russia[20]—two areas where the unity of political power and capitalism didn't occur until the twentieth century. Great Britain, nevertheless, had coal in appreciable amounts[21] and this played a considerable role in its production and advancement of armaments.[22] Later, British coal supplies would power its navy.[23] The point is that control of (especially scarce, vital) natural resources became a prime function of the state under Capitalism— arguably the most important natural resources being fossil fuels (i.e., energy).

While the French[24] and especially the British[25] surged forward under the regime of Capitalism (as would the United States), Germany (among others) faltered. I emphasize Germany because it has the largest reserves of coal in Central and Western Europe[26] but was hampered in that it didn't have a unified state until the late nineteenth century.[27] Coal, of course, has more than military applications. The Second Industrial Revolution, for instance, was powered by coal—more on that later. Coal made Germany a center of knowledge of science, chemistry, and engineering.[28] Without a centralized strong state to capture markets and other natural resources, however, Germany's relatively advanced economy was dependent on a system of world trade that was frequently manipulated by those powers that held large territories (France, Great

Britain, the United States). Thus, Germany was part of the networks of northwestern Europe where scientific knowledge and its practical application were greatly advancing,[29] but it was hampered in that it was economically dependent on the likes of Britain and France.

Germany didn't begin to pursue overseas possession until it was unified in 1871. By this point it had to contend with the fact that the world was mostly either effectively under the control of existing imperial powers (mostly, France and Britain) or had gained national independence (most of the Western hemisphere). There has virtually been endless debate on what specifically caused World War I (1914–1918), and I will not engage this expansive, multifaceted literature.[30] Nevertheless, focusing on the question of energy, Great Britain in a proximate sense is primarily culpable for precipitating the Great War. Again, due to its significant coal deposits, Germany in important ways had a modern, cutting-edge economy. Its advanced exporting industries included (at the beginning of the twentieth century) electrical engineering, pharmaceuticals, chemicals, metals, finished goods, and machine-tool production.[31] While Germany domestically had the energy to grow economically, it lacked secure access to international markets and the other raw materials needed to reliably economically expand. Reflective of this reality, leading into the Great War capital flight was a salient political issue facing Germany—as holders of capital seemingly perceived limits to Germany's medium-to-long-term economic prospects. Hence, instead of reinvesting their profits into Germany's economy, investors moved their money elsewhere.[32]

Great Britain saw Germany as an immediate, unacceptable threat to its global hegemony. It was particularly concerned with Germany's aggressive naval-building effort, which did suggest that it was going to challenge Great Britain's hold over its vast colonial possessions.[33] Great Britain was determined—even to the point of going to war—to hem in Germany, regardless of the effect this would have on the German economy. For instance, when Germany and France came into dispute over Morocco in 1905, Great Britain blocked Germany's effort to institute an "open door" policy in Morocco.[34] Great Britain was motived by a strong anti-German bias,[35] which made war a virtual inevitability. British antipathy toward Germany was ostensibly predicated on the fact that Germany, due in significant part to its domestic coal reserves, was a major geopolitical threat—particularly if it could gain secure, robust, reliable access to the international system. In the aftermath of World War I, a new energy source—oil—began to shape the global system.

A New Global System and Oil

While World War I was not about oil, by the early twentieth century this resource was beginning to shape global politics. The significance of Great Britain's dominant position in the world system leading up to World War I is evident with its decision on the eve of the war to switch its naval fleet to oil.[36] Such a switch was possible because of its presence in Iran and the government's financial sponsorship of the Anglo-Iranian oil firm.[37] Thus, given its imperial system, Great Britain was able to engage the next generation of naval technology, whereas Berlin (who had naval ambitions of its own[38]) could not make this leap due to Germany's paucity of colonial possessions and influence.

The big winner, however, of World War I was the United States. It became the world's top economy. This is because of its copious fossil fuels and its strong central government. The issue of centralized political authority resulted from its civil war, where the forces of political decentralization (the South) were defeated.

The victory of the North had a pronounced effect in the realm of trade policy. An underappreciated aspect of the American Civil War (1861–1865) was the trade question. The South sought a dependent relationship with Europe, whereby it would provide raw materials (primarily cotton) to this region in exchange for finished goods. This required low tariffs. The North desired high trade duties to protect domestic industry from cheaper and better-made European industrial products.[39] The first secessionist crisis in the U.S. was in the 1830s with South Carolina's threat to withdraw from the country in response to national trade tariffs.[40] With the victory of the North, the U.S. set a policy to in effect utilize its coal supplies to forward its national industry.[41] The prime global reserves of coal are in the U.S.—close to 30 percent of total supply.[42] The U.S. also holds significant supplies of natural gas.[43]

The rise of the U.S. (broadly speaking) is a story of energy and sovereignty. Shortly after the American Revolution, the First Industrial Revolution was predicated on hydro-power, with the rivers of the northeast harnessed for industrial production[44] and the American system of production—that is, interchangeable parts.[45] The Second Industrial Revolution was centered in the U.S. because of its tariff policy and its massive coal supplies. The heat generated by coal allowed for the economies of scale that characterized this industrial revolution.[46]

While the United States greatly advanced because of the Second Industrial Revolution, so did the economies of northwestern Europe and

Japan. Where the U.S. economy entered a plateau of its own was with the advent of what should be rightly recognized as the Third Industrial Revolution. This revolution is commonly referred to as the automobile revolution or the consumer durables revolution. These revolutions are viewed as resulting from Fordism, or the moving assembly line, which initiated the age of mass producing sophisticated technologies (most saliently the automobile).[47] More accurately, the Third Industrial Revolution was the result of oil. The 1920s is the beginning of the age of oil.[48]

This Third Industrial Revolution was monopolized by the U.S. for two key reasons. First, and most obviously, the U.S. was the world's largest producer of oil from the late nineteenth century to the post–World War II period. Second, the other advanced regions of the world did not have appreciable amounts of oil. Here is where World War I had a significant impact. The war left Britain and France deeply indebted to the U.S., which financed the Allied war effort through loans. Germany was punished with heavy war reparations and was further punished by efforts to deny it any international influence. Hence, one of Europe's advanced economies was left entirely dependent on a world trading system it had no direct role in shaping.

Arguably, this is most significant on the issue of the carve-up of the Middle East after World War I, where prior to the war German interests had a direct role in developing Iraqi oil fields. This was particularly important because in the early twentieth century Germany was an important pioneer in the advent of the automobile.[49] Germany's piece of Iraqi oil fields went to U.S. oil firms. The consortium of oil firms that controlled these fields blocked their development during the interwar years in an effort to bolster world petroleum prices.[50]

With Europe financially prostrate because of the war, and one of the continent's most technologically advanced automobile producers cut off from a reliable source of oil, the automobile revolution essentially bypassed this region. Investors in the U.S. could finance ever technologically advancing and expanding automotive production with the knowledge that there was ample, domestically available inexpensive gasoline to power a growing automobile fleet. The result was that the U.S. in the 1920s produced 85 percent of all automobiles.[51]

Automotive production in the U.S. had broad implications for its entire economy. Automobiles require the input of glass, steel, and rubber, so growing automotive production meant an expanding industrial base. Perhaps more importantly, the sophisticated manufacturing techniques developed to produce automobiles (Fordism) spread throughout the industrial sector. This made the U.S. industrial base in the 1920s the most advanced in the world; moreover, by the 1920s the U.S. economy accounted for fully 25 percent of the world's GDP (gross domestic product); also, the U.S. became the globe's largest creditor nation, with European countries (as noted) heavily indebted to the U.S.[52]

Economic historian Peter Fearon observes of the other leading industrial power in the 1920s, Great Britain, that its "economy was retarded by the weight of the old staple industries such as cotton textiles, coal, shipbuilding and iron and steel . . ." He explains that this is "in contrast to the striking advance of the consumer durables sector in America."[53] Thus, the U.S. economy excelled in the production of such commodities as household appliances.[54] Indeed, economic historian Alexander J. Field contends that "almost all of the [technological] foundations for [U.S.] postwar prosperity were already in place by 1941."[55]

I argue in *Energy and the Politics of the North Atlantic* that World War II was primarily caused by energy issues.[56] The global energy imbalance, whereby the United States was surging ahead and the other advanced economies were quickly falling behind, created a profound political instability in the world political system. This imbalance was exacerbated by the fact that the U.S. was actively seeking to limit the Third Industrial Revolution to itself. It did so through a high tariff that was reinstituted just as the automobile revolution was being established in the early 1920s (chapter 3).

The state played a more salient role in the Third Industrial Revolution than in earlier such revolutions.[57] The success of the U.S. economy in the 1920s depended on changing consumer spending patterns. Most glaring, urban zones in this period were not adapted to the automobile because cities were densely organized, as well as lacking automobile-friendly roads and parking. Beginning in the 1920s the American federal government, through the Commerce Department, began promoting urban sprawl. Urban sprawl necessitates public road building and appropriate zoning rules. Such urban sprawl is built around the automobile and, indeed, fosters automobile dependency. Additionally, urban sprawl tends to create large single-family homes, which can accommodate significant amounts of furniture and appliances (i.e., consumers durables—retail items expected to last three years or more).

The Great Depression of the 1930s deepened the global political crisis from the concentration of the Third Industrial Revolution in the U.S. Most saliently, the U.S. turned further inward with the Smoot-Hawley protectionist tariff and by abandoning the gold standard. The federal government employed a national strategy to counter the economic downturn by creating financial incentives to move people into suburban communities that were automobile dependent (chapter 4).

Perhaps following the lead of the U.S., other countries took destabilizing unilateral actions in the context of the depression. Japan responded to its dependent position in the global system by invading China in 1937. By 1930, the German government stopped looking to the U.S. for global leadership and adopted a truculent outlook—ultimately, with the rise of Hitler in January of 1933. Hitler looked with envy at the automobile revolution in the U.S. and sought to replicate it. This required bringing Soviet oil reserves within the orbit of Germany (Europe), which, of course, resulted in World War II. In the Pacific theater an American oil embargo against Japan resulted in the U.S. militarily engaging Japan, as Japan responded to the embargo with the attack on Pearl Harbor.[58] A key factor that resulted in the Axis Powers' defeat was their lack of oil—with 75 percent of the German military being horse drawn.[59] In contrast, the Allies were amply supplied with petroleum, provided predominately by the U.S. (nearly six billion of the seven billion barrels of petroleum used in the Allied war effort from 1941 to 1945).[60]

In the aftermath of World War II and the onset of the Cold War, the U.S. adopted the leadership position of the capitalist camp. The Cold War itself was seemingly the result of the West's (especially America's) opposition to the Soviet Union's effort to form an industrial state based on copious energy reserves while ideologically opposed to the profit motive.[61] During the Cold War, the U.S. consistently sought to prevent its allies from purchasing Soviet oil.[62] After the oil shocks of the 1970s, Saudi Arabia pursued an aggressive oil production strategy, which played a key role in the sharp decline of world oil prices in the 1980s.[63] Arguably, a prime goal of Saudi Arabia (a solid American ally[64]) in undercutting world petroleum prices during this period was to end the financial windfall that the Soviet government was garnering through the export of oil at the time.[65]

At the center of American Cold War leadership and the capitalist alliance was urban sprawl. The postwar economic boom in the U.S. was a direct result of government sponsoring of urban sprawl. The countries of West Germany and Japan geared their industrial development to the reliable access they had to the expanding consumer demand taking place in America. This worked to cement the pro-capitalist Cold War alliance.[66]

This international relations formula of relying on urban sprawl to forward the capitalist alliance and the capitalist economy (more broadly) was fundamentally threatened with the oil shocks of the 1970s. By 1973 the U.S. was no longer the leading oil producer, as production in America peaked in 1970 at just under ten million barrels a day. Moreover, the U.S. was importing roughly 35 percent of its oil needs. The center of global petroleum production shifted to the Persian Gulf—with Saudi Arabia, Iraq, Iran, and Kuwait being the prime global producers. Saudi Arabia in 1973 showed a willingness to use its oil as a political instrument—announcing a selective embargo directed at Israel's allies. This roiled the global oil market. This market was even more severely shaken by the Iranian Revolution in 1979, which brought an anti-U.S. government to power. Additionally, there were concerns that this anti-West, anti-U.S. revolution could spread to other Persian Gulf countries.

The countries of Western Europe and Japan never adopted the urban sprawl that the U.S. had. Nevertheless, Western Europe had predicated industrial and electricity production on oil. But with the 1970s oil shocks, France and Germany announced plans to shift to nuclear energy to power their respective economies. Popular political pressure prompted Germany to essentially abandon this plan, whereas France went ahead—today, 75 percent of electricity in this country is drawn from nuclear power. Moreover, France powers the other countries of Western Europe, as the largest exporter of electricity in the world. Elsewhere I explain that the European Union and its precursors were formed to deal with the reality that Western Europe had comparatively little domestic fossil fuel and as a result were reliant on an international energy system it essentially had no influence over.[67]

The United States responded to the oil shocks of the 1970s in a decisively different way (chapter 6): not by curbing its automobile/oil dependency but by focusing its political and military power upon the Persian Gulf. Similarly, in the early 2000s, as concerns arose about global petroleum supplies, the U.S. invaded the oil-rich country of Iraq. A trade embargo had been in place against Iraq since 1991 (as a result of the First Persian Gulf War). Thus, Iraqi oil fields were being underutilized in 2003 when the U.S. invasion took place. Today, American saber rattling against Russia and the Putin regime coincides with the reassertion of Russian sovereignty over its oil fields. In the immediate aftermath of the collapse of the Soviet Union the Yeltsin government privatized control of Russian petroleum. Under the Putin government, the state has taken back control of Russian oil.[68]

Something else in U.S. energy politics occurred during the 1970s that is curious. The U.S. turned away from nuclear power. American utility firms stopped ordering new nuclear power plants in the late 1970s. This raises a different facet of American energy politics. Up to this point I have emphasized the role of energy in propelling forward the U.S. economy and how this economy had a central role in the Cold War. Next, I turn to alternative energy—including nuclear. American policies on alternative energy can only be fully comprehended by considering how energy for the U.S. is a hegemonic device. The U.S. seeks to control the energy systems of other countries, and this has driven American policy on alternative energy. I take up this issue next.

Alternative Energy and the American-Led World System

Perhaps it will turn out that the most historically significant policy by the American government will be its indifference to clean renewable sources of energy.[69] Additionally, as other countries have sought to expand their use of clean renewable energy (most significantly Germany), the U.S. government is manifesting hostility to these efforts.

In 1952 a U.S. presidential commission (the Paley Commission) advised the federal government to aggressively sponsor research into solar energy. The U.S. has the advantage of the sun-drenched desert Southwest and the warm and sunny South. Moreover, America has a windy Midwest and Northwest.[70] Thus, unlike Europe or Japan the United States has a meteorology whereby significant amounts of surplus energy can be generated through wind and solar power. Presidents from Truman to Nixon mostly ignored the Paley Commission's recommendations.[71]

In the aftermath of the 1979 Iranian Revolution, the Carter administration did commit political and financial capital to developing solar power—taking the high-profile step of placing solar panels on the White House. Once oil prices declined in the first half of the 1980s, the Reagan administration drastically cut spending on alternative energy and took down the solar panels from the White House.[72]

Even now in the era of global warming, the U.S. government manifests an unserious attitude, at best, to clean renewable energy sources.[73] The Obama administration's $70 billion allocated to clean energy in 2009 was a one-off expenditure.[74] Maybe more significantly, the administration did not use this money to finance government research but instead utilized it to issue loan guarantees for entrepreneurial projects. Five hundred million of this money was dispensed in an irregular manner, and the result was that a Barack Obama campaign finance donor was reimbursed on a bad investment.[75]

The Donald J. Trump administration has publicly cast itself as indifferent (even hostile) to the issue of climate change and as pro fossil fuels.[76] The Trump White House website, for instance, declares the president's "commitment . . . to reviving America's coal industry."[77] Additionally, President Trump approved the Keystone XL Pipeline project, which was canceled by his predecessor (President Obama). (The pipeline would ostensibly accelerate petroleum production from the carbon-intense Canadian oil sands located in the province of Alberta.)[78] Finally, President Trump withdrew the U.S. from the voluntary 2015 Paris global warming accord.[79]

Why has the U.S. manifested an indifferent, unserious stance on clean renewable energy? This, despite historically and still today consuming massive amounts of energy—due in significant part to its sprawled urban zones. Clean renewable energy cannot serve as a hegemonic device. Most everyone has access to the wind and sun. Also, startup costs for solar panels and wind turbines manufacturing are not high.[80]

In *Energy and Empire* I juxtapose U.S. policy and politics on clean renewable energy with America's stance on nuclear energy.[81] Unlike solar energy, whose potential the government virtually ignored, the U.S. aggressively researched and promoted civilian nuclear energy in the 1950s and 1960s. Unlike solar energy, U.S. policymakers thought civilian nuclear technology could be monopolized. Thus, the U.S. classified its nuclear energy know-how and selected a fuel for nuclear power plants that it could monopolize. On the fuel question, instead of using heavy water technology, the government selected enriched uranium for the nuclear technology it exported to its allies. Heavy water can be used as a medium to ignite unprocessed uranium. Heavy water and unprocessed uranium are more broadly available than enriched uranium. Uranium enrichment involves increasing the amount of uranium-235 (^{235}U) in nuclear fuel. Uranium enrichment is a process that requires an expensive and sophisticated infrastructure. Going into the 1970s, the U.S. was virtually the only source of enriched uranium in the world outside of the Soviet Bloc. Hence, America's allies depended on it to fuel their nuclear power plants.[82]

The Nixon administration (1969–1974) made a misstep when it sought to privatize the U.S.'s uranium enrichment facilities. As part of the privatization process, the administration significantly raised the cost of enriched uranium. With concerns that the U.S. was now going to use its monopoly of enriched uranium to maximize price, Europe and Japan initiated their own enrichment facilitates, and with that the U.S. lost its civilian nuclear monopoly.[83]

With the loss of this monopoly, the U.S. government in the late 1970s turned against nuclear energy (chapter 7). The American government abandoned nuclear energy under two pretenses: nuclear weapons proliferation and the Three Mile Island nuclear plant incident in 1979. Of course, nuclear weapons proliferation had always been possibility, but in the late 1970s this somehow became a top concern. It is also noteworthy that internationally the U.S. came out against nuclear energy before the Three Mile Island incident. Additionally, in the first decades of the 2000s there was a resurgence of activity in the planning of nuclear power plants, with significant progress made toward completing two new plants.[84] (More on this later.) Next, I turn to the question of plutonium power.

Plutonium Politics

The U.S. damaged civilian nuclear energy with it policies on plutonium (chapter 7). Plutonium held the promise of a virtually inexhaustible energy source, with few of the liabilities of fossil fuels (e.g., scarcity, air pollution, greenhouse gas emissions). Moreover, plutonium use would "close" the nuclear energy cycle. (Nuclear waste could be almost perpetually recycled, as the "waste" produced in nuclear reactions would be used over and over again in the form of plutonium.) Thus, in withdrawing support from plutonium and actively opposing it, the U.S. as a result lowered the utility of nuclear power and sustained its liabilities (i.e., nuclear waste and a reliance on an international trading system of raw uranium potentially dominated by producing countries). Therefore, the implication of the U.S. international opposition to plutonium was not solely maintaining the utility of its huge stockpile of nuclear weapons[85] (i.e., limiting international access to nuclear weapons material), but this opposition also had the effect of maintaining the world's dependency on fossil fuels.

The U.S. opposition to plutonium as an energy source took the form of the Nuclear Non-Proliferation Act of 1978.[86] Empowered by this legislation, the Carter administration established a policy of preconditions for the U.S. transfer of enriched uranium and nuclear technology to other countries. The U.S. sought guarantees that nations receiving

American nuclear materials would not engage in fuel recycling, nor could they export any nuclear materials to those who did. (France and Great Britain were not penalized for their recycling facilities, but any exporting of recycled fuel would require U.S. approval.)[87]

Also damaging to the idea of a plutonium-powered economy was the ending of the U.S.'s effort to perfect nuclear fuel recycling and the commercial breeder reactor. The U.S. government was financing the construction of the Barnwell recycling/reprocessing facility and the Clinch River breeder reactor. The Carter administration suspended political support for both projects. Reprocessing nuclear fuel involves the extraction of plutonium from nuclear waste, and the breeder reactor can run on the plutonium retrieved from reprocessing. Breeder reactors generate more plutonium than they consume (by converting uranium-238 [^{238}U] into plutonium).[88] Thus, both the Barnwell reprocessing center and the Clinch River breeder reactor were potentially key to a virtually never-ending fuel cycle and unlimited energy. The U.S. ended its reprocessing/recycling and breeder reactor projects to set moral examples to stop the proliferation of plutonium.[89]

Since plutonium could be used to manufacture weapons, the U.S. argued that its proliferation represented a nuclear weapons risk. There are reasons to question that this was the prime reason that motivated the U.S.'s anti-plutonium policy. First, nuclear weapons proliferation can take place in the absence of plutonium production for civilian purposes. This was the central point of the International Nuclear Fuel Cycle Evaluation, a 1980 study sponsored by the International Atomic Energy Agency (chapter 7). Second, the U.S. has not acted very harshly toward friendly states that have pursued nuclear weapons programs or actually adopted nuclear weapons. The most obvious cases are India and Pakistan—which have nuclear arsenals and have openly tested their weapons. The less evident cases are Israel (which is believed to have a secret nuclear weapons program) and apartheid South Africa (which is believed to have had a nuclear weapons program).[90] The case of India is particularly glaring. India never signed the Nuclear Non-Proliferation Treaty (NPT), but in 2008 the U.S. nonetheless sponsored it into the civilian nuclear trading system.[91] Under the NPT (negotiated in the late 1960s)—outside of the United States, Russia, Great Britain, France, and the People's Republic of China—countries that possess or pursue nuclear weapons are excluded from the trade in civilian nuclear power.[92] The only countries the U.S. aggressively opposes attaining nuclear weapons are those countries with which it already has a hostile relationship: the clearest examples being Iran and North Korea.[93] (Despite being outside of the NPT framework, Pakistan has received tens of billions of dollars in military and economic aid from the U.S.[94]—nor does the U.S. object as Pakistan is attaining a nuclear power capacity.[95])

Third, the idea that the U.S. would use the fear over the spread of so-called weapons of mass destruction (WMDs) to forward an ulterior agenda is bolstered by the Bill Clinton (1993–2001) and George W. Bush (2001–2009) administrations' WMD allegations against Iraq—including claims that Iraq under Saddam Hussein had an active nuclear weapons program. As became especially evident with the American 2003 invasion of Iraq, U.S. allegations of Iraqi WMD programs were motivated by the American objective of regime change.

Fourth, the U.S. in pursuing its campaign against plutonium elided proposals for the internationalization of the nuclear fuel cycle. With a backlog of orders for enriched uranium, the Nixon administration put forward an offer to create an international uranium enrichment cartel. The offer, however, did not go beyond allowing foreign governments to invest in future privately controlled U.S. enrichment facilities.[96]

In light of the current threats of peak oil production[97] and climate change,[98] the U.S.'s opposition to civilian plutonium production and use beginning in the late 1970s may ultimately serve as the undoing of the international energy system and the biosphere (by means of global warming). Of course, plutonium production does present significant safety problems[99] and, as already noted, a nuclear weapons proliferation threat. Internationalization of plutonium production could have worked to meaningfully address the safety and weapons proliferation issues surrounding plutonium. Through internationalization, the countries of the world could have worked together to overcome the technical and safety barriers to large-scale plutonium production/use. (A global market for plutonium could have provided the incentives to resolve the significant technical/safety issues that currently serve as considerable obstacles to robust plutonium civilian utilization.) The U.S. government reaffirmed its hostile stance toward plutonium in 2012 with the Obama administration's Blue Ribbon Commission on America's Nuclear Future (chapter 7).

Additionally, a fully effective anti-nuclear weapons proliferation regime could be envisioned through internationalization of nuclear fuel production (including plutonium), as countries that deviate from the nuclear fuel regime could be punished with an absolute worldwide economic/energy embargo. Hence, internationalizing the global energy system (via nuclear power) could have worked to move humanity toward a world regulatory system to manage such momentous issues as conflict, weapons proliferation, and the environment (e.g., global warming).[100]

As noted earlier, in the first decade of the twenty-first century the U.S. appeared to be on the cusp of a nuclear energy renaissance, with numerous new nuclear power plants in the planning stages. Writing in 2017, all but one of these planned facilities were abandoned.[101] This is because of the hydrofracking revolution—whereby oil and gas shale are processed into commercially viable petroleum and natural gas. By the early 2000s North American natural gas supplies were declining. As the cost for this resource increased, nuclear power was viewed as a price-competitive alternative. Hydrofracking radically changed the energy terrain in the U.S., with natural gas prices dropping precipitously. Natural gas stocks are now so voluminous in the U.S. that it is now exporting liquified natural gas overseas.[102] Not only did hydrofracking ostensibly destroy the market for nuclear power,[103] but it creates a substantial barrier to clean energy alternatives.[104] This is not true only within the U.S., as low and declining energy prices draw investment from Germany—as its decisive move to clean renewables have pushed up its energy prices.[105]

Noteworthy is the fact that the hydrofracking revolution in America would not be occurring but for the U.S. government, which went to great lengths to identify gas and oil shale deposits for producers. European governments have not done the same.[106] As a result there is great uncertainty as to whether shale deposits exist in this region in appreciable amounts. American policymakers continue to support and champion the hydrofracking revolution despite its deepening of the world's dependency on fossil fuels, making any significant move in preventing catastrophic global warming a seeming impossibility. The world in 2015 missed perhaps the last meaningful opportunity to curb climate-changing emissions[107] when, under the leadership of the Obama administration,[108] the Paris global warming conference failed to produce a treaty to regulate and reduce emissions.[109] Central to this failure was American hydrofracking and the continued development of the Canadian oil sands (chapter 6)—which primarily serve the U.S. market.[110] Additionally, the *New York Times*, in 2014, reported that the U.S. State Department created in 2011 a Bureau of Energy Resources "for the purpose of channeling the domestic energy boom into a geopolitical tool to advance American interests around the world."[111]

Conclusion

The modern state and energy have a dialectic relationship, with this state first arising from the successful military harnessing of energy (wind). This began a centuries-long process of increasing access to and use of energy, which ultimately resulted in the entirety of the globe being divided into nation-states. Through energy, state power can be expanded without the need for a massive military. Moreover, the advancement of the modern economy is predicated on sufficient access to energy and this has salient public (foreign) policy implications. State decisions over what energy sources (e.g., solar, oil shale, plutonium) to pursue or not pursue has a profound impact on the use and development of these sources. The final theoretical supposition of this study is that with energy tending to be a zero-sum resource, throughout the twentieth century and into the twenty-first, energy has been an acute source of geopolitical tension and conflict. As noted in the theoretical overview, these suppositions can only be fruitfully applied in specific historic contexts and circumstances.

The modern state arose in Western Europe with the Netherlands and England first successfully tying together wind and cannons (derived from molding iron ore with intense heat). This region of the world operated through capitalism—with a sophisticated trade regime, based on firms and networks of broad scope. Hence, the first states projected capitalism—thereby creating what we recognize as modern Capitalism. The fact that Great Britain was victorious in its competition with the Netherlands meant that the modern state and international Capitalism were founded on aristocracy, as opposed to republicanism.

Another happenstance that had a profound effect on the development of the modern world system was the fact that Germany had relatively significant coal reserves and was within the orbit of the science and technological development of Western Europe. The result was great technological and industrial advancement for the German economy. Germany's national government formed late (1871) relative to those in Great Britain and France. By the time Germany had a pressing need to secure foreign markets and raw materials for its advanced economy, the globe was either divided predominately between Great Britain and France or already had national governments (mostly, the Western hemisphere). Great Britain determined that Germany not gain secure access to foreign markets and raw materials, and this caused World War I.

Happenstance intervened again and the United States quickly rose to the top of the world system in the early twentieth century. The U.S., which had a centralized government, was the first major oil producer and it contains the largest coal reserves in the world. The U.S., like Germany, was part of the network of science and technological development that was centered in northwestern Europe throughout the seventeenth, eighteenth, and nineteenth centuries. With the Third Industrial Revolution predicated on copious amounts of oil, this network was not only now centered in the United States but monopolized by it. American dominance of the Third Industrial Revolution was facilitated by World War I, which left France and Great Britain deeply in debt and Germany politically prostrate. Thus, these otherwise leading countries were in no position to engage the Third Industrial Revolution and thereby compete with the U.S. With the automobile revolution firmly entrenched in America, the U.S. government took the destabilizing step of turning inward during the 1920s and the 1930s (e.g., the Smoot-Hawley tariff). One result was Germany and Japan undertook their own destabilizing actions to cope with the Great Depression and their otherwise dependent economies. This resulted in World War II. Arguably, the prime goal of Germany during World War II was to compete with the United States by replicating the automobile revolution. This necessitated the incorporation of Soviet oil fields within the German (European) sphere of control.[112]

In the aftermath of World War II and in the context of the Cold War, the United States assumed a global leadership position— specifically of the capitalist alliance. The U.S. government used its domestic urban sprawl to establish its leadership and to cement its alliance with Western Europe and Japan. Its allies are given access to the robust, massive economic demand created by American urban sprawl. One fundamental flaw in this formula is that it is predicated on the massive consumption of oil. Ultimately, the U.S.'s consumption of oil outstripped its ability to domestically produce oil, and this meant the U.S. became dependent on the global petroleum system. This became an obvious political, economic liability in 1973 when Saudi Arabia demonstrated a willingness to use its role as the major exporter of oil as a political tool. America's significant oil dependency was further called into question with the Iranian Revolution of 1979. The U.S. government responded to its salient energy vulnerability by seeking to militarily, politically dominate the Persian Gulf—the world's primary oil-producing region. This strategy culminated with the 2003 invasion of Iraq. Additionally, the U.S. has come into political conflict with Russia over the Putin government's unwillingness to turn over Russia's oil reserves to private capital.

Whereas the U.S. adopted urban sprawl as an economic stimulus strategy as well as a Cold War strategy, Japan and Western Europe did not.[113] Western Europe in the postwar period did rely on oil to power industry and generate electricity. With the oil shocks of the 1970s, Western Europe (under the auspices of the French state) shifted to nuclear power. Also, Germany today is seeking to center its economy on clean renewable energy sources (wind and photovoltaic solar). Doing so will serve to insulate it from volatility in the world energy system—particularly as the decline of conventional oil production is a general concern.

In sharp contrast, the U.S. has turned anti-nuclear and only in the immediate aftermath of the Iranian Revolution did it seriously pursue clean renewable energy. Otherwise, the U.S. actively works to maintain the global dependency on fossil fuels. This results from the American strategy of dominating global politics through the dominance of energy. Thus, its takes an aggressively hostile stance toward plutonium and undermines clean renewable energy by sponsoring the hydrofracking revolution and the development of the Canadian oil sands. This strategy both directly contributes to the global warming phenomenon and prevents the formation of an international treaty to prevent catastrophic climate change.

American energy politics profoundly shaped the twentieth and the twenty-first centuries, as evidenced by World War II (chapters 3 and 4), the Cold War (chapter 6), nuclear energy in the 1950s and 1960s (chapter 5), and the momentous decision to turn away from plutonium in the 1970s (chapter 7). These politics were and continue to be decisively determined by economic elites in the U.S., the subject of the next chapter.

Chapter Two

The Political Economy of Energy

As outlined in chapter 1, during the first half of the twentieth century, the U.S.'s abundant supply of petroleum, and its subsequent urban sprawl, gave America a decisive economic/political advantage over Western and Central Europe (chapter 3). Germany, under the Nazis, sought to counter this advantage through its own automobile-centered development program. Unlike the U.S., however, Germany has little domestic oil (chapter 4).

During the height of the Cold War in the 1950s and 1960s, U.S. urban zones became increasingly sprawled. In contrast to the interwar period, when the U.S. maintained the economic benefits of urban sprawl for its domestic manufacturers, during the Cold War America liberalized access to its economy (chapter 6). This served to integrate the economies of the capitalist camp. The U.S. government also tried to tie its economy to that of its Cold War allies through civilian nuclear power (chapter 5).

In part because of its copious supplies of fossil fuels and in part because of the weakening of Europe by World Wars I and II, the U.S. has had the initiative throughout the twentieth century relative to Europe. (The Hitler regime attempted unsuccessfully to regain European global predominance by reorganizing the continent under German auspices.) Consistent with economic elite theory, the American initiative has been shaped and propelled by U.S. economic elites—both as special interest politics and the advocacy and imposition of broad (or general) policies on the state.

U.S. Energy Policy as Special Interest Politics

Urban Sprawl

A salient argument deployed to account for U.S. urban sprawl is that particular economic interests (e.g., large landholders) have been successful in instituting pro–urban sprawl polices in order to benefit their bottom line. This view of the politics of urban sprawl is consistent with the plural elitism take on policymaking in the U.S. Plural elitism grew out of the pluralism theory of the policymaking process.

Pluralism arose as the dominant political science paradigm in the post–World War II period. Pluralist theorists, most prominent among them being Robert Dahl, hold that various interest groups, including major corporations and labor unions, exercise influence over government.[1]

The near-total dominance of the theory of pluralism in American political science ended in the late 1960s and early 1970s with the social movements of this period (e.g., the antiwar movement, the civil rights movement, and the environmental movement). What came into full relief during the later 1960s and early 1970s was that government was not a neutral arena whereby different interest groups brought their political resources to bear (i.e., money, votes, prestige) as held by early pluralist thinkers. Nor was the successful mobilization of interest groups all that was needed to influence/shape the policymaking process.[2] Instead, political influence in the U.S. came to be viewed as consistent with plural elitism.

Plural elitism theorists hold that certain interests are entrenched and exercise dominant influence over policy formation. Theodore Lowi explains that the allocation of policymaking authority to specific agencies within the executive branch leads to the "capture" of those agencies by special interests—and thus the establishment of what he calls "subgovernments." The practice of ceding policymaking authority to executive branch agencies is named by Lowi "interest-group liberalism."[3]

Grant McConnell, like Lowi, attributed the diffusion of state power to a dominant political philosophy. This political philosophy according to McConnell is rooted in discourses developed during the Progressive Era. These discourses posit that democracy is most effectively applied in small bureaucratic units. In turn, this fracturing of the federal government into a multitude of small units allows the capture of significant amounts of state power by special interests.[4] Hence, while both McConnell and Lowi trace the public philosophy that has predicated the creation of a governmental structure that promotes capture by special interests to different philosophical precepts, both their conclusions are similar.

While Lowi and McConnell attribute the creation of subgovernments to the institutional structure of the federal government, especially the executive branch, and the legislative practice of delegating policy-making authority to executive branch agencies, Dahl and Lindblom, in a 1976 modification of early pluralist thought, argue that business groups in particular are going to have privileged access over the policymaking process. Subgovernments, they aver, are less the result of happenstance and more the result of the fact that businesspeople are directly responsible for running the economy. The result of this responsibility is the "privileged participation of business" in government:

> Businessmen are not ordered by law to perform the many organizational and leadership tasks that are delegated to them. All these societies operate by rules that require that businessmen be induced rather than commanded. It is therefore clear that these societies must provide sufficient benefits or indulgences to businessmen to constitute an inducement for them to perform their assigned tasks.
>
> The consequence of these arrangements—peculiar as they would appear to a man from Mars—is that it becomes a major task of government to design and maintain an inducement system for businessmen, to be solicitous of business interests, and to grant to them, for its value as an incentive, an intimacy of participation in government itself. In all these respects the relation between government and business is unlike the relation between government and any other group in the society.[5]

Therefore, subgovernments are the logical outcome of an economic system that relies on private elites to deliver economic prosperity. By giving businesspeople dominant influence over those government agencies that shape the behavior of the economy, this helps to ensure that the policies of these agencies will lead to economic growth and stability. Arthur Selwyn Miller refers to this arrangement as the "fusion of economic and political power."[6]

Dahl and Lindblom's argument that political authority over economic policies must be ceded to economic interests in order for those policies to be successful is consistent with the history of Federal Housing Authority (FHA). The FHA was given responsibility over the federal government's prime housing program beginning in the 1930s, and policymaking positions within the FHA were granted to prominent individuals from the housing industry as well as from the financial sector.[7] As indicated by Dahl and Lindblom, the fact that individuals with such backgrounds were given responsibility to set the federal government's housing policy is logical since it was the housing industry and the financial sector that were ultimately entrusted with building and financing the nation's housing, even housing that was sponsored by the FHA. From the post–World War II period into the late 1960s, the FHA played the key governmental role in subsidizing and encouraging urban sprawl in the U.S.[8]

U.S. international oil policy in the 1920s is also consistent with plural elitism. Joan Hoff Wilson, in her history of U.S. foreign policy during this period, found that American petroleum companies were ceded the authority to negotiate oil agreements with other countries on behalf of the U.S.[9]

The profound global implications of urban sprawl in the U.S. challenges the notion that it is solely a function of special interest politics. Today, urban sprawl remains a means to prop up the world economy. To this end, petroleum and natural gas supplies in the Middle East and Central Asia remain key prizes.

Civilian Nuclear Power

There is a wealth of literature that casts U.S. civilian nuclear power policies as a product of the nuclear industry itself.[10] Perhaps the best and most widely cited example of this literature is Mark Hertsgaard's *Nuclear Inc.: The Men and Money Behind Nuclear Energy*.[11] Hertsgaard argues that the leadership of the U.S. nuclear power industry is integrated into what he refers to as the Atom Brotherhood, and due to the finite nature of fossil fuels and the "greenhouse effect,"[12] this brotherhood foresees the inevitability of a nuclear-powered America (and world). Through its deep pockets, as well as corporate and political connections, nuclear reactor manufacturers have garnered huge sums in subsidies (for research, including demonstration nuclear power plants) and have been extended preferential protection from lawsuits resulting from the accidental release of radioactivity.[13] Moreover, the government has taken ultimate responsibility for the long-term storage of nuclear waste.[14] Hertsgaard wrote his seminal book in 1983, when the U.S. nuclear power industry still appeared capable of recovering in the short term from the setbacks of the late 1970s (most prominently, the Three Mile Island accident).

Rick Eckstein's *Nuclear Power and Social Power* identifies a different component of the special interest politics surrounding nuclear power in the U.S.[15] Eckstein specifically points to local growth coalitions as potential opponents to nuclear power plants.[16] According to Eckstein, it was local business interests that successfully defeated the start-up of the completed Shoreham nuclear power plant on Long Island, New York. Nuclear plants are potential threats to public health and, hence, to local real estate values, as well as the local business climate, as people and firms can be reticent to locate in the vicinity of such a plant. Despite the potential opposition that Eckstein notes, in the contemporary period the federal government has reinitiated nuclear power plant building.[17]

U.S. policies toward nuclear power cannot be the sum of special interest politics. Most glaringly, there is no evidence that the politically potent fossil fuel industry (i.e., oil, natural gas, and coal) has ever politically stood in the way of the federal government's development and promotion of nuclear power. This, even though a hugely successful civilian power program would have eliminated the need for fossil fuel as a source of energy (especially coal). While nuclear power is not a direct economic threat to petroleum for the powering of automobiles (i.e., gasoline), nuclear power, in theory, held the potential of generating so much cheap surplus energy that electrically powered automobiles, or those propelled by hydrogen, could be feasible.[18]

Far from manifesting opposition, the fossil fuel industry demonstrated significant political support for nuclear power in the 1950s. This support was shown through the 1956 report *Peaceful Uses of Atomic Energy* (the McKinney report), submitted to the Congressional Joint Committee on Atomic Energy. The McKinney report was compiled by the Panel on the Impact of the Peaceful Uses of Atomic Energy. To write its report, the panel drew upon "qualified individuals, organizations and study groups, each operating autonomously and submitting their independent findings of fact and their conclusions to seminar discussion groups. . . . All in all, 327 people, all authorities in their field, took part in this work."[19] As outlined in chapter 5, this panel recommended public financial support for civil nuclear power. Numerous fossil fuel firms and trade associations helped write the panel report. Among them were the American Petroleum Institute (trade association); the American Gas Association (trade association); Appalachian Coals, Inc.; Gulf Oil; National Coal Association (trade association); National Petroleum Council (trade association); Shell Oil; Texas Co. (oil firm); Standard Oil of California; Standard Oil of Indiana; and Standard Oil of New Jersey.[20]

The panel showed indifference to the adverse impact that a nuclear power program could have on the fossil fuel industry. It wrote: "Disruptive influences, even on specific industries most directly affected [by nuclear power], are likely to come—if at all—over periods of time long enough to permit orderly adjustment." The report goes on that with regard to those "specific industries popularly assumed to be most vulnerable to atomic inroads—coal, for example—such dislocations as appears possible would come from a welter of forces more complex and more overriding than atomic energy alone." The panel adds that "if atomic power is exploited as a source of electric power at a rate consistent with sound technological, economic and public policy considerations, the impact will be totally beneficial at home and abroad."[21]

Therefore, neither the federal government's policies on urban sprawl nor nuclear civilian power can be accounted for by simply looking at special interest politics. Instead, we must look at those political processes where the general interests of the U.S. polity and economy are identified and acted upon. As noted earlier, there are two different theoretical camps that seek to identify and analyze the processes whereby the general political interests of the U.S. are formulated and implemented: 1) state autonomy theory and 2) economic elite theory.

State Autonomy Theory

At the core of state autonomy theory is the notion that officials within the state can and do behave autonomously of all social groups.[22] Officials within the state have special theoretical significance because they are often looked upon to deal with political and economic matters. Moreover, they are also provided in many instances with the resources, such as legal authority and a budget, to do so.[23] Indicative of the argument that autonomous officials within the government drive state behavior, Adam Rome, in his book linking the rise of modern environmentalism in the U.S. to urban sprawl,[24] holds that the federal government beginning in the 1920s viewed low-density housing development as the means to attain broad-based home ownership.[25] Also consistent with the state autonomy position is Stephen Krasner's argument that U.S. foreign policy as it relates to raw materials, including petroleum, has historically been shaped by the ideology of officials within the state.[26]

In this context, autonomous policymakers can and do draw upon different public interest advocates, scientists, and economists to determine how to prioritize various imperatives and how to address them.[27] In this way, public interest groups, for instance, are incorporated into the policymaking process. Scientists and economists have specific importance within state autonomy theory. This is because they offer the technical know-how to instruct public officials. Scientists and economists also orient state officials to the political, economic, environmental, and social issues that must be addressed in order to avoid more serious difficulties.[28] According to Theda Skocpol, the legitimacy and usefulness of experts (i.e., scientists, economists, among others) is enhanced by the fact that they "most often . . . attempt to act as 'third-force' mediators, downplaying the role of class interests and class struggles and promoting the expansion of state or other 'public' capacities to regulate the economy and social relations."[29]

On the question of climate change, however, the federal government has historically shunned the advice and activism of numerous scientists and environmental groups.[30] A strong consensus has developed among scientists that the continuing uncontrolled emission of carbon dioxide holds seemingly dire consequences for the earth's biosphere.[31] This consensus includes the Intergovernmental Panel on Climate Change, a panel composed of leading climate scientists.[32] The U.S. government's resistance to climate science is particularly evident with the 2009 Copenhagen Climate Change Conference. At this conference, the Obama administration was unable to reach agreement with other governments of the world on the issue of a binding global warming agreement. At the heart of this failure was the U.S.'s inability/ unwillingness to specify how it would address its massive greenhouse gas emissions (with the U.S. Senate not passing climate change legislation on the eve of the conference).[33] As I noted in chapter 1, the 2015 Paris Climate Change Conference (under American leadership) again did not result in a substantive treaty.

Similar to the U.S. government presently eliding scientists' advice on the global warming issue, the Carter administration set aside leading nuclear scientists' reasoning on the matter of civilian use of plutonium.

Nuclear scientists posited their argument through the International Nuclear Fuel Cycle Evaluation report (officially released in 1980), put out by the International Atomic Energy Agency. The writers of the report held that civilian plutonium production, contrary to the position ultimately taken by the Carter administration, did not pose a special nuclear weapons proliferation threat (chapter 7).

It is my contention that to understand why the U.S. ignored the advice of the world's leading nuclear scientists on civilian plutonium as offered in the International Nuclear Fuel Cycle Evaluation we must look to economic elite politics (i.e., economic elite theory). Economic elite theory is treated next.

Economic Elite Theory

While plural elite theorists describe how individual corporate decision makers dominate specific and narrow policy areas,[34] economic elite theorists contend that these corporate decision makers, along with other individuals of wealth, develop and impose broadly construed policies on the state. Additionally, while plural elite theory views the business community as socially and politically fragmented, proponents of the economic elite approach hold that the owners and leadership of this community can be most aptly characterized as composing a coherent social and political unit or class.[35]

Clyde Barrow points out that "typically, members of the capitalist class [or the economic elite] are identified as those persons who manage [major] corporations and/or own those corporations." He adds that this group composes no more than 0.5 to 1.0 percent of the total U.S. population.[36] This group as a whole is the upper class and the upper echelon of the corporate or business community. The resource that members of the economic elite possess that allows them to exercise a high level of influence over government institutions is wealth. The wealth and income of the economic elite allow it to accumulate superior amounts of other valuable resources, such as social status,[37] deference,[38] publicity,[39] prestige,[40] organization,[41] campaign finance,[42] lobbying,[43] political access,[44] and legal[45] and scientific expertise.[46]

Within the economic elite approach, despite the segmentation of the economic elite along lines that are related to their material holdings, most policy differences that arise due to differences in economic interests can and are mediated. There are social and organizational mechanisms that exist that allow business leaders to resolve difficulties that develop within a particular segment and between different segments of the corporate community. For specific industries, or for disagreements between different industries, trade or business associations can serve as organizations to mediate conflict. William Appleman Williams, in his extensive history of the U.S. politics during the nineteenth century surrounding economic, foreign, and trade policies, explains that agricultural interests throughout the country formed business associations to address their common problem: how to gain access to new markets to profitably absorb the agricultural surpluses produced in the U.S. Williams writes:

> [Agribusinesses] participated in the general movement to
> create agricultural clubs and societies. Whether formed on
> a national scale, like the American Shorthorn Association
> (1846) and the Agricultural Society (1852), or organized
> on a state basis, like the Indiana Horticultural Society
> (1841–1842) and the Wisconsin Agricultural Society (1851),
> such groups . . . totaled 621 by 1849.[47]

Williams notes that these organizations "helped ease some" of the regional, economic, and political "conflicts" that emanated from the immense and varied U.S. agricultural sector.[48]

Social institutions, such as social and country clubs, can also serve as means through which to develop political consensus among the upper echelon of the business community on various economic, political, and social issues.[49] Michael Useem, based on his extensive study of large American and British corporations, argues that corporate directors who hold membership on more than one board of directors tend to serve as a means through which the corporate community achieves consensus on various political issues.[50]

On broad issues, such as urban sprawl, international oil policy, and civilian nuclear power, business leaders are also able to arrive at policy agreement and consensus through "policy-planning networks." According to G. William Domhoff, the policy-planning network is composed of four major components: policy discussion groups, foundations, think tanks, and university research institutes. This network's budget, in large part, is drawn directly from the corporate community. Furthermore, many of the directors and trustees of the organizations that comprise this policy-planning network are often drawn directly from the upper echelons of the corporate community and from the upper class. These trustees and directors, in turn, help set the general direction of the policy-planning organizations, as well as directly choose the individuals that manage the day-to-day operation of these organizations.[51]

Domhoff describes the political behavior of those members of the economic elite that manage and operate within the policy-planning network:

> The policy-formation process is the means by which the power elite formulates policy on larger issues. It is within the organizations of the policy-planning network that the various special interests join together to forge, however slowly and gropingly, the general policies that will benefit them as a whole. It is within the policy process that the various sectors of the business community transcend their interest-group consciousness and develop an overall class consciousness.[52]

Therefore, those members of the economic elite that operate within the policy-planning network take on a broad perspective and act on behalf of the economic elite as a whole. Within this policy-planning network, members of the economic elite are interested in general positions on such issues as foreign policy, economic policy, business regulation, environmental policy, and defense policy questions.[53] David A. Wells, a well-known figure in business and political circles during the last third of the nineteenth century, argued that the growing U.S. industrial base needed access to external markets in order to maintain stability and profitability. In a similar vein, Captain Alfred T. Mahan during the same period famously held that the U.S. needed to greatly enhance its naval capacity in order to secure vital shipping lanes to foreign markets.[54] As described in chapter 5, the Rockefeller Foundation in the 1930s provided the initial financial support for the research of nuclear energy.

This broad perspective also allows the policy-planning network to develop plans and positions to deal with other groups and classes. The network, for example, develops positions and plans concerning such policy areas as welfare and education. These plans can take several forms depending on the scope and level of the problems facing the business community and the state.[55]

Domhoff argues that the focal point in the policy-planning network is the policy discussion group. The other components of the policy-planning network—foundations, think tanks, and university research institutes—generally provide original research, policy specialists, and ideas to the policy discussion groups.[56] Policy discussion groups are largely composed of members from the corporate community and the upper class. Examples of policy discussion groups are the Council on Foreign Relations, the Committee for Economic Development, the National Association of Manufacturers, and the U.S. Chamber of Commerce. Overall, policy discussion groups are the arenas where members of the economic elite come together with policy specialists to formulate policy positions, and where members of the economic elite evaluate policy specialists for possible service in government.[57] For instance, as outlined in chapter 7, a number of the Ford Foundation experts that participated in the composition of the foundation's civilian plutonium report were appointed to key foreign policymaking positions in the Carter administration. Also described in chapter 7 is how, in the 1970s, the Committee for Economic Development, a policy discussion group (composed of economic elites and policy experts), formulated an argument for the internationalization of the nuclear/plutonium energy cycle.

Certain environmental groups, in terms of their leadership and/or financing, have the characteristics of economic elite-led policy-planning organizations. These groups include the Sierra Club prior to the 1960s, the Save-the-Redwoods League, and the Environmental Defense Fund. The Environmental Defense Fund, for instance, receives significant financing from large foundations, and it has several corporate executives on its board of directors.[58] Susan R. Schrepfer in her survey of the Sierra Club's early charter members, found that approximately one-third were academics, and "the rest of them were almost all businessmen and lawyers working in San Francisco's financial district."[59] The club was founded in 1892. Schrepfer goes on to explain that businesspeople continued to compose a substantial portion of the club's membership and leadership until the 1960s.[60] Unlike the Sierra Club, the high level of economic elite participation on Save-the-Redwoods League's governing council has been maintained throughout its history. The closed governance structure of the league created the "tendency for the council and board to be increasingly dominated by businessmen and patricians, while fewer academics were drawn into the organization's leadership in the 1950s and 1960s."[61]

Economic elites can use their relationships with environmental and natural resources groups to gain information and policy proposals in their efforts to shape public policies on environmental and natural resource questions when deemed necessary.[62] In 2007, the Natural Resources Defense Council, along with Environmental Defense Fund, the World Resources Institute, and the Pew Center on Global Climate Change, formed the United States Climate Action Partnership with ten major businesses: DuPont, General Electric, Alcoa, Caterpillar, Duke Energy, PG&E of California, the FPL Group of Florida, PNM Resources of New Mexico, British Petroleum, and Lehman Brothers. The political goal of the partnership is to reduce climate-changing emissions through the development and deployment of energy-efficient and abatement technologies.[63]

Similarly, the president of World Resources Institute (an environmentally oriented think tank) was a member of the Department of Energy Blue Ribbon Commission on America's Nuclear Future, which operated from 2010 to 2012. Also on this commission was the former President of PSI Energy, Inc., "Indiana's largest electric utility and subsidiary of the holding company Cinergy Corp., now Duke Energy." Additionally, the chairman and chief executive officer of Exelon Corporation sat on this Obama administration nuclear energy commission. Exelon "is one of the nation's largest electric utilities."[64] As noted in chapter 1 and described in chapter 7, the Blue Ribbon Commission on America's Nuclear Future issued a recommendation against plutonium energy.

Economic elite–led policy discussion groups have also been formed for the purpose of shaping decision-making on the urban level. One prominent example of such an entity is the National Municipal League.[65] From the nationwide effort of this organization came the Progressive Era urban reforms of the civil service "to regulate personnel practices, competitive bidding to control procurement, the city manager form of government to systematize decision making, and at-large elections to dilute the voting power of the working classes."[66]

Returning to the issue of the "general interests" of the capitalist polity and economy, the economic elite approach would suggest that the conceptions of the general interest that dominate the state are not determined within the state in response to different shifts in the operation of the political economy and/or public opinion. This view is implicit in the neo-Marxist view of politics,[67] as well as in state autonomy theory.

Instead, it is economic elites and producer groups, operating through policy-planning networks, that determine which issues within capitalism are to be addressed by the state and how.

Locally oriented economic elites (e.g., large land owners, land developers, owners of utilities and local media outlets, as well as real estate attorneys) have historically imposed the objective of local economic growth on local and state governments in order to inflate land values and expand the local consumer base. Together these particular elites have been labeled *local growth coalitions* by Harvey Molotch.[68] In the U.S. it was locally oriented economic elites (especially large land owners and developers) that developed the techniques and impetus for early urban sprawl. The techniques of urban sprawl were spread and standardized through economic elite–led policy-planning groups—most prominently, the Home Builders and Subdividers Division and the City Planning Committee of the National Association of Real Estate Boards (NAREB).[69] In chapter 3 I outline how, as the broad economic benefits of urban sprawl became apparent to economic elites in the 1920s, the federal government began promoting urban sprawl.

Conclusion

The empirical record indicates that throughout the twentieth century two markedly different political processes were occurring in the United States and in Western and Central Europe. In Europe, political elites (i.e., public officials) ostensibly predominated in determining public policy formation on energy questions. Economic elites in the U.S. were more central in shaping state policies on energy. Determining why is outside the scope of this study.

Energy politics, however, may provide insight into the divergent political processes on both sides of the Atlantic (political elite centered vs. economic elite centered). The ability of the U.S. to access copious amounts of energy allows for easier political unity and action among economic elites, whereas Europe's comparative dearth of energy creates harder political/economic choices for the continent and this necessitates a greater reliance on (opportunity for) political elites in Europe to arrive at a specific energy strategy. Reflective of these divergent energy politics on both sides of the Atlantic, U.S. economic elites operating through policy discussion groups successfully championed urban sprawl in response to an economic downturn after World War I and in direct response to the Great Depression of the 1930s. Whereas in Europe, the Hitler dictatorship broke through a political impasse/stalemate among German business elites in instituting a policy of automobile-centered economic development (chapter 4). Significantly, as discussed in the next chapter, the Hitler dictatorship was established because it became evident that the U.S. was not going to share the economic bounty with Europe derived from its sizable fossil fuel supplies. This "bounty" was being realized through automobile dependency/urban sprawl.

Chapter Three

Urban Sprawl in the U.S. and the Creation of the Hitler Regime

A central argument of this book is that the copious amounts of fossil fuels in the U.S. gave it a definite strategic advantage over the countries of Western and Central Europe. The U.S. was able to use this advantage to develop urban sprawl, which greatly expanded domestic demand for consumer durables—especially automobiles. In the interwar period, the U.S. adopted the position that the benefits of urban sprawl would accrue exclusively to its domestic industry. This had the effect of alienating the countries of Europe (especially Germany) and allowing the continent to lapse into political and economic crisis—ultimately leading to the installation of Adolf Hitler as dictator of Germany.

Hitler perceived the rise of the United States as a political/economic threat to Europe. He foresaw the American century, and he believed that the only way that Europe could effectively compete with the U.S. was through a geopolitical reorganization of the continent under the control of Germany. Significantly, Hitler identified two key factors that gave the U.S. a decisive advantage over the countries of Western and Central Europe: its natural resource base (including petroleum) and the advanced capacity of the Americans to manufacture consumer durables—especially automobiles.[1] Thus, as I explain in this chapter and the next, energy and the politics of urban sprawl were key causal factors in igniting World War II on the European continent.

The U.S. Federal Government and Urban Sprawl in the 1920s

Real estate interests in U.S. at the turn of the twentieth century were disseminating the techniques of automobile-centered urban sprawl. In addition to enhancing the economic value of land on the urban periphery, automobile-centered urban sprawl expanded the market for automobiles, as well as created demand for appliances and furniture to fill the relatively large homes built on urban outskirts.[2] During the 1920s the federal government began to promote urban sprawl as a way to stimulate the economy.

In 1921, a presidential advisory conference was convened to recommend proposals that could deal with the economic downturn, and specifically the unemployment, that followed World War I. The conference was titled the President's Conference on Unemployment and comprised an economic elite–led policy discussion group. Among the corporate elites that were conference members were: the president of the U.S. Chamber of Commerce, the president of the Pittsburgh Coal Company, president of the Pelham Oil & Trust Company, president of the Illinois Central Railroad Company, president of the American Steamship Owners Association, chairperson of the Bethlehem Steel Corporation, and president of the National Implement & Vehicle Association. The conference was presided over by Secretary of Commerce Herbert Hoover, who, himself, was a wealthy mining engineer/businessperson.[3]

One of the conference's twelve recommendations to combat unemployment was road building. The conference argued that "a congressional appropriation for roads . . . would make available a large amount of employment."[4]

The President's Conference on Unemployment formulated its recommendations through committees. It was the Committee on Public Works that developed the conference's recommendation on road building. On this committee was James Couzens, a former vice president of the Ford Motor Company. Also on this committee was Evans Woollen, president of the Fletcher Joint Stock Land Bank and member of the Economic Policy Committee of the American Bankers' Association (a trade association).[5] The committee report stated that "it is the judgement of this committee that the country should put itself behind the *better roads—more work program*, insisting that it be pushed at once to the last dollar of money that is available."[6]

This road building recommendation was consistent with the automobile industry's political agenda, which beginning in the first decade of the twentieth century promoted the reorganization of the nation's transportation infrastructure, fostering automobile dependency. In 1903 automobile manufacturers were supporting the American Road Builders Association and the national movement to have governments at all levels pay for roads and highways that could accommodate automobiles.[7] In 1911 the American Automobile Association sponsored the first American Road Congress.[8] At this congress, Hugh Chalmers, president of the Chalmers Motor Company, conceded that "the automobile industry is, of course, in favor of good roads and would be greatly benefitted by them," but he went on to stress that "since the roads are for all the people, they should be built by all the people, or all the people should contribute to the building of them."[9] Chalmers concluded his speech by arguing:

> I believe when the people are thoroughly aroused on this question [of the quality of the U.S. road system] and realize that the benefits of [good roads] are not for one class of people alone, but for all the people alike, that they will rise up some day and demand of the national Congress, to start with, and the State assemblies, in the second place, that they cooperate to the end that we keep pace in road improvement with all other transportation improvements of this century.[10]

Another recommendation put forward by the President's Conference on Unemployment related to home building. The conference averred that "the greatest area for immediate relief of unemployment is in the construction industry." The one type of construction the conference specifically referred to was housing, where the authors of the conference report claimed that "we are short more than a million homes." The conference advised "organize[d] community action . . . to the end that building may be fully resumed."[11]

The conference's Committee on Construction Industries advised that Secretary of Commerce Hoover take a leading role to promote construction (house building) nationwide:

> It is therefore recommended that Secretary Hoover appoint a committee selected from the various elements interested in

construction, such as financiers, labor, engineers, architects, contractors, material manufacturers, and others to be known as the Committee on Construction Development.

The conference's Committee on Construction Industries went on to suggest that its proposed Committee on Construction Development work "in cooperation with the Secretary of Commerce." The committee explicitly argued for "the prompt removal of unnecessary or inequitable [local] limitations and restrictions which have retarded real construction activity."[12]

Consistent with the President's Conference on Unemployment Committee on Construction Industries' recommendations, in 1921 Secretary of Commerce Herbert Hoover appointed an Advisory Committee on Zoning. It put out in 1924 *A Standard State Zoning Enabling Act.* Renamed Advisory Committee on City Planning and Zoning, it disseminated *A Standard City Planning Enabling Act* in 1928. "Together these two documents outlined the basic principles for state and local governments to follow in implementing the comprehensive urban land-use planning agenda. Many state legislatures adopted one or both of the model enabling acts almost verbatim." Marc Weiss, in his history of suburban land planning, goes on to report that "NAREB [National Association of Real Estate Boards] President (1922) and community builder [i.e., suburban developer] Irving B. Heitt served on both Advisory Committees, along with nine men closely associated with the newly emerging city planning profession."[13]

Historian Adam Rome describes how the Department of Commerce under Hoover promoted urban sprawl.[14] Specifically,

> throughout the 1920s, the Commerce Department also worked with a private philanthropic organization—Better Homes for America—to promote the ideal of homeownership. The organization produced a film entitled "Home, Sweet Home" and distributed thousands of copies of the Commerce Department's *How to Own Your Own Home* booklet. By the end of the decade, Better Homes for America had over 7,000 local chapters, and each sponsored a variety of lectures and demonstrations, including construction of model homes.[15]

These Better Homes for American chapters were consistent with the President's Conference on Unemployment Committee on Construction

Industries' recommendation that "in continuation of the policy of the creation of local organizations inaugurated by the Department of Commerce, the National Federation of Construction, the U.S. Chamber of Commerce, etc. . . . the time is ripe for their more definite and extensive organization." The Committee on Construction Industries added that "such local committees as have already been organized in the country have had a profound value in readjusting the construction situation."[16]

Historian Greg Hise notes that Secretary of Commerce "Hoover served as titular chairman of the Better Homes in America movement."[17] Moreover, Marc Weiss reports that "with the accession of Herbert Hoover as secretary of commerce in 1921, NAREB became an important and highly favored trade association working closely with the Commerce Department's new Division of Building and Housing, as well as with other federal agencies."[18]

Urban Sprawl and Consumer Durables

Urban sprawl beginning in the 1920s significantly affected the U.S. manufacturing sector. This is especially evident with automobile production, where the automobile dependency created by urban sprawl spurred automotive consumption.

A specific difficulty facing the automobile industry in the 1920s and leading into the Depression Era was that most cities during this period were highly centralized and congested,[19] and this meant that automobiles were either impractical for a large segment of the U.S. populace or not needed because places of employment, as well as goods and services, were within walking distance. Additionally, those neighborhoods that were well outside of city centers were normally close to inexpensive trolley service.[20] As a result, automobiles were mostly a luxury item. Prior to the Depression, automobiles were purchased largely for the purpose of recreational outings.[21]

The production and marketing strategies of most automobile firms during the first two decades of twentieth century reflected the fact that for most the automobile was a luxury. Historian Donald Davis outlines the production activities of early automotive manufacturers. He points out that early automobile manufacturers mostly produced automobiles that emphasized aesthetics, amenities, and engine power. Hence, they generally shunned the low-end automotive market, wherein automobiles were primarily built for utility and aesthetic considerations and amenities were not prioritized. Davis argues that automobile manufacturers during the early part of the century tended to produce automobiles of higher expense because Detroit's early automotive elite primarily came from an upper-class background and they wanted to make automobiles that were commensurate with their class position.[22] By pursuing the middle and upper price range of the automotive market, however, automotive makers were competing for suburban consumers whose homes could most readily accommodate an automobile and who would find most use for such a commodity. Such consumers were predominately middle and upper class.[23] Therefore, suburban consumers seemingly made up the most lucrative and stable segment of the automobile market.

Henry Ford, among early automotive producers, was the exception. Unlike other early automobile manufacturers, Ford's primary goal was to build an automobile that maximized utility and was as inexpensive as possible, and he stuck to this goal.[24] Significantly, Ford did not necessarily have a specific consumer in mind when he built his low-end automobile. One of his early partners quoted him as saying in 1916 that "you need not fear about the market, the people will buy them all right, because when you get to making them in quantities, you can make them cheaper, and . . . the market will take care of itself."[25] To the extent that Ford thought about who was the likely consumer for his product, it was not urban or suburban dwellers but farmers.[26]

One factor that allowed Ford's low-cost automobile strategy to succeed was the fact that urban land developers by the 1920s were developing homes away from city centers and trolley lines and, instead, around the automobile. As a result, automobiles became less of a luxury item, and more of a necessity.

This was most evident in the case of Los Angeles, where land developers were particularly aggressive in building entire communities predicated on automobile ownership. As a result, by the end of the 1920s, the Los Angeles area had become the U.S. region most adapted to the automobile, whereby "residents of Los Angeles purchased more automobiles per capita than did residents of any other city in the country." During this period "there were two automobiles for every five residents in Los Angeles, compared to one for every four residents in Detroit, the next most 'automobile oriented' American city."[27] Historians of Los Angeles take these statistics to assume a particular affinity among the city's residents for the automobile.[28] A more likely cause, however, for the relatively high level of automobile ownership in Los Angeles is that much of the new affordable housing stock was being constructed in areas only accessible by automobile. Moreover, as businesses responded to the increasing mobility of suburban residents, employment, retail outlets, and services were increasingly offered away from the city center and areas serviced by trolleys. This created further incentives for Los Angeles residents to obtain an automobile.[29]

Overall, urban sprawl significantly bolstered the consumption of consumer durables in the U.S. In her historical analysis of U.S. consumption patterns, economic historian Martha L. Olney finds that

> between 1919 and 1928, [U.S. households] spent annually an average of $267 each on durable goods—$172 for major durables (now mostly automobiles and parts rather than furniture) and only $96 for minor durables (still mostly china and tableware, house furnishings, and jewelry and watches).[30]

After several decades of urban horizontal growth,[31] "by 1979–86, households annually spent an average of $3,271 each for durable goods, with $2,230 for major durables (still predominantly automobiles and parts) and $1,041 for minor durable goods (now house furnishings, miscellaneous other durable goods, and jewelry and watches)."[32] Conveyed in constant dollars, households between 1919 and 1928 spent an average of $955 on consumer durables, and $3,353 between 1979 and 1986.[33] Olney adds that "strong growth in purchases of automobiles and parts remains evident: *average annual purchases for 1919–28 were four times greater than the average for 1909–18*, and growth continued through the post–World War II years." Additionally, "purchases of household appliances and the 'entertainment complexes'—radios, televisions, pianos, and other musical instruments—showed a similar pattern."[34]

Utilizing statistical analysis, Olney demonstrates that the dramatic increases in the consumption of durable goods exceeded overall increases in income during the pre-Depression Era and the post–World War II period.[35] It is for this reason that Olney contends that the 1920s marks the beginning of the consumer durables revolution in the U.S. She attributes the surges in the consumption of consumer durables to two factors: advertising and the availability of consumer credit. She acknowledges, however, that advertising,[36] and especially consumer credit,[37] were not as widespread during the 1920s as they were after World War II.[38] What was evident during both periods was an increasing trend of urban sprawl, expanding demand for consumer durables. This expanding demand for consumer durables, especially automobiles, brought about the expansion and technological sophistication of the U.S. industrial sector.[39]

Economic historian Peter Fearon notes of the other leading industrial power in the 1920s, Great Britain, that its "economy was retarded by the weight of the old staple industries such as cotton textiles, coal, shipbuilding and iron and steel . . ." He explains that this is "in contrast to the striking advance of the consumer durables sector in America."[40] Thus, the U.S. economy excelled in the production of such commodities as household appliances.[41] Indeed, economic historian Alexander J. Field contends that "almost all of the [technological] foundations for [U.S.] postwar prosperity were already in place by 1941."[42]

The most prominent feature of the consumer durables–geared U.S. industrial base was automobile production. In 1920 U.S. automobile factories sold 1.9 million automobiles, and in 1929 4.4 million. American automobile manufacturers' passenger car output represented 85 percent of the global total.[43] Fearon explains that "the influence of the automobile [on the U.S. economy] was pervasive." For example "it provided one of the chief markets for the steel industry and for the manufacturers of glass and tyres."[44] During much of the 1920s "nearly 17 percent of the total value of fully and semi-manufactured goods was accounted for by automotive products."[45] It is statistics like these that prompt economic historian Elliot Rosen to regard the automotive industry as the "nation's principal industry" by the 1920s.[46] Economic historian Maury Klein adds that "during the 1920s the automobile industry became one of the main pillars of the American economy."[47] Another economic historian, Richard B. Du Boff, notes that "during the 1920s, the [automotive] industry became the nation's leader in manufacturing."[48]

A 1929 government report, titled *Recent Economic Changes in the United States*, noted the impact that urban sprawl during the 1920s was having on the U.S. economy. The report was an extension of the 1921 President's Conference on Unemployment. The *Recent Economic Changes* report was the last of three generated as a result of the conference. It was composed by the Committee on Recent Economic Changes. On the committee was Owen D. Young, chairperson and president of major appliance manufacturer General Electric;[49] John J. Raskob, chief financial officer of both General Motors and the chemical giant DuPont; as well as Daniel Willard, president of the Baltimore and Ohio Railroad.[50] As described in its report, the Committee on Recent Economic Changes "was directed to make a critical appraisal of the factors of stability and instability; in other words, to observe and to describe the American economy as a whole." The committee produced an "analysis of post-war developments in American economic life, particularly those since the recovery from the depression of 1920–21."[51]

The committee took note of the sprawling of urban zones during the 1920s: "the private automobile and bus, with improved roads, have greatly enlarged the area within which dwellings may be located, and have permitted comparatively open developments in attractive locations, to an extent that would not have been possible before the war." Moreover, "The family's enlarged radius of movement due to the automobile . . . strengthens the call toward the suburbs."[52] The committee report authors made the explicit point that "the extension of residential areas in and about cities, made possible by the automobile and improved streets . . . has resulted in a remarkable suburban growth of detached houses."[53] Finally, the committee observed that "the automobile has been one of the pervasive influences affecting . . . production during recent years." "In addition to its direct influence on demand" the automobile "has facilitated changes in demand in many communities," and "these changes . . . have enhanced the prosperity of some groups of manufacturers."[54]

U.S. Foreign Policy and the Radicalization (or Nazification) of the German Government

While government-promoted urban sprawl in the U.S. was successfully growing and technologically advancing the American economy, the countries of Europe were in an economically untenable situation in the 1920s and leading into the 1930s. What is perhaps most glaring about the U.S.'s relationship to European economic/political instability during this period was that the U.S. was mostly the cause of this instability. The Allied war effort during World War I was largely financed by U.S. creditors, and this huge debt continued to malign the European allies into the 1930s. Additionally, Germany incurred large debts from the U.S. in the effort to cover the massive war reparations that were imposed upon it. Even after the reparations were cancelled, Germany's dollar-denominated debt to the U.S. continued to stifle its economy. Historian Adam Tooze, in *The Wages of Destruction: The Making and Breaking of the Nazi Economy*, explains that in 1933 its "debt burden . . . threatened Germany's standard of living no less seriously than the reparations that had now been removed from the table." The United States was "by far" Germany's "largest creditor."[55]

It was the unwillingness of the U.S. to forgive Europe's debt, as well as the unwillingness of the U.S. to integrate its economy with that of Europe during the 1920s, that seemingly led to the rise of the Nazis in Germany and subsequently to the onset of World War II. Tooze argues that historians need to "focus squarely" on "the consequences of America's flawed hegemony in the 1920s," and on the reality that "the exogenous causal factor [prompting the creation of the Hitler regime] was the failure of American policy to do what could have been done."[56] Historian E. J. Feuchtwanger, in *From Weimar to Hitler*, holds that "it would have been wiser if . . . the United States had made the saving of the precarious German democracy their first priority."[57] A historian of American external relations writes, with a tone of disapproval, that the "foreign policy of the United States in the 1920s and 1930s consisted not so much of dirty political deals as it did of selfishly shortsighted commercial and financial transactions that reflected its inexperience as the world's leading economic power."[58]

Arguably more damaging to international economic and political stability than the debt matter was the trade policies of the U.S. Tooze explains that "American tariffs . . . , compounding America's competitive advantage in virtually every area of manufacturing, made it difficult, if not impossible, for America's debtors to repay their debts."[59] Worse still, by denying secured access to its sizable economy to other industrialized countries, the U.S. was adversely affecting the development of these countries. This was especially evident of Germany, which did not possess much by the way of external or internal colonial territories. A bilateral or multilateral trade treaty designed to encourage international economic integration with the U.S. would have encouraged investment in industrial expansion and technological advancement in countries like Germany. This is essentially what happened in the post–World War II period, when the German and Japanese economies grew through export-led development.[60]

German politics ultimately came to mirror the U.S.'s economic nationalism. The German election of 1928 maintained in power a government supportive of the existing international order, with an expressed commitment to an "Atlanticist" economic strategy, anchored by freer and secured international access to the U.S. economy. From 1923 to 1929 successive German governments were based on the idea of positioning "Germany as a key ally of the United States."[61] Feuchtwanger explains that Gustav Stresemann, who was foreign minister from 1923 to 1929, was "strongly convinced of the interdependence of nation-states in the conditions of modern industrialism." Stresemann further held that "in Europe this interdependence required institutionalized cooperation and it would also have to include the United States."[62]

At the end of 1929, however, "German foreign policy quickly changed towards greater assertiveness and independent action."[63] Tooze reports that, by 1932,

> the governments of Franz von Papen, General Kurt von Schleicher and finally Adolf Hitler adopted a contrary position. Rather than seeking prosperity and security in multilateral arrangements guaranteed by the power of the United States, they sought to secure unilateral German advantage, if necessary even in the opposition to America's efforts to restore the international order.[64]

Tooze adds that in German political circles by the early 1930s "the voices of liberalism were drowned out by the deafening clamor of economic nationalism."[65] Among the factors that did "damage to trans-Atlantic economic relations" was that by 1929 "Europeans knew . . . that the new [Smoot-Hawley] tariff [of 1930] would in all likelihood make it harder for America's European debtors to earn the dollars they needed to service their obligations to Wall Street."[66]

My contribution to understanding the collapse of the Germany polity's faith in the Atlanticist strategy in the 1920s, and the subsequent predominance of confrontational/radical/warmongering nationalist politics in that country, is the argument that urban sprawl in the U.S. had a role in the failure of the Atlanticist approach. First, and most obvious, the economic prosperity in the U.S., in significant part resulting from urban sprawl, meant that Europe's economic and political problems were less of a concern for American policymakers. In her book *American Business and Foreign Policy: 1920–1933*, Joan Hoff Wilson asserts that "between 1925 and 1929 an aura of prosperity, again especially in the United States, made international cooperation seem less urgent than in the immediate postwar years."[67] More damaging, however, to the U.S.'s willingness to make sufficient policy adjustments (e.g., opening up its economy to foreign industrial producers) to address destabilizing global economic imbalances was that urban sprawl gave American policymakers a clear formula of how to grow the U.S. economy without having to expose it to foreign competition. (U.S. import duties increased substantially, with the Fordney-McCumber tariff of 1922, when the federal government began its pro–urban sprawl actions.[68])

It is noteworthy that Owen D. Young (chairperson and president of General Electric) was on the Committee on Recent Economic Changes (which documented the positive effect of U.S. urban sprawl in the 1920s on manufacturing) and was one of the principal authors of the 1929 Young Plan (named after him). The Young Plan was a program to restructure the inter-Allies' war debt and Germany's reparations. As part of the plan, the U.S. refused to eliminate the Allies' debt in exchange for the abrogation of German reparations.[69] Historian Richard J. Evans in *The Coming of the Third Reich* notes that "reparations still loomed over the German economic scene, even though they had been rescheduled and in effect substantially reduced by the Young Plan in the summer of 1930."[70] Tooze holds that "the disappointment that followed in the wake of the Young Plan was devastating to the credibility of the Atlanticist strategy."[71]

Conclusion

U.S. urban sprawl in the 1920s was not merely the product of happenstance, but the result of producer groups' and economic elites' conscious efforts to use diffuse urban development to grow the economy. This is evident in the 1921 President's Conference on Unemployment. It was a business-led policy discussion group that recommended road building and new housing construction to revive the U.S. economy. The result of these recommendations was urban sprawl. This urban sprawl was noted by the Committee on Recent Economic Changes. The committee also reported on the positive relationship between U.S. urban sprawl and the consumption of manufactured goods. The economic success related to urban sprawl in the 1920s meant that the U.S. was ostensibly less dependent on international markets, and, as a result, this facilitated U.S. protectionist policies. Not only did urban sprawl help to ostensibly insulate the U.S. from Europe's economic troubles, but the kind of binding free trade treaties that could have economically/politically stabilized Europe, particularly Germany, would have meant that American manufacturers would have had to share the wealth being generated through urban sprawl. Urban sprawl in the U.S.

was predicated on an asset that was somewhat unique at the time to America: abundant production of oil.[72]

This nationalistic posture on the part of the U.S. during the 1920s was particularly corrosive to German politics, which during this period was explicitly looking to the U.S. for economic and political leadership. The U.S., however, was unwilling to take the steps necessary (total debt forgiveness and trade liberalization) to pull the countries of Europe into an effective coalition. This unwillingness ultimately greatly contributed to the political radicalization of Germany (i.e., its Nazification) and the onset of World War II.

The eliding of the international marketplace, and a reliance on urban sprawl (and domestic petroleum supplies) to foster economic growth in the U.S., is, as described in the next chapter, even more evident during the Franklin D. Roosevelt administration (1933–1945) in the 1930s. While requests for the U.S. to coordinate its economic policies with those of Europe were ignored, the New Deal used governmental power to directly sprawl the development of U.S. urban zones in an explicit effort to revive the U.S. economy from the Great Depression.

Chapter Four

Urban Sprawl, the Great Depression, and the Start of World War II

As the Great Depression set in during the early 1930s, the U.S. rejected an internationalist approach to coping with it. Under Franklin Roosevelt's government, the U.S. continued its nationalist attitude toward foreign economic affairs. Its response to the Depression was centered on domestic policies, not on using the nation's considerable economic resources to directly lead the world out of the severe downturn of the 1930s.

Arguably, the most important of the Roosevelt administration's domestic responses to the Great Depression was the subsidization of urban sprawl. The government's pro–urban sprawl policies in the 1930s were an effort to use the economic assets of the U.S. to revive the American economy. These assets were 1) surplus capital, 2) an industrial base geared toward the production of consumer durables (especially automobiles), and 3) large reserves of domestic petroleum. Economic elites and producer groups formulated and implemented the public policies that deployed these assets in the form of U.S. urban sprawl.

It is noteworthy that in the late 1920s and the 1930s Germany also sought to foster automobile consumption to promote economic stability and growth. Hitler, in particular, thought that in order to compete with the U.S., Germany (and Europe) had to replicate America's automobile-centered economy. Germany and Hitler, however, were limited in this effort by the fact that Germany lacked oil.

The International Community
and the Early Roosevelt Administration

In historian Robert Dallek's *Franklin D. Roosevelt and American Foreign Policy, 1932–1945*, part 1 is titled "The Internationalist as Nationalist, 1932–1934."[1] What Dallek outlines in the first part (four chapters) of his political biography is that while Roosevelt prior to entering the White House stood on international, multilateral pretenses, his administration rejected internationalism and adopted a nationalist, domestic tack in dealing with the Depression.

After the election of 1932, President Herbert Hoover took an openly internationalist stance in seeking to counter the Depression, but as Dallek explains, during the presidential transition period, Roosevelt "made clear to the Congress and the public" that his "administration would not follow Hoover's ideas of curing the Depression from abroad."[2] Roosevelt's "determination to keep international economic reform in the background until domestic legislation could work registered clearly enough at the White House conference on January 20."[3] Roosevelt "did not want discussions of foreign affairs . . . to overshadow domestic reforms."[4]

As President, Roosevelt pursued "nationalistic monetary and economic policies," which "seemed to preclude meaningful international talks" on a global response to the Depression.[5] Dallek reports that Roosevelt "committed himself to a policy of 'intranationalism'—the reorganization of American economic institutions without interference from the outside."[6] Roosevelt's decision in 1933 to unilaterally withdraw from the gold standard was an explicit rejection of the harmonizing of currencies to promote global trade. This "action infuriated the British and the French."[7] Moreover, as part of the Roosevelt administration effort to stabilize the agricultural sector, it authorized tariffs on agricultural products.[8] Similarly, the administration's plan (the National Industrial Recovery Act) to revive the U.S. industrial sector through domestic actions implied tariffs on imported industrial goods.[9] In the summer of 1934, Roosevelt "told a press conference that with the self-sufficiency in both agriculture and industry now the policy of other nations, the United States also would have to be economically self-contained."[10]

Writing about U.S. external economic policies during the Great Depression, historian Joan Hoff avers:

> Although the Smoot-Hawley tariff was modified by New
> Dealers with the 1934 Reciprocal Trade Agreements in order
> to give the president more power to negotiate and reduce
> import duties, this legislation should not be confused with
> the adoption of the Wilsonian idea of free trade. Despite
> its unconditional most-favored-nation provision . . . the
> purpose of the 1934 act was to expand the foreign markets
> of the United States, not to increase imports.

Hoff adds that "this meant commitment to unilateral Open Door expansionism prevailed in Washington even during the Great Depression."[11] Dallek explains that "Roosevelt's . . . reciprocal trade program chiefly served American rather than world economic interests."[12]

Even prior to Roosevelt's election in 1932, leading members of the U.S. financial community put forth a plan to revive the U.S. economy by investing America's substantial surplus capital into domestic real estate. This strategy was manifest in the President's Conference on Home Building and Home Ownership held in 1931. This conference's proposals were incorporated into the Federal Housing Authority's (FHA) pro–urban sprawl policies. The FHA, itself, was the result of the 1934 President's Emergency Committee on Housing, another economic elite–led policy discussion group.

Surplus Capital

By the 1920s the U.S. economy held a substantial amount of surplus capital. In 1929 approximately $52 billion was held in bank savings and other deposits. As one observer notes, funds in banks, savings and loans, and other commercial lenders from 1900 to 1929 "grew about three times as fast as the overall economy."[13]

Much of this excess capital was utilized to underwrite the Allied war effort during World War I through loans. In the post-armistice aftermath, the U.S. was the primary source of funds for the European economies seeking to recover from the war and pay war reparations. As a result of this lending activity, the U.S. became the world's largest creditor nation. With the onset of the Depression in 1929, however, the international flow of capital collapsed, as countries, including those in Western and Central Europe, found it difficult to impossible to cover outstanding debts.[14] Moreover, with the crash of the stock market, brokerage loans declined substantially. Loans that were issued against stocks dropped from a high of $7 billion in June 1929 to $1.6 by June of 1931, and later to $335 million by June 1932.[15]

Within the context of the Depression, leading members of the U.S. banking and investment community sought to make domestic real estate into a more reliable outlet for capital. This was reflected in the President's Conference on Home Building and Home Ownership held in 1931. A Committee on Finance (which ostensibly became an economic elite policy-planning group) was convened as part of the conference. Among the committee's members were executives from the United States Building and Loan League (a trade organization); Dillon, Read, and Company (a key investment firm); Metropolitan Life Insurance; New York Title and Mortgage Company; Southern Trust Company; American Loan and Savings Association (a major mortgage lender); and the American Bankers Association (a trade organization). Also on this committee was the president of the National Association of Real Estate Boards (NAREB).[16]

The committee's report focused on the residential real estate market. Its authors noted that "instability in home property values was confirmed as a major difficulty by the committee's studies." Importantly, "financial institutions have a vital stake in the stability of real estate values in any territory where they operate."[17] The committee made two key recommendations in order to bring stability to the residential real estate market: an appropriate down payment and long-term amortized loans.

The committee advised "that a down payment of about 25 per cent of the purchase price should be established as the basis of a sound home purchase transaction."[18] The committee authors noted that at the time "most of the savings institutions that lend on first mortgages operate on conservative principles, and it has been customary for them to limit their loans to from 40 to 60 per cent of appraised value."[19] A down payment of 25 percent of appraised value would expand the pool of potential home purchasers.

On the question of home mortgage repayment, "mindful of the problems presented on the maturity of short term 'straight' mortgages" the committee advised "to all home buyers the advantages of long term amortized loans."[20] Up to this time, standard mortgages had a three-year term.[21] Arguing against this mortgage maturation term, the committee explained that "it has been demonstrated that a long term mortgage, say from 11 to 18 years, that provides amortization of the entire principal, is the most satisfactory to both borrower and lender."[22]

The terms of the standard mortgage loan were mostly the result of the structure of the U.S. banking system. Most U.S. banks and savings institutions were what are known as unit banks. In other words, they had no branches and operated exclusively out of one office. Throughout the nineteenth century and into the early decades of the twentieth century, branch banking was largely prohibited by the states, or severely limited—such as only allowing bank branches within the city limits of the home branch.[23] By the 1920s branch banking was in greater practice, but it was still limited as twenty-two states forbade bank branches and another nineteen placed varying degrees of restrictions on them. Even in California, where branch banking was politically well established, in 1923, unit banks were successful in having the state superintendent of banks review the opening of new branch offices.[24] With savings and deposits fragmented throughout a national system of individual banks operating out of one office, most banks and savings and loans could not afford to have their capital tied up in long-term home loans. In other words, the vast bulk of banks and other savings institutions were simply too undercapitalized to have their assets vested in multidecade home loans. Hence, the mortgage terms of 60 to 40 percent loaned on appraised value, with a three-year maturity period.

These standard mortgage terms tended to create instability in residential real estate markets. As already noted, high down payments constricted the pool of potential home purchasers. More importantly, relatively short-maturation loan terms could work to adversely affect housing markets. While such loans where often renewed, short mortgage terms could serve to depress a real estate market if a local bank needed to increase its liquidity. Since most banks only made direct loans in their community,[25] a bank that was threatened with insolvency could call in a significant number of its home loans in a community to shore up its finances. Such activity could lead to frequent defaults in a particular area or for many homeowners to prematurely place their homes up for sale. Additionally, if a significant number of homeowners served by a community bank suspected that the bank was not going to renew their mortgage, they may seek to sell. Finally, if bankers sensed a drop in the real estate market in a particular locality, they may choose not to renew mortgages in that locality or ask for higher down payments upon renewal. Logically, in the context of the worsening economic conditions of the Depression,[26] the inherent instabilities embedded in the standard lending and home purchasing practices of the period were exacerbated. The committee report noted that "in some states . . . [it was] found that mutual savings banks made their loans for one year, or payable on demand."[27]

Therefore, the longer loan amortization period called for by the Committee on Finance would serve to stabilize the residential real estate market nationally and make such real estate a more reliable and profitable commodity to place investment funds. Created in 1934, the Federal Housing Authority (the unofficial name of the Federal Housing Administration) instituted a policy whereby the federal government guaranteed home loans. Under this program, home mortgages were underwritten if they required 20 percent down and their maturation period was twenty years. Later, this guarantee was modified to 10 percent and twenty-five years.[28]

The Production of Consumer Durables

As noted in the last chapter, by the 1920s the U.S. was experiencing a consumer durables revolution. (Consumer durables are retail goods that are expected to last at least three years.) Thus, the U.S. economy excelled in the production of such commodities as household appliances.[29]

As also noted in the last chapter, the most prominent feature of the consumer durables–geared U.S. industrial base was automobile production. While the overall trend in automotive production during the 1920s was upward, market downturns caused significant production declines in 1921, 1924, and 1927.[30] Additionally, during earlier depressions, automobile output "contracted severely."[31] During the Great Depression, among industrial producers "the collapse in the motor vehicle sector was especially pronounced." By the end of 1929 "the reduction in automobile output was the greatest in the entire manufacturing sector."[32] Jane Holtz Kay, in her history of the automobile in the U.S., entitled *Asphalt Nation*—reports:

> By 1932 half the auto plants in Michigan had closed. The saturation of the car market combined with the Depression shut down one out of three dealers. Within a year after the stock market crash, the number of auto workers had

shrunk to 100,000, reflecting and accelerating the dwindling car sales.[33]

To overcome the depression in the automotive industry, in the mid-1930s the federal government subsidized the outward development of urban areas, thus making the automobile a necessity for increasingly greater numbers of people. Moreover, the horizontal expansion of cities pushed up demand for other consumer durables, such as household appliances,[34] because this expansion brought with it larger homes that necessitated more consumer durables to fill such homes.

The U.S. Federal Government's Promotion of Urban Sprawl

As noted earlier, the federal government, beginning in the mid-1930s, initiated a program to underwrite home mortgages. It did so through the Federal Housing Authority (FHA). The FHA's legislative authority is found in the National Housing Act of 1934. The committee that composed this act was headed by Marriner Eccles, a wealthy Utah businessperson who was an official in the Department of Treasury. Also on this five-person committee was Albert Deane, executive "assistant to the president" of General Motors—Alfred Sloan.[35] Eccles's committee was actually a subcommittee of the President's Emergency Committee on Housing. The president's committee included W. Averell Harriman, who was asked to participate on this issue because of "his national standing as a businessman."[36] As historian Sidney Hyman explains, "When the terms of the new housing program were finally agreed to, [Harriman] was expected to 'sell' the program to . . . the business community at large."[37] Also on the President's Emergency Committee on Housing was John Fahey, chairman of the Federal Home Loan Bank Board.[38]

The presence of Sloan (through his assistant) on a presidential housing committee is noteworthy. By this time General Motors was selling half of all automobiles in the U.S. As explained in the last chapter, from the first decade of the twentieth century automobile firms were promoting a reorganization of the nation's transportation infrastructure and spurring automobile dependency.

Automobile manufacturers were not the only supporters of a national system of automobile-friendly roads and highways. Frederic Paxson, a historian of the U.S. highway movement, notes that many early highway "proposals had money behind them, for chambers of commerce, automobile associations, and industrial organizations" contributed politically to their fruition.[39] Nevertheless, automobile firms were persistently aggressive in promoting automobile-dependent infrastructure (i.e., roads and highways).[40] In the early 1930s, for example, when cash-strapped states began using their gasoline taxes for programs other than road building, "General Motors banded two thousand groups into the National Highway Users Conference to lobby against the practice."[41] This lobbying effort yielded the Hayden-Cartwright law of 1934, which determined that "states which diverted the [gasoline] tax to other than road use should be penalized by a reduction in their share of federal aid."[42] Stan Luger, author of *Corporate Power, American Democracy, and the Automobile Industry*, explains that at the 1939 World's Fair, General Motors "presented a model of the future based on suburbs and highways."[43] Finally, numerous automotive-related companies, among them General Motors, Standard Oil of California, and Firestone Tire and Rubber, were found by a federal grand jury to have successfully conspired to dismantle electric streetcar (trolley) systems in forty-five U.S. cities, including Los Angeles, San Francisco, and New York during the 1940s.[44]

Marriner Eccles's biographer (drawing from extensive interviews with Eccles) outlines the thinking underlying the formulation of the National Housing Act of 1934. "A program of new home construction, launched on an adequate scale, would not only gradually provide employment for building trade workers but," more importantly, "accelerate the forward movement of the economy as a whole." It was anticipated that

> its benefits would extend to everyone, from the manufacturers of lace curtains to the manufacturers of lumber, bricks, furniture, cement and electrical appliances. Transportation of supplies would stimulate railroad activity, while the needs generated for the steel rails and rolling stock would have spin-off effects on steel mills.[45]

Moreover, "if banks with excess reserves made loans for home construction, the effect would be to create the basis for new money."[46] Therefore, the purposes of the legislation that authorized the FHA were seemingly to spur consumption, including that of consumer durables, and to prompt the profitable movement of capital out of banks and into the housing sector. Urban sprawl would presumably help accomplish these goals since suburban developers already by 1920s demonstrated a predilection for building large, relatively expensive homes on undeveloped tracts of land, far from trolley lines.[47]

Upon its creation, the FHA was placed under the stewardship of prominent officials from the real estate sector, and they used their authority to promote the horizontal growth of urban American. Created in 1934,

> FHA's staff was recruited almost entirely from the private sector. Many were corporate executives from a variety of different fields, but real estate and financial backgrounds predominated. For example, Ayers DuBois, who had been a state director of the California Real Estate Association, was an assistant director of FHA's Underwriting Division. Fred Marlow, a well-known Los Angeles subdivider, headed FHA's southern California district office, which led the nation in insuring home mortgages. National figures associated with NAREB, such as real estate economist Ernest Fisher and appraiser Frederick Babcock, directed FHA operations in economics and in underwriting.[48]

Significant for this discussion is the fact that the first administrator of the FHA was an executive from Standard Oil. Also among the FHA's initial leaders were two individuals from the automotive sector: Albert Deane of General Motors (deputy administrator of the FHA) and Ward Canaday, "president of the U.S. Advertising Corporation of Toledo, with a reputation for sales promotion in the automobile industry." Canady was the FHA's director of public relations.[49] Jeffrey Hornstein, a historian of the U.S. real estate industry, notes that the industry generally "welcomed the FHA . . . both because it promised greatly enhanced general demand for housing and because the agency was run largely by Realtors and their allies in the banking world."[50]

To encourage housing sales, the FHA underwrote home purchases. As explained earlier, it would guarantee 80 percent of home mortgages for qualified homes and buyers for a twenty-year term. (Later, this guarantee was modified to 90 percent and 25 years.) Up to this time, standard mortgages covered about 50 percent of the home purchase price and had a three-year term.[51]

This program gave the FHA the ability to influence the types of homes purchased and, subsequently, housing development patterns. Weiss notes:

> Because FHA could refuse to insure mortgages on properties due to their location in neighborhoods that were too poorly planned or unprotected and therefore too "high-risk," it definitely behooved most reputable subdividers to conform to FHA standards. This put FHA officials in the enviable position, far more than any regulatory planning agency, of being able to tell subdividers how to develop their land.[52]

With this power, the FHA promoted the building of large-scale housing developments in outlying areas. Weiss explains that the Federal Housing Administration's "clear preference . . . was to use conditional commitments [for loan guarantees] specifically to encourage large-scale producers of complete new residential subdivisions, or 'neighborhood units.'' Thus, the FHA, through its loan program, encouraged and subsidized "privately controlled and coordinated development of whole residential communities of predominately single-family housing on the urban periphery."[53]

With federal housing policy firmly under the control of the FHA, Kay writes that it "decentralized housing out of the city and did little to help slum dwellers."[54] In his comprehensive analysis of U.S. suburban development, geographer Peter O. Muller explains that "the nearly complete suburbanization of the [urban middle class] . . . was greatly accelerated by government policies . . . the most important being the home loan insurance programs launched by the Federal Housing Administration in 1934."[55] Kay adds:

> Cities remained the center of Depression malaise and neglect. Their expansion ceased or declined compared to suburbs. Twenty-five percent of Detroit's growth was on its periphery, only 3 percent within the city. Likewise, Chicago's suburbs swelled 11 percent, the downtown less than 1 percent. Vast acreage in the central business districts fell for parking spaces.[56]

Kenneth Jackson, in his important history on the suburbanization of urban development in the U.S., concurs with Weiss's, Kay's, and

Muller's assessments of the bias within the FHA for new housing stock in outlying areas. Jackson writes that "in practice, FHA insurance went to new residential developments on the edges of metropolitan areas, to the neglect of core cities." As a result, Jackson notes that between the years 1942 and 1968 the "FHA had a vast influence on the suburbanization of the United States."[57]

As argued earlier, urban sprawl in the U.S. spawned a consumer durables revolution beginning in the 1920s. This revolution was sustained throughout the postwar period, with the consumption of consumer durables (especially of automobiles) substantially exceeding income growth.[58] Today, U.S. urban sprawl has international economic ramifications. The U.S. is the world's largest consumer.[59] (U.S. consumers, excluding government and businesses, purchase close to 20 percent of the world's total economic output.[60]) Importantly, European, Japanese, and South Korean automakers count heavily on access to the huge U.S. automobile market to attain profitability.[61] With a third less population than Western and Central Europe, before the 2008 recession the U.S. consumed on average two million more new automobiles annually (during peak years, fifteen million versus seventeen million), and, even today, half of all new automobiles purchased in the U.S. are of the highly profitable SUV and light truck varieties.[62] The Japanese automakers Honda and Toyota (the world's largest automobile manufacturer), for instance, derive two-thirds of their overall profits from sales in the U.S.[63] It is also noteworthy that General Motors, the second largest manufacturer of automobiles, registers about 40 percent of its sales in the U.S. market.[64] (The U.S. contains less than 5 percent of the world's population.)

German Automobile Policies in the Early 1930s

During the 1930s, the U.S. was not alone in having government directly promote the country's automobile industry. Germany, in particular, sought to foster automotive consumption. (General Motors was a common link between the American and German governments' automotive-related activities in the 1930s.) The Nazi regime embraced the automobile. Hitler viewed domestic automotive production as a necessary component of great power politics.

Historian R. J. Overy, in his article entitled "Cars, Roads, and Economic Recovery in Germany, 1932–8," describes how the German government just prior to the installation of the Hitler regime began to promote automobile consumption as a means of attaining economic recovery.[65] These policies included the reduction of the tax on automobile purchases, aggressive road-building projects (including the autobahn), and government propaganda touting the automobile. The Hitler government continued these policies. Countering most historians' claims that Germany's economic recovery under the early part of Hitler's rule was attributable to rearmament, Overy ascribes this recovery more so to the regime's pro-automobile policies than to its rearmament activities. He further holds that the diversion of resources to the military in fact undercut the economy's growth by conflicting with the government's pro-automotive stimulus policies. Describing the impact of Germany's pro-automotive policies on automobile consumption and production, Overy notes that "car sales shot up during 1933, and helped to accelerate a trend that had already been noticeable in late 1932."[66] (Hitler attained power in early 1933.) Neil Gregor, in his history of automobile manufacturer Daimler-Benz, notes that the German automotive industry's "recovery can be said to have been not only tentatively but strongly underway prior to the appointment of Hitler as Chancellor on 30 January 1933."[67] Overy goes on to explain that "the index of production of cars rose very much faster than for industry as a whole, from 100 in 1932 to 250 in 1934 as against 100 and 140 for all industry."[68]

Glenn Yago, author of *The Decline of Transit: Urban Transportation in German and U.S. Cities, 1900–1970*, points out that German businesses took the leading role in advocating increased automobile consumption:

> By 1929, the activities of the RDA (Reichverband der Automobilindustrie—Reich Association of the Automobile Industry), the HAFRABA (Verein für Vorbereitung der Autobahn Hanasastädte—Frankfurt–Basel—Association for Promoting the Hansa Cities–Frankfurt–Basel Autobahn), and others were creating political support in German industry for a shift away from the exclusive use of railroads [and toward the automobile].

Nonetheless, there was a spilt among German firms over the expanded use of the automobile: "By the end of the twenties, industry and trade associations were split between the traditional rail enthusiasts and those supporting motorization and highway building." The question dividing these factions was over which mode of transportation would better serve Germany's macroeconomic perform:

> It is evident from the German business press and the "Denk-schriften" (policy papers) of [industry and trade] associations that any mode of transportation was supposed to be able to meet the needs of both transportation-consuming and transportation-producing industries. By helping to increase profits, a given transportation mode would maximize employment, be a countercyclical source of government spending (without competing with private capital), and assist capital accumulation in other important branches of industry (e.g., military industries).[69]

A key factor that tilted the German polity toward the automobile was the entrance of General Motors (GM).[70] Yago argues that "the GM takeover of Opel was the turning point in the history of the German automobile industry."[71] Henry Ashby Turner Jr., in his history of General Motors in Germany during the 1920s, 1930s, and 1940s, describes the significant investment that General Motors made in taking over Opel: "In acquiring Opel, GM not only entered the German auto industry at the very top but also became the owner of one of the country's most venerable and best-known manufacturing companies." Turner explains that in 1929

> General Motors bought 80 percent of the shares of Opel stock and secured the rest two years later when the owners exercised an option to sell the reminder. The total purchase price came to slightly over $33.3 million, a sum equivalent to more than a third of GM's overall after-tax profits in the depression-plagued year of 1931. At a time when the American economy was contracting drastically, Opel represented a significant commitment of GM's financial resources.[72]

Moreover, GM, after its takeover of Opel, paid for "costly plant expansion and modernization projects." By 1932, GM had invested $42 million in its German subsidiary.[73] From March 1930 to May 1932 (around the time of GM's purchase and modernization of Opel), the German government instituted its pro-automobile policies, including reducing the tax on automobile purchases and instituting road building.

According to Yago, the Hitler regime, by embracing the automobile, became an ally of those within the German business community that championed automobile dependency. Yago explains:

> With the Nazis' takeover of state power, a concerted attempt was made by auto-linked capitalists to break the resistance to the automobile by rail-related capitalists and state bureaucrats. A community of interest was established between the automobile industry and the German fascists who pursued a national transportation policy encouraging motorization.[74]

Hitler "in late March" of 1933 "pledged to use his new powers to promote automotive travel and transport." In April 1933, the government eliminated all taxes on new vehicle purchases. Moreover,

> in June [of 1933] the new regime, drawing on preparations begun by the republican government, announced plans for a nationwide network of four-lane, median-strip highways to augment Germany's antiquated road system. In September construction on the first stretches of this autobahn commenced amidst much fanfare.[75]

Hitler thought that the establishment of a German automobile industry was a "national matter."[76] As a result, he designated a German (Ferdinand Porsche) as manufacturer of the official automobile of the Third Reich (i.e., the Volkswagen), despite General Motors' aggressive effort to garner that moniker for an Opel model.[77]

Hitler's championing of Germany's automobile industry was consistent with the strategic thinking he articulated in his 1928 posthumously published *Second Book*. Hitler perceived the United States as Europe's greatest threat. He held that America was "the stiffest competitor in many areas."[78] Hitler argued that the "danger arises" that Europe would be dominated by "a new determination of the fate of the world by the people of the North American continent." He went on to explain that "[a] few already recognize that this danger is threatening all of Europe. . . . In the context of the future international state hierarchy, [Germany, in particular] will be at most what Switzerland and Holland were in the previous Europe."[79]

Hitler specifically pointed to the U.S. dominance of the automotive sector as a worrying development: "We must watch how American vehicles are proliferating even in our own country." Hitler accurately noted that "this is only possible because the size of the internal American market and its wealth of buying power and also, again, raw materials [e.g., oil] guarantee the American automobile industry internal sales figures that alone permit production methods that would simply be impossible in Europe. . . .The result of that is the enormous export capacity of the American automobile industry." Hitler identified the automobile sector as having great strategic importance: "At issue is the general motorization of the world—a matter of immeasurable future significance. Because the replacement of human and animal power with the engine is just at the beginning of its development; the end cannot yet be assessed at all today. . . . For the American union . . . today's automobile industry leads all other industries." In contrast to the U.S., "taking all factors into consideration, particularly in view of the inadequacy of our own raw materials . . . the future of Germany must appear very bleak and sad."[80]

Another factor that was seemingly decisive in the formulation of Germany's pro-automobile policies during the early 1930s was the perfection of the Haber-Bosch coal hydrogenation process—a process through which coal could be liquified. (Germany has very little by way of domestic oil production.) The chemical and engineering firm IG Farben developed this coal liquefying process during the 1920s,[81] and by 1930–1931 it could produce 100,000 tons of liquid coal,[82] whereby it could only produce 48,000 in 1929.[83] Around the time IG Farben reached this 100,000-ton level of production (March 1930 to May 1932), the German government began its initial pro-automotive consumption policies. Tellingly, as it was cutting taxes on automobile purchases, the German government was substantially raising taxes on gasoline—making it the highest taxer of gasoline in Europe. Consequently, liquefied coal became more price competitive with oil-derived gasoline, which was at a depressed price at the time.[84] Historian Adam Tooze explains in *The Wages of Destruction: The Making and Breaking of the Nazi Economy* that during the Nazi period, a high tax on imported fuel was continued as it was "indispensable to sustaining the momentum of the synthetic fuel programme."[85]

There was, however, an inherent limitation in the Haber-Bosch coal liquefying process—namely, it consumed more coal-derived energy than it yielded in the form of liquid fuel. Thus, large-scale coal liquefying would have an adverse effect on the domestic coal market, and in the long term accelerate the time at which Germany would have to begin to import coal (and other fuels) to maintain its economy. Ultimately, despite the technical success of the Haber-Bosch process, securing petroleum supplies remained a Nazi military objective throughout the war,[86] as Germany's military suffered from continual and chronic fuel shortages.[87] Moreover, neither of the German states after World War II utilized coal liquefying as part of their energy strategies.[88]

Conclusion

The Great Depression did not change the U.S.'s orientation to the global economy. The depression did not prompt significant moves to integrate the American economy with the rest of the world. Just like its response to the economic downturn of 1920–1921, the U.S. government responded to the Great Depression by promoting urban sprawl. It did so, however, in the 1930s more directly than it did so in the 1920s. Thus, under the auspices of the New Deal and a more aggressive role for the federal government in the economy, the central government subsidized urban sprawl explicitly as a way to counter the Depression.

The strategy to respond to the Depression through domestic real estate was manifest through the Committee on Finance of the President's Conference on Home Building and Home Ownership, made up of leading members from the financial and land development sectors. The committee in 1931 put forward proposals to enhance home ownership and the flow of capital into domestic real estate. This was key because U.S. financial institutions had significant amounts of surplus capital but few profitable outlets for it in the context of the Depression.

The Committee on Finance proposals were incorporated into the Federal Housing Authority's policies during the 1930s and beyond. In addition to promoting home ownership, the authority's policies served to aggressively sprawl urban development in the U.S. during the 1930s and throughout the postwar period. This had the positive economic effect of greatly expanding demand for consumer durables (i.e., automobiles, appliances, furniture, etc.). By the 1920s, the U.S. industrial sector excelled at the production of consumer durables, in particular automobiles. The Federal Housing Authority (FHA) was the product of the President's Emergency Committee on Housing. It is noteworthy that the president of General Motors (the largest manufacturer of automobiles at the time)—through his assistant—was on this committee that created the FHA, which subsequently played such a key role in expanding the U.S. market for automobiles.

Also noteworthy was General Motors' role in the pro-automobile policies of the German government during the early 1930s. GM's sizable investment in Germany served to spur these policies. The Hitler regime continued and expanded these pro-automobile policies by eliminating all taxes on new automobile purchases and making road building a national priority. The official car of the Third Reich (i.e., the Volkswagen) was supposed to be a low-cost automobile for the German of average means. Hitler ultimately believed that a thriving European automotive sector was central to its competition with the U.S. (Of course, Hitler hoped that Germany would guide/control Europe in this competition.)

Germany, however, was limited in its automotive policies by the fact that it has little by way of domestic petroleum production. As a result, it sought to rely on coal liquefying to power the country's automotive fleet. Germany, under the Hitler government, tried to overcome its oil dependency through foreign policy—that is, World War II and its invasion of the Soviet Union (a major producer of petroleum).

The U.S. possessed huge amounts of domestic petroleum, and this allowed its pro–urban sprawl policies to proceed in high gear. In chapter 6 I explain how in the postwar period the demand created by American urban sprawl served as a lynchpin of the Cold War alliance headed by the U.S. By the early 1970s it was evident that American urban sprawl could not be sustained by U.S. domestic oil production. The U.S. addressed this issue through its foreign policies, and it continues to do so. Before moving on to global oil politics, in the next chapter I outline how the American government in the 1950s and 1960s pursued nuclear energy as an additional means to cement the Cold War alliance. Because solar power could not serve this purpose, the U.S. state ignored the potential of solar energy. Economic elites in the U.S. would take the lead in setting both nuclear and solar power policies.

Chapter Five

U.S. Economic Elites, Nuclear Power, and Solar Energy

Historically, U.S. urban sprawl and U.S. nuclear policy have been linked, but not in the way one might think. As explained in chapters 3 and 4, urban sprawl beginning in the 1920s was embraced as a means to stimulate the economy. Nuclear power in the 1950s was not necessarily intended to meet the growing energy demand created with the sprawling of the U.S.'s urban zones. Instead, nuclear energy was initially developed by the U.S. as a hegemonic policy. The link between urban sprawl and nuclear power is that they were initiated and politically sponsored in the U.S. by economic elites.

U.S. economic elites championed nuclear power. In addition to the efforts of Atomic Energy Commission chairperson and investment banker Lewis Strauss, economic elites supported nuclear energy through the policy discussion groups of the Rockefeller Foundation and the Panel on the Impact of the Peaceful Uses of Atomic Energy. Conversely, at about the same time that the Panel on the Impact of the Peaceful Uses of Atomic Energy was strongly advocating for public financing of nuclear power, the economic elite leaders of the Association for Applied Solar Energy (based in Arizona) in 1955 expressed opposition to government support for solar energy.

U.S. Economic Elites and Nuclear Power

In a 1956 report the Rockefeller Foundation leadership outlines the foundation's early and leading role in the development of nuclear science:

The Rockefeller Foundation had . . . taken a lively interest in nuclear research . . . [I]ts funds had provided fellowship assistance to many whose prepared minds were to play a significant role. Among those . . . were such scientists as Robert F. Bacher (1930–32), Hans Bethe (1930–32), Arthur Compton (1919–20), Ernest O. Lawrence (1925–27), J.R. Oppenheimer (1927–28), Henry DeW. Smyth (1921–24), Edward Teller (1933–34), and John A. Wheeler (1933–35).

The authors of 1956 report go on to note:

In addition to opportunities for further study by individuals, Foundation funds assisted a number of laboratories with buildings, such items of equipment as electrostatic generators, cyclotrons, and betatrons, and free research funds for nuclear investigations. One notable group of laboratories was at the University of Copenhagen, where the physicist Niels Bohr, the chemist George von Hevesy, and the physiologist August Krogh led a distinguished company of scientists in pooling the resources of their several disciplines to work at such questions as the biological uses of isotopes. Another was the Radiation Laboratory of the University of California at Berkeley, where Ernest O. Lawrence devised and rapidly developed the cyclotron. The list would include the Collège de France, the University of Minnesota, Rochester, Stockholm, Washington University at St. Louis, the Massachusetts Institute of Technology, Columbia, Chicago, Princeton, the University of Sao Paulo. Two of the last grants made by the Foundation before the field of nuclear research was swept up into the wartime Manhattan Project provided $60,000 in 1942 to expedite the winding of the armature of the giant magnet of Lawrence's new 184-inch cyclotron, and a sum of $100,000 at about the same time to the Metallurgical Laboratory for the University of Chicago for research in problems of industrial hygiene arising from the handling of radioactive materials.[1]

The Rockefeller Foundation was founded in 1909 with a $50 million endowment by John D. Rockefeller Sr. and has been led by the Rockefeller family ever since.[2] The foundation has been a leading financial sponsor of scientific and public policy research throughout the twentieth century and into the contemporary era.[3] Edward H. Berman, in his history of the relationship of the Carnegie, Ford, and Rockefeller foundations to America's international relations, writes that these "foundations have consistently supported the major aims of United States foreign policy, while simultaneously helping to construct an intellectual framework supportive of that policy's major tenets."[4]

Within the Roosevelt administration, atomic research (i.e., the Manhattan Project) was overseen by Vannevar Bush.[5] Bush was a leading scientific administrator for the corporate community. Bush's biographer notes:

> In January 1938, Bush wooed a group of leading corporate researchers at a meeting in New York City, offering his revamped [MIT] engineering division as a forum for the benefit of corporate laboratories. In attendance were nearly 50 executives from some of the nation's leading companies: Procter & Gamble, Champion Paper, Colgate-Palmolive, Swift, Lilly Research, Burroughs Wellcome and Dodge.[6]

In 1939 Bush became president of the Carnegie Institution, which was "founded by wealthy industrialist Andrew Carnegie in 1902. The institution had an endowment of $33 million and spent $1.5 million annually on research." Bush's biographer described the institution's board of trustees as "larded with rich and influential members," which included Herbert Hoover, Frederic Delano (Franklin Roosevelt's uncle), and W. Cameron Forbes ("a member of a wealthy Boston family").[7]

The Atomic Energy Commission

In the 1950s and into the late 1960s the institutional support for nuclear science came predominately from the Atomic Energy Commission (AEC). A federal independent regulatory commission, the AEC funded virtually all research that went into nuclear energy during this period.[8]

Significantly, the AEC's general advisory committee advised against civilian nuclear in 1947.[9] This committee (made up of nine members) was "the top scientific" adviser to the AEC.[10] Headed at the time by arguably the top nuclear scientist in the world, J. Robert Oppenheimer, the general advisory committee concluded that "it does not appear hopeful to use natural uranium directly as an adequate source of fuel for atomic power." In a revised report, the committee nevertheless held that it did "not see how it would be possible under the most favorable circumstances to have any considerable portion of the present power supply of the world replaced by nuclear fuel before the expiration of twenty years."[11]

Ignoring the advice of its science advisory committee, the AEC, under the chairpersonship of Lewis Strauss, aggressively sponsored nuclear power. Strauss was a wealthy investment banker, who by his twenties was "accepted into the prestigious American Banking Association and New York Chamber of Commerce and his name appeared in *Who's Who* beginning in 1924."[12] By the time of his initial appointment to the AEC, Strauss's "wider circle of acquaintances included nearly all the powerful men who dominated American business, finance, and politics."[13] During his investment banking career, Strauss had become acquainted with the nuclear science community. Strauss's biographer holds that "by the middle of 1939, Strauss knew many of the leading [nuclear] physicists. They accepted him into their fraternity, if not as a fellow scholar, then as more than a mere financier."[14] In 1946, he was among the first five appointees to the AEC.[15] It is noteworthy that when Strauss left the AEC, he went to work for the Rockefeller family as a financial adviser.[16]

In 1953 Strauss was appointed chair of the AEC by the Eisenhower administration. As chair of the AEC, Strauss became a leading champion of nuclear energy. He personally brokered the first nuclear reactor used for the generation of electricity in the U.S. As his biographer reports, "Strauss had persuaded Philip Fleger, chief executive of Duquesne Light Company, to provide the site [in Shippingport, Pennsylvania], build the generator to be linked to the reactor, and connect the plant into Duquesne Light's network. . . .The AEC contributed a substantial portion of the capital cost." Strauss's biographer explains that Strauss "saw in [the reactor] an opportunity to demonstrate the potential for nuclear power":[17]

> Already he could see that in Europe, where the cost of producing electricity in conventional power plants was far greater than in the United States, atomic power could become cost-effective more quickly. An American firm had sold a reactor to Belgium in 1957, and Strauss expected other orders from European countries to follow quickly.

Strauss's biographer adds that "he knew that the design, manufacture, and operation of such plants [e.g., Shippingport] by American firms was the best way to insure the technological advances that would reduce the costs [of nuclear power] to a competitive level."[18] The Shippingport reactor was completed and operating in 1957.

Another prominent economic elite on the Atomic Energy Commission in the 1950s was Thomas E. Murray. According to the historians of the commission, Murray was

> a highly successful engineer and business executive in New York . . . and by the time he was appointed to the Commission in March 1950 he had been president of his own company, board member of his family company and several large corporations, trustee of several banks, and a receiver of the Interborough subway system.[19]

In 1953 Murray gave a speech before an "electricity utility convention" where he argued that "attaining economical nuclear power was just as vital to national security as the United States' preeminence in nuclear weapons." Murray went on to assert that "friendly nations were counting on the United States not only to protect them from Soviet aggression but also to supply them with nuclear power technology."[20]

As noted in chapter 2, during 1956 the report *Peaceful Uses of Atomic Energy* was submitted to the Congressional Joint Committee on Atomic Energy. The report was compiled by the Panel on the Impact of the Peaceful Uses of Atomic Energy. To write its report, the panel drew upon "qualified individuals, organizations and study groups, each operating autonomously and submitting their independent findings of fact and their conclusions to seminar discussion groups. . . . All in all, 327 people, all authorities in their field, took part in this work."[21] Numerous fossil fuel firms and trade associations helped write the panel report. Among them were the American Petroleum Institute (trade association); the American Gas Association (trade association); Appalachian Coals, Inc.; Gulf Oil; National Coal Association (trade association); National Petroleum Council (trade association); Shell Oil; Texas Co. (oil firm); Standard Oil of California; Standard Oil of Indiana; and Standard Oil of New Jersey. Other notable firms/institutions that participated in compiling the panel report included Chase Manhattan Bank, Ford Motor Co., DuPont Chemical, General Dynamics, General

Electric, General Motors, Monsanto Chemical, Pacific Gas & Electric, the Rockefeller Foundation, Sullivan & Cromwell (prominent New York law firm), and the *Washington Post*.[22]

This panel strongly recommended public financial support for civilian nuclear power. It asserted

> that, in the event that industry does not take on the full risks and burdens, the Commission [i.e., the AEC] should support a program to bring atomic power to a point where it can be used effectively and widely on a competitive basis, even to the construction with public funds of one full-scale 'demonstration' plant of each major reactor size and type.

The panel pressed that "the urgency associated with this [atomic power] program requires that the technological resources of atomic power be fully explored with *high priority*." The panel's concluding recommendation was that "atomic power be exploited as a source of electric power at a rate consistent with sound technological, economic and public policy considerations." The panel added that "if atomic power is exploited as a source of electric power at a rate consistent with sound technological, economic and public policy considerations, the impact will be totally beneficial at home and abroad."[23]

Under the heading "International Consequences of the Growth of Atomic Power," the panel speculated that "in the uncommitted areas of the world, American leadership in making atomic power available could be a strong influence in guiding these areas toward the course of freedom" (i.e., the American camp). Thus, "in this sense, atomic power acquires great importance in international relations," and "this consideration should strongly influence our national policy as to the rate at which the development of atomic power suitable for such purposes is pressed." The panel argued that "there is urgency for the development in the United States of atomic powerplants suited to the needs of the other nations of the free world."[24] The panel went on to argue that "atomic power may be the most tangible symbol of America's will to peace through the peaceful atom." Moreover, "If we fail to bring atomic power to the free world, other countries [i.e., the Soviet Union] will do so ahead of us."[25]

General Electric official Everett L. Hollis, writing in a 1957 political/legislative survey of civilian nuclear power in the U.S., reported that "the policy that atomic energy be developed as a Government monopoly was to some degree the result of the desire to maintain America's international monopoly." He also reported that "for reasons of foreign policy it was contended that the United States must have a vigorous peacetime atomic program."[26] During the 1950s, 1960s, and 1970s, General Electric was the U.S.'s leading builder of nuclear reactors.[27]

Solar Power

In contrast to nuclear power, which received substantial research support from the Rockefeller Foundation, and later gained the political endorsement of the U.S. corporate community, solar energy was historically starved of institutional help in the U.S. This lack of support was devastating to the science, engineering, and knowledge base of solar power.

Frank T. Kryza, in *The Power of Light: The Epic Story of Man's Quest to Harness the Sun*, outlines efforts in the late nineteenth and early twentieth centuries to develop industrial-scale solar power projects. Kryza, in particular, documents Frank Shuman's ingenuity in tapping the power of the sun during the first and second decade of the twentieth century. Shuman was a successful and wealthy Philadelphia inventor, who became interested in solar power. He conducted experiments demonstrating the promise of solar power—including the use of water to store ample amounts of heat energy that can be used at night or during cloudy days. Kryza describes the results of Shuman's initial solar power experiments:

> A good-sized coal-fired boiler in the first decade of the twentieth century—the time Shuman was conducting his experiments—would have been capable of generating 100,000 pounds of steam per hour, consuming 2 or 3 tons of coal to do so, to run a 3000-horsepower steam engine.
>
> Shuman's first full-scale demonstration project produced an average of 600 pounds of steam per hour, less than 1 percent of what a large coal-fired boiler might produce. He was tapping from sunlight the amount of energy per hour contained in about 30 pounds of coal. Given this was his first try, Shuman thought these results respectable.[28]

Kryza goes on to note that the problem of running a solar plant at night or during cloudy days "was not difficult to solve":

> For 6 hours of every 24-hour cycle, while the sun was shining at its brightest, the heat absorber [or solar collector] delivers water at 212 degrees Fahrenheit to both the steam turbine and the [water] tank. For the remaining 18 hours of the day, the engine would draw off hot water from the surplus stored in the tank, permitting engine operation round the clock.[29]

Kryza adds that "factoring in liberal figures for heat loss, a tank of the size proposed would still comfortably permit overnight operation of the plant at full throttle—and, with better insulation, even operation during a string of 1 or 2 cloudy days—without interruption."[30]

As Shuman was making gains with his solar experiments, he turned to the "financial oasis that had funded all his earlier ventures— the 'big-money' men of Philadelphia." However, "Pennsylvania was America's premier coal country, and these tycoons were already committed to fossil fuels." Shuman's "former backers reached modestly into their deep pockets, or not at all, to support his new venture . . . . He needed support from people who were not heavily invested in coal."[31]

Shuman was able to find political and financial support from the governments of Great Britain and Germany, both of which were interested in using industrial-scale solar power infrastructure to economically develop their African colonies:

> Practical demonstrations of Frank Shuman's solar technology in the years before World War I would win the enthusiastic support of Lord Kitchener of Khartoum, the British proconsul of Egypt; Sir Reginald Wingate, the iron-fisted ruler of neighboring Sudan; and earn Shuman an invitation from the German Reichstag to accept the equivalent in [German Marks] of $200,000 in venture capital—a colossal sum equivalent today to millions of dollars—to bring solar power to Germany's growing colonial possessions in Africa.[32]

Shuman's effort at solar powered irrigation of the Nile River was not entirely successful, but the British and German government remained committed to sun energy on the African continent. Unfortunately, World War I scuttled further attempts to perfect solar engineering in Africa, or elsewhere. Kryza notes solar power research "would not recover until the early 1980s."[33]

Solar Power and U.S. Economic Elites in the Post–World War II Period

While the corporate community was expressing its strong support for government (i.e., the AEC's) financial aid for the development and deployment of atomic power through the 1956 report *Peaceful Uses of Atomic Energy*, economic elites in November 1955 were noting their hostility toward government support of solar power. This opposition was outlined at the World Symposium on Applied Solar Energy. The symposium was organized by the Association for Applied Solar Energy (AFASE) and financed in part by the Rockefeller Foundation and Ford Foundation.[34] Historian Harvey Strum explains that the AFASE (founded in 1954) "initially, . . . consisted of a group of businessmen, lawyers, financiers, and educators from Arizona and California, with funds being raised in the Phoenix area." Among the founders were "Walter Bimson, chairman of the board of Valley National Bank in Phoenix." Strum notes that the "organizers of the AFASE shared . . . [a] free-enterprise approach to energy development, and they believed that 'practical utilization' of solar energy was contingent on American industry's getting involved in solar development."[35]

General chairman of AFASE Lewis W. Douglas gave the opening remarks to the symposium. Douglas at the time was chair of the board and director of the Southern Arizona Bank and Trust Company. In his remarks Douglas condemned the idea that "it is the responsibility of the state to distribute scarcities according to the range of priorities of purpose which the state should have the power to determine." In contrast, he spoke in positive tones about "a free and unrestrained application of scientific knowledge, functioning within the dominion of a free society, including the market place in which most economic claims are freely adjusted."[36]

Henry B. Sargent was president of AFASE. Sargent spent his entire professional career in the utility industry and was executive vice president of Central Arizona Light and Power and later president of Arizona Edison Co. By 1955 Sargent was president and director of the

American and Foreign Power Company.[37] Sargent, speaking as head of
AFASE, declared that the "ultimate success or failure" of solar energy
"lies largely with the business man." He added that "it is he who trans-
lates technological advances into the practical accomplishments which
benefit mankind and raises the standard of living and brings about a
better understanding among people."[38]

The seeming result of this laissez-faire attitude toward solar power
was that this form of energy received scant research support from
the federal government. In the article "American Solar Energy Policy,
1952–1970," historians of U.S. solar research policy Harvey Strum and
Fred Strum explain that "between 1952 and 1970 the National Science
Foundation (NSF) conducted almost all solar energy research, averaging
about $100,000 per year."[39]

AFASE changed its name in 1963 to the Solar Energy Society
(SES) and went defunct in 1970 (moving from Tempe to Melbourne,
Australia). Harvey Strum explains that "a relatively small number of
people were working in the [solar energy] field, and the general lack
of interest on the part of the federal government handicapped the
organization." He reports that "at the end of the 1960s, SES officials
concluded that solar energy would not replace fossil fuels until a great
deal of additional research had taken place and the cost of equipment
had been brought down to a competitive level."[40]

Harvey Strum and Fred Strum note that "even after the 1973 oil
crisis solar energy did not obtain funding in proportion to that given
to nuclear and fossil fuels. In 1974 the federal government spent $15
million on solar research and in 1975 spent $30 million."[41] Federal solar
policy was hobbled by a pronuclear bias within federal energy research
agencies, and by the opposition to certain types of solar research by
the electric utility industry.[42] The utility industry was opposed to the
development of solar power technology that would allow consumers
to generate their own electricity.[43] It was only during the last two years
of the Carter administration (1979–1980) that solar research attained
political and financial priority.[44] These years coincide with the oil crisis
brought on by the Iranian Revolution. Given the special interest politics
historically surrounding solar power, Strum and Strum writing in 1983
conclude that "with the exception of the last two years of the Carter
Administration, American energy policy has ignored the potential of
solar energy while relying on nuclear energy as the only real alternative to fossil fuels."[45]

Conclusion

Through the Panel on the Impact of the Peaceful Uses of Atomic Energy and its 1956 report, *Peaceful Uses of Atomic Energy*, the corporate community in the U.S. manifested broad support for civilian nuclear power, as well as public financing for it. In the 1950s and 1960s the federal government (through the AEC) financially sponsored nuclear science and engineering—including the building of nuclear facilities. The AEC annual spending on civilian nuclear power "rose from a cost of less than $20 million in 1954 to over $100 million five years later; and the scope was greatly expanded toward reactor construction and demonstration."[46] U.S. economic elites ostensibly embraced nuclear power for strategic and geopolitical reasons. Industrial-scale solar power, in contrast, had no obvious strategic advantages. In other words, it was not evident that U.S. development/deployment of industrial-scale solar power could enhance its geopolitical/hegemonic position. The result is that throughout the late nineteenth and twentieth centuries research into the industrial-scale collection/use of solar power received virtually no governmental (nor institutional) support in the U.S.

A key thesis of this book is that the U.S. is not a "normal" country when it comes to the question of energy. On the demand side, the U.S. fosters increased energy consumption through urban sprawl. In chapter 3 I outlined how economic elites, through the 1921 President's Conference on Unemployment, successfully championed urban sprawl as a means to counter the economic downturn in the aftermath of World War I. Through the Federal Housing Authority, economic elites further propagated urban sprawl in an effort to address the Great Depression (chapter 4).

On the supply side, the U.S. historically drew upon its sizable fossil fuel supplies to fill the energy demand of urban sprawl. As shown in the following chapter, when its domestic supply proved inadequate, the U.S. sought to dominate the petroleum supplies of the Persian Gulf. Indicative of the fact that the U.S. pursued nuclear power primarily for hegemonic reasons, and not to meet domestic energy demand, is the fact that the U.S. stopped ordering new nuclear reactors after the oil shocks of the 1970s. This is in contrast to other countries, particularly Germany and France (next chapter), which sought to greatly expand their nuclear power capacity in response to these shocks.

Chapter Six

Global Oil Politics

Doug Stokes and Sam Raphael in their volume, *Global Energy Security and American Hegemony*, point to the overtly hegemonic dynamics of U.S. foreign policy in relationship to oil.[1] The U.S's dominance of the world's petroleum gives it strategic leverage over virtually every country in the world. America's tar (or oil) sands policy is consistent with this.

In *Urban Sprawl, Global Warming, and the Empire of Capital*, I argue that there is a less obvious, but ostensibly as important, hegemonic component to U.S. international oil policies—namely, urban sprawl.[2] A prime idea that has driven U.S. oil policy has been to sustain urban sprawl in America (at seemingly all costs). This becomes particularly evident in the aftermath of the oil shocks of the 1970s, where instead of curbing demand (i.e., urban sprawl) the U.S. government sought to cement its dominance over the petroleum supplies of the Middle East. The U.S. is also bringing Canadian oil sands online.

The countries of Western and Central Europe, in contrast, have tried to bolster their energy security by limiting their exposure to the international energy market. First, by limiting automobile dependency; second, by expanding domestic nuclear power in the aftermath of the 1970s oil shocks; and third, by growing its capacity to capture energy from the sun (solar and wind power).

Therefore, this chapter is divided into two parts. First, I describe the U.S. response to the oil shocks of the 1970s. Second, I outline European energy policy—with a specific emphasis on France's nuclear power policy and the European Union's clean energy program. What comes into relief is the U.S's and Europe's divergent approaches to energy security—with the U.S. trying to facilitate more fuel fossils (especially oil) onto the world market (including the Canadian tar sands) and Europe undertaking an effort to minimize/eliminate its fossil fuel consumption.

The Oil Shocks of the 1970s

In 1973 the Persian Gulf region of the Middle East took on particular importance for the Western allies. What came into relief in 1973 is that the region contained the key supplies of petroleum for the Western world. The petroleum-bearing countries of the region are Iran, Iraq, Kuwait, Saudi Arabia, United Arab Emirates, and Qatar, with Iran, Iraq, Kuwait, and Saudi Arabia being the primary producing countries for the world's oil market. The Persian Gulf nations today possess the majority of the world's known petroleum reserves—Saudi Arabia alone is estimated to hold 20 to 25 percent of the world's proven reserves of petroleum.[3]

The Persian Gulf's strategic importance is in significant part the result of U.S. oil policies. This is particularly apparent on the demand side. As U.S. cities became increasingly sprawled,[4] and as a result more automobile dependent,[5] U.S. oil consumption steadily climbed.[6] Between 1946 and 1953, for instance, U.S. gasoline usage went from thirty billion gallons annually to forty-nine billion, amounting to a yearly growth rate of slightly over 7.2 percent. In 1958 U.S. gasoline consumption exceeded fifty-nine billion gallons.[7]

U.S. consumption had a detrimental effect on its petroleum production. This was important because the U.S. was historically capable of reducing world petroleum prices through increased production. By 1970, however, U.S. oil production had peaked, and it was no longer capable of regulating world prices.[8] When Saudi Arabia imposed a selective embargo on countries favorable to Israel in 1973, the U.S. was importing about 35 percent of its oil needs, and it could not respond to the shortfall created by the embargo with domestic production.[9]

Therefore, leading up to the oil shocks of the 1970s U.S. oil reserves were depleted predominately because of high levels of domestic consumption. What is theoretically and historically significant, however, is the response of the U.S. government when the dependency and vulnerability of the U.S. economy on foreign sources of petroleum came into stark relief in 1973. No effort was put forward by the U.S. government to rollback or limit urban sprawl and the automobile dependence that it spawned.

The U.S. responded militarily to its apparent dependency. U.S. policymakers used the country's superior political and military position to ensure that Persian Gulf oil remained in the U.S. sphere of influence, and that the region's petroleum sufficiently flowed. Until 1979, the U.S. amply supplied the Iranian government with military equipment and training to militarily safeguard the petroleum reserves of the region against any Soviet aggression. After the U.S.'s client regime in Iran collapsed (which brought on a second oil crisis), the U.S. sought to directly build up its military capabilities in the region, culminating with a direct military presence after the first Persian Gulf War in 1991.[10]

This emphasis on the supply side to deal with the U.S.'s energy problems of the 1970s is reflected in two reports put out by the Twentieth Century Fund (now the Century Fund). This organization is a foundation that in the 1950s and 1960s sponsored studies on the natural resource needs of the U.S.'s expanding economy.[11] The Twentieth Century Fund created two policy-planning groups in the early 1970s composed largely of economic elites that put forward proposals to deal with the U.S.'s petroleum situation. One task force, convened in 1973, was titled "The Twentieth Century Fund Task Force on United States Energy Policy." On this task force was a director and senior vice president of Exxon, a vice chairman of the board of the American Electric Power Company, Walter J. Levy (a consultant to most major oil firms[12]), a vice chairman of the board of Texas Commerce Bancshares (a major Texas bank[13]), and the chairman of the board of Carbomin International Corporation (an international mining firm). The other task force, formed in 1974, was known as "The Twentieth Century Fund Task Force on the International Oil Crisis." Walter J. Levy and the executives from Carbomin and Texas Commerce Bancshares also served on this task force. Also on this Twentieth Century Fund task force was the chairman of the board from Atlantic Richfield (an oil firm), a managing director from Dillon, Read & Co. (a leading New York investment management firm), the chairman of the board from the Louis Dreyfus Corporation (an investment management firm), the chairman and president of The First National Bank of Chicago, and a consultant to Wells Fargo Bank (a major California bank). Also on these task forces were academics (mostly economists) from Princeton, Harvard, MIT, and the University of Virginia, as well as the presidents of Resources for the Future (which was on the two task forces) and the Carnegie Institution (only on the energy policy group)—both of which are economic elite–led research institutes.[14]

In the wake of the 1973 oil shortage and the Organization of Petroleum Exporting Countries (OPEC) seeking to maintain high oil prices, both of the Twentieth Century Fund's task forces advised the U.S. to strive to develop sources of oil and energy outside of the OPEC countries. This would serve to reduce the strategic positioning of OPEC countries over petroleum and petroleum prices. OPEC includes all the Persian Gulf oil producers, plus Algeria, Angola, Ecuador, Equatorial Guinea, Gabon, Libya, Nigeria, Venezuela, and Indonesia. The Twentieth Century Fund's task force on the international oil crisis advised that "the best remedy for the problems caused by the increased price of oil [brought about by OPEC members] would be, simply, to lower the price" of petroleum. "The Task Force believes that this remedy should be sought through reliance on market forces."[15] The task force goes on to explain in its report that *"the most effective means of exerting market pressure will be to accelerate exploration for crude and develop producing capacity from"* areas outside of OPEC.[16] The task force on U.S. energy policy averred

> *that it is essential that the nation take firm and forceful action to implement a comprehensive near-term energy program designed to assure greater availability of domestic supplies of oil and other sources of energy.*[17]

The authors of this task force's report went on to explain:

> Our present dependence on OPEC cannot be eliminated, but it can—and should—be lessened, thus reducing the competition for OPEC supplies and consequently the political and economic power of the cartel. While we cannot achieve independence, a lessening of our dependence can make a disruption of supplies or a more aggressive price policy on the part of OPEC much less likely.[18]

Therefore, the key recommendations put forward by these policy-planning groups, made up in large part of economic elites, in light of U.S. oil dependency on OPEC countries was to expand the supply of available energy free from OPEC control, and not necessarily to reduce energy consumption.

In addition to calling for greater oil production outside of OPEC control, both these groups, in their reports, called for greater energy efficiency, or what they labeled in their reports as "conservation." The difficulty is that increased energy efficiency does not necessarily reduce overall consumption levels.[19] The energy policy group, in a section of its report entitled "Measures to Promote Conservation," *"endorse[d] the use of special incentives to encourage further investment in energy-saving capital goods and consumer durables because conserving energy is as important as increasing the supply."*[20] It specifically suggested in its report the use of a "luxury" tax to discourage the purchase of large, less efficient, automobiles. Moreover, the implementation of "excise taxes levied annually and collected with state registration fees also might serve to encourage quicker scrapping of cars that consume above-average amounts of gasoline."[21] Finally,

> the Task Force favor[ed] the continuation of such energy-conserving measures as reasonable speed limits on highways, building standards that reduce the use of energy for heating and cooling, and requirements that appliances bear tags disclosing their energy-utilization efficiency.[22]

The task force on the international oil crisis did not set out specific conservation proposals. Instead, it deferred to the energy policy task force on this.[23]

The Committee for Economic Development in a 1974 "National Policy Statement" titled *Achieving Energy Independence*, also prioritized efficiency as a conservation strategy: "Opportunities to improve efficiency of energy use should be exploited now and should receive as much attention as opportunities to increase supply."[24] This policy statement was directly overseen by the Subcommittee on Problems and Potentials of Economic Growth: The Energy Problem. On this subcommittee were executives from Exxon; Detroit Edison Co.; Pacific Power & Light; Southern California Edison Co.; Atlantic Richfield; Sears, Roebuck; Fidelity Bank; Princess Coal; General Electric; Westinghouse; Morgan Stanley; Trans World Airlines; and Aluminum Company of America (ALCOA). Also on this subcommittee was Walter J. Levy (who, as noted, served on both of the Twentieth Century Fund task forces).[25]

Increased energy efficiency can lead to overall lower levels of petroleum consumption. Energy savings from increased efficiency, however, can be offset by increased economic growth.[26] This is especially the case within sprawled urban regions, where greater levels of economic activity can lead to a larger workforce driving to and from work and increased demand for spacious homes on the urban periphery. So whereas automobiles may become more fuel efficient, in the context of diffusely organized cities more automobiles and longer driving distances can lead to greater overall gasoline/oil consumption—despite gains made in fuel efficiency.[27] This is precisely what has transpired in the United States. The current U.S. automobile fleet is more efficient than the U.S. automotive fleet of the early 1970s.[28] Because, however, of a substantially enlarged automobile population and ever-increasing amounts of driving, gasoline/diesel consumption in the U.S. today substantially exceeds that of the 1970s. According to energy economist Ian Rutledge, in 1970 driving in the U.S. consumed 7.1 million barrels per day of petroleum, whereas by 2001 that figure increased to 10.1 million.[29] Today, according to the U.S. Department of Energy, driving in the U.S. consumes about 15 percent of total global oil production.[30]

In large part because of the steady growth of gasoline/diesel consumption in the U.S.,[31] its economy consumes 20 to 25 percent of the world's total petroleum production (with less than 5 percent of the global population).[32] This is especially glaring, because in the aftermath of the spike in oil prices in the 1970s, U.S. factories and utilities shifted from petroleum-based fuels to other sources of energy (mostly, coal, natural gas, and nuclear power).[33]

U.S. Energy Security and Unconventional Oil

Thus, the U.S. has historically sought to establish its energy security by expanding the pool of available fossil fuels—with a focus on petroleum. This thinking extended to unconventional fossil fuels—and specifically to the Canadian oil sands. This conception of unconventional petroleum (synthetic fuel) as part of North America's energy security was reinforced by the oil shocks of the 1970s, with the Twentieth Century Fund's task force on "United States Energy Policy" in 1977 "*recommend[ing] an extensive program of government-supported research and development for new energy sources.*" The task force specifically pointed to oil shale and synthetic gas derived from coal as potential alternatives to petroleum-based gasoline.[34] The CED, in *Achieving Energy Independence*, argued in 1974 "that to the extent necessary the government fund research, development, and demonstration pilot plants for synthetic fuels from oil shale and coal."[35]

The onset of the twenty-first century has witnessed a new energy shock of sorts—as oil prices spiked at $147 a barrel in 2008. Following 2008, petroleum prices on the world market tended to persist at around $100 a barrel (i.e., historic highs).[36] With concerns about oil prices and, more broadly, available supplies of petroleum, the Council on Foreign Relations (CFR) sponsored a 2009 study on the Canadian oil sands—titled *The Canadian Oil Sands: Energy Security vs. Climate Change* (authored by Michael A. Levi). The Advisory Committee overseeing this study included officials from the oil behemoths Exxon Mobil and Chevron.[37] Also on this committee was Tara Billingsley, who at the time was a staff member on the Energy and Natural Resources Committee of the U.S. Senate. John Deutch, CIA director under the Clinton administration,[38] served on this advisory committee—as did individuals representing the Natural Resources Defense Council, the Pew Center on Global Climate Change, and the World Resources Institute. Steven Mufson, who regularly reports on energy issues for the *Washington Post*, was on the advisory committee. In addition to Exxon Mobil and Chevron, private firms represented on this committee included PIRA Energy Group, ARC Financial Corp., and Louis Capital Markets.[39]

In the "Foreword" to the Canadian oils sands report, the president of the CFR summarizes its recommendations. The summary identifies tar sands production as bolstering America's energy security—noting that the report observes that the "security benefits" of the oil sands "cannot be ignored." The CFR president goes on to explain that "the report's recommendations focus on policies that would provide incentives to cut the emissions generated in producing each barrel of crude from the oil sands, but in a way that is careful to avoid directly discouraging increased production."[40] It is noteworthy that oil exports from Canada (including oil sands petroleum) to the United States have already increased 3.8 million barrels per day from 2.5 million barrels in 2008—while imports from OPEC countries have significantly declined.[41]

Since its inception in 1921 the CFR has been an economic elite–led policy discussion group designed to treat questions of foreign affairs.[42] During its early history the CFR received significant financial contributions from Chase National Bank, Standard Oil of New Jersey, IBM, General Motors, General Electric, Texaco, and the National City Bank of New York.[43] Inderjeet Parmar, who has written extensively on the CFR,[44] describes in the following the corporate director positions held by the fifty-five CFR directors for the years 1921–1946:

> The fifty-five leaders held at least seventy-four corporate directorships. . . . The corporations concerned were among the

largest in the United States: Myron C. Taylor of U.S. Steel and AT&T; Leon Fraser, Owen D. Young and Philip D. Reed of General Electric; Clarence M. Wooley and Lewis W. Douglas of General Motors; R.C. Leffingwell of J. Morgan and Co.; and Frank Polk, Douglas, John H. Finley, David F. Houston, and Reed of Mutual Life Insurance Company of New York.[45]

Reflective of the elite social standing of CFR directors during this period, the fifty-five directors of Parmar's study "held, on average, at least three [elite social club] memberships, with the Cosmos and Metropolitan clubs in Washington, DC, and Century and Knickerbockers of New York, being the most popular. In all, 170 club memberships were reported."[46]

The CFR's seeming identification of the Canadian oil sands as part of America's energy security strategy is significant insofar as this organization has historically played a key role in the making of U.S. foreign policy. Perhaps most significant, CFR was central in formulating American grand strategy (i.e., U.S. containment policy) for the post–World War II period.[47]

Next, I turn to Western and Central Europe's response to the energy crises of the 1970s. Unlike the U.S., Europe never developed the automobile/oil dependency that the U.S. did. Moreover, when the 1973 oil crisis struck, Europe turned to nuclear power as a means to reduce its exposure to the world petroleum market. Additionally, in the present era of persistently high oil prices, the European Union is making a significant push toward the development and deployment of solar and wind power technology.

European Post–World War II Oil Policies

The advanced industrialized countries of the Federal German Republic (i.e., West Germany) and France responded to the oil crises of the 1970s by trying to severely limit their oil use. These nations had little appreciable domestic petroleum production. Due to major oil strikes in 1966 along its northern coast, Great Britain had less immediate need to reduce its oil use. Nevertheless, the nations of Western Europe had not developed the petroleum vulnerability that the U.S. had by the 1970s. This is particularly because urban zones in these countries were not as sprawled and automotive dependent as the U.S.'s.[48]

Postwar Western European concerns about energy security were manifest in the 1955 Armand report and the 1956 Hartley report, both sponsored by Council of Ministers of the Organisation for European Economic Co-operation (OEEC). Primarily because of fear over trade imbalances, the Armand report, entitled *Some Aspects of the European Energy Problem: Suggestions for Collective Action* and named after its author, Louis Armand (a French government official), advised against dependency on foreign sources of oil. Instead, Armand advised Western European countries to rely on domestic sources of energy, on sources of energy that were in Europe's African colonies, and especially on nuclear power.[49]

Shortly after receiving the Armand report, the OEEC created a Commission for Energy. The commission sponsored what became known as the Hartley report, named after its chairperson, Harold Hartley of Great Britain. The authors of this report extended their concerns over oil imports beyond trade imbalance issues and expressed fears about oil security. According to the Hartley report, "there are inevitable risks in the increasing dependence on Western Europe on outside [oil] supplies, particularly when most of them must come from one small area of the world" (i.e., the Persian Gulf).[50] Accordingly, Western Europe by 1975 should only draw 20 percent to 33 percent of its energy from imported petroleum, and the rest should predominately come from coal.[51] The Hartley report authors averred that "coal must remain the mainstay of the Western European energy economy."[52] They recommended that Western European domestic coal production satisfy half of the region's energy needs, and the rest could be met with hydropower, natural gas, oil, imported coal, and nuclear energy.[53]

Both the Hartley and Armand reports counseled that Western European governments should intervene to ensure the region's energy stability. The Hartley commission suggested that

> in order to deal effectively with the urgent problems involved in the supply and demand of energy, each member country will require an energy policy suited to its own circumstances and its needs and resources. This policy should include some measure of coordination between the different forms of energy.[54]

The Armand Commission held that OEEC countries should avoid "a situation in which competition between the various forms of energy acts to the detriment of the community as a whole."[55]

Subsequent to the Armand and Hartley reports, the OEEC formed the Energy Advisory Commission, under the chairpersonship of Professor Austin Robinson. In 1960 this energy commission put forward a new report on European energy, entitled *Towards a New Energy Pattern in Europe*. Unlike the Armand or Hartley reports, which advocated government promotion of domestic coal (Hartley) or nuclear power (Armand) in order to limit imported oil use, the Robinson Commission argued that Western Europe should rely on inexpensive imported petroleum for much of its energy needs. As to the security of oil supplies, new discoveries in Venezuela, West Africa, and Libya, and "in particular, discoveries of oil and natural gas in the Sahara [e.g., Algeria] have created new possibilities of important supplies in an area more closely integrated into the economy of Western Europe." Therefore, "as a result, there has been made possible a wider diversification of oil supplies to Western Europe."[56] The Robinson energy commission went on to argue that "it does not seem likely that shortages of oil or other supplies will make themselves felt in acute form by 1975."[57] With regard to the region's balance of payments, the commission asserted that "if Western Europe can maintain its share of world markets for manufactures, the import of the increased proportions of the total supplies of energy that have emerged from our study may reasonably be expected to be within the probable limits of its capacity."[58] Hence, the way to cover the costs of imported energy is to maintain or expand Western Europe's world market share of industrial products. A key means to do this is to keep the cost of energy inputs low. Thus "when formulating a long-term energy policy, the paramount consideration should be a plentiful supply of low-cost energy." Additionally, "the general interest is best served by placing the least possible obstacles in the way of economic development of the newer and cheaper sources of energy."[59] In other words, Western European governments should not subsidize nuclear power or coal to the detriment of abundant and inexpensive petroleum supplies.

Especially in the areas of electricity and industrial production, as well as home heating, Western European countries did pursue the more liberal course advocated by the Robinson Commission. As a result, by the early 1970s, 60 percent of this region's energy needs were met through imported oil.[60] In the case of automobile transportation, however, Western European countries have historically instituted more restrictive policies. Haugland and his associates, experts on European energy, point out that in Western and Central Europe "the share of taxes in transport fuel—in particular for gasoline—is generally the highest of all end-use prices. In Europe the tax share in unleaded gasoline [for example] is substantially above the actual production costs, ranging from 50 to 75 percent of the end-user price." They go on to assert that "not surprisingly, in the United States, where gasoline taxes are the lowest in the OECD [Organisation for Economic Co-operation and Development], the average fuel consumption ranks among the highest."[61] By way of comparison, according to a study of the Energy Information Administration (a U.S. government agency), while the average cost of gasoline was recently $2.68 per gallon in the U.S., it was $7.00 in Britain, $7.19 in Germany, $6.97 in Italy, and $6.89 in France. These price differences are mostly, if not solely, attributable to taxation.[62] On a per capita basis, the U.S. uses more than twice as much gasoline as these other countries.[63]

There is a strategic advantage to limiting oil use in the realm of transportation while allowing it to expand in such areas of the economy as electricity and industrial production. There are readily available substitutes for petroleum products in these latter activities: coal, natural gas, nuclear power, wind power, solar, among others.[64] This is not the case for automotive transportation. Thus, if there is a severe shortage of crude, the housing stock, industrial infrastructure, and retail outlets that are only accessible via automobile can become virtually worthless overnight.

With the oil shortages of the 1970s the governments of France and West Germany sought to slash their petroleum consumption by greatly expanding the use of nuclear power. This strategy, however, sparked the Green environmental movement on the continent,[65] as the question of what to do with the highly radioactive waste from nuclear power production has never been satisfactorily answered.[66] This movement was more successful in Germany than in France in derailing plans to center industrial and electricity production on nuclear energy. Political scientist Michael Hatch contends that these different outcomes can be attributed to each country's respective political system. The French employ a presidential system, where policymaking power is in large part insulated from the public in the executive branch. The German parliamentary form of government is more sensitive and responsive to social movements and strong shifts in public opinion.[67] Nevertheless, France's shift to nuclear power,[68] the more modest increase of nuclear power in other countries of the region,[69] greater use of coal and natural gas, and increases in energy efficiency did result in a decline in petroleum consumption in Western Europe, whereas oil consumption in the U.S. increased after the energy shocks of the 1970s.[70]

It is worthwhile outlining France's move toward a nuclear-centered economy in the mid-1970s. In 1974 the French government announced a plan to expand its nuclear program, projecting thirteen nuclear plants of 1,000 Mw each to be completed by 1980. The long-term plan was to build by 1985 fifty reactors in twenty locations providing 25 percent of France's energy and by the year 2000 two hundred reactors in forty nuclear parks providing more than half of France's projected energy needs. In the 1980s, France became more nuclear than any other country, deriving 75 percent or more of its electricity from this one source. Today, fifty-nine nuclear power reactors operate in France. Nuclear electricity produced in France is used in other European Union countries. France is the largest exporter of electricity in the world.[71]

In a move that will economically protect its nuclear industry, France in 2011 banned the mining (hydrofracking) of oil and gas shale.[72] Significantly, France "is viewed as having some of the most promising shale oil and gas prospects."[73] Another observer explains that France "has some of the largest deposits of unconventional gas in Europe."[74] The countries of Western and Central Europe have generally resisted the practice of hydrofracking.[75]

Among EU nations, Poland has aggressively pursued hydrofracking, but the hoped-for production of natural gas from shale there has not materialized. The prospect of hydrofracking in Europe is hampered by the fact that "European governments had not been willing to make the necessary investment in research and development that helped companies figure out how to extract natural gas and oil from impermeable rock formations in the United States."[76]

In the first decade of the 2000s, as world energy prices were rising,[77] the EU in 2007 adopted the 20/20/20 policy.[78] One goal of this policy is for the region to derive 20 percent of its energy from "clean" renewable sources by 2020. (This target in 2014 was revised to 27 percent of total EU energy to be drawn from clean renewable sources by 2030.[79]) In an effort to promote solar power in particular, countries in the EU have instituted "feed-in-tariff" programs, where power companies pay high rates for electricity generated from photovoltaic cells. These cells, placed on the rooftops of homes, directly convert sunlight into electricity.[80] There are also plans for the EU to draw solar- and wind-generated electricity from North Africa.[81] Another goal is a 20 percent reduction of energy consumption in the EU by 2020 (through efficiency gains).[82] The EU's 20/20/20 policy is cast as an effort to combat global warming (with one goal being a 40 percent reduction in greenhouse gas emissions by 2030 compared to 1990 emission levels).[83] Nevertheless, the 20/20/20 policies would have the effect of reducing the EU's fossil fuel usage and enhancing the region's energy security and autonomy.[84] Consonant with the EU's 20/20/20 energy goals, Germany, as part of its 2011 plan to dismantle its domestic nuclear power plants, is making it a political priority to expand its wind and solar power capacity.[85]

Consistent with its effort to move away from fossil fuels and toward more secure energy sources (nuclear, wind, solar), the EU has instituted a permit trading system intended to drive up the price of carbon-based fuels (oil, natural gas, coal). Permits are required by firms that emit carbon dioxide[86]—an inevitable outcome when burning fossil fuels for energy. Importantly, the EU recently adopted a plan to reduce the number of permits in circulation in the hope that such an action would drive up the price of permits and by implication the cost of using fossil fuels as energy.[87]

Conclusion

The U.S. undermined its national energy security by promoting, fostering, and maintaining sprawled urban zones. Even when it was patently evident that the U.S. was dependent on foreign petroleum to meet its energy needs (i.e., the oil shocks of the 1970s), no effort was undertaken to curb the key source of America's energy vulnerability—urban sprawl. Instead, the U.S. responded by seeking to dominate those regions of the world where surplus petroleum is located—most importantly, the Persian Gulf area. During the decades of the 2000s and 2010s, oil prices have gone significantly upward. The U.S. responded to this "tight" oil reality by developing unconventional fossil fuels in North America (oil and gas shale, as well as oil sands). America adopted this tack despite the severe environmental effects of doing so (global warming).

In contrast to the U.S., the countries of Western and Central Europe have tried to limit their exposure to the world energy market by limiting automobile dependency. After the oil shocks of the 1970s, France, in particular, significantly expanded its nuclear capacity as a means of bolstering energy security and the economic stability of the region. Moreover, in the present environment of high oil prices, the countries of the EU have aggressively fostered solar and wind power (e.g., the 20/20/20 program). This includes a permit trading program intended to create positive economic incentives for the use of low/no carbon energy. Importantly, in sharp contrast to the U.S., EU countries, for the most part, have foregone hydrofracking. Most glaringly, France (despite the significant energy potential of its shale rock deposits) has banned hydrofracking. The prevention of hydrofracking helps to maintain a favorable economic milieu for low/no carbon energy sources (nuclear, solar, wind).

A component of my thesis is that economic elites played the key role in shaping the U.S. policy on alternative energy. In chapter 5 I showed how economic elites led on the questions of nuclear energy and solar power. The next chapter focuses on the alternative energy of plutonium.

After it was clear that the U.S. no longer held a monopoly on nuclear fuel/technology in the 1970s and that a global plutonium market was seemingly on the cusp of being established, economic elite policy-planning groups engaged in discussions over American nuclear policy. One strand of thought among these groups was the internationalization of the nuclear fuel cycle. The other strand can be characterized as nationalist in outlook, with the argument posited that the U.S. should shut down its civilian plutonium efforts and strongly work to prevent the development of a worldwide market in plutonium. This hostile view toward plutonium was reiterated in 2012 by the Obama administration's Blue Ribbon Commission on America's Nuclear Future.

One of the ironies of the U.S. decision to end its pursuit of civilian plutonium use in the late 1970s is that the U.S. government (since the 1920s) has been domestically fostering energy-profligate urban sprawl (chapters 3 and 4). The result of the U.S. government's pro–urban sprawl policies is that America is by far (among countries with populations higher than forty million) the largest per capita consumer of energy (especially oil) and per capita emitter of the key greenhouse gas (i.e., carbon dioxide).[88]

Thus, U.S. nuclear/plutonium policies coupled with its urban sprawl policies have significantly contributed to placing humanity on an unstable, unsustainable energy/climate trajectory. The U.S.'s walking away from nuclear and plutonium energy in the aftermath of the oil shock of 1973 indicates that the U.S. pursued these energy sources primarily for foreign policy purposes, and not for reasons related to domestic energy demand.

Chapter Seven

Plutonium and U.S. Foreign Policy

The International Energy Agency in 2010 concluded that half of the world's known oil supplies have been exhausted.[1] As a result humanity is pursuing petroleum in increasingly remote areas—such as the Arctic Ocean and deep sea locations (e.g., in the farthest depths of the Gulf of Mexico).[2] Conventional natural gas supplies in North America are rapidly declining, and producers are now turning to the gas extraction technique known as hydrofracking—using massive amounts of water and other chemicals to force gas trapped deep below up to the earth's surface.[3] Coal mines are being burrowed great distances underground (and mountain tops are being destroyed) to access existing supplies.[4]

Moreover, the heavy reliance on fossil fuels has created the global warming phenomenon. Ironically, the decline in fossil fuel supplies is potentially accelerating climate change.[5] As conventional sources of petroleum decline, "dirtier" or higher carbon forms of liquid energy are being used—most glaringly the tar or oil sands of Canada.[6] Part of the methane released by hydrofracturing (aka, fracking) is lost into the atmosphere.[7] (Methane is a potent heat-trapping gas.[8]) Also, coal remains a mainstay for electricity generation.[9] (Coal is the most carbon intense of the fossil fuels.)

While fossil fuel depletion and global warming are well understood by scientists and the energy supply industry, humankind remains on its current track of using fossil fuels (and emitting greenhouse gases) at unsustainable levels. As a result, there are real questions as to whether civilization and humanity itself will survive to the next century.[10]

Environmental activists and scientists are focusing on "green" energy sources to resolve our energy and climate crises.[11] Perhaps rightly so, but we must engage in historical analysis to fully understand why humanity has come to so heavily rely on fossil fuels. Going into the 1970s, governments in the U.S., Western Europe, and Japan were actively looking at plutonium as an alternative to fossil fuels—particularly as a source for electricity.[12] In the West, the U.S. was initially the strongest champion of nuclear power. During the 1970s, however, the U.S.'s Carter administration was instrumental in undermining the pursuit of plutonium-fueled nuclear power plants. By the late 1970s, it became evident that the U.S. could no longer dominate Western Europe's and Japan's nuclear energy systems, and these countries were beginning to export plutonium-making capacity (see chapter 1).

The proliferation of plutonium-producing technology threatened America's global hegemonic position. If plutonium could have been successfully produced by numerous countries, the U.S.'s global political leverage as a result of its fossil fuel policies would have been greatly diminished.

Consistent with economic elite theory, economic elites were central in the development of the U.S. nuclear/plutonium policies. As noted in chapter 5, initial economic elite support for nuclear science came at its earliest inception through the Rockefeller Foundation and later through Lewis Strauss and the Atomic Energy Commission (AEC). Additionally, in the 1950s the Panel on the Impact of the Peaceful Uses of Atomic Energy was a visible conduit of economic elite political support for civilian nuclear energy. Ultimately, in the late 1970s decisive opposition to civilian plutonium would be expressed through the Ford Foundation. It is worthwhile, however, to outline the internationalization position (with regard to civilian plutonium) cast by the economic elite–led Committee for Economic Development (CED). This would parallel the position conveyed in the International Nuclear Fuel Cycle Evaluation report (sponsored by the International Atomic Energy Agency), composed by nuclear scientists and government officials from throughout the world. In 2012 the Blue Ribbon Commission on America's Nuclear Future (formed under the auspices of the U.S. secretary of energy) recommended against reinitiating the U.S. civilian plutonium program.

Plutonium Politics in the Late 1970s

As noted in chapter 1, by the late 1960s and early 1970s, the U.S. lost its lead in the civilian nuclear energy field, and what remained of U.S. nuclear dominance was the capacity to enrich uranium. (The enrichment of uranium refers to the process of increasing in nuclear fuel the amount of uranium-235 [^{235}U]—the most readily/easily fissionable kind of uranium.) What pushed nuclear power to the top of the international agenda was the 1975 agreement between Germany and Brazil, which would have had the former transfer to the latter enrichment and nuclear waste recycling infrastructure.[13]

With the German agreement to transfer the entire nuclear fuel cycle to Brazil, and concerns being raised about weapons proliferation, the Committee for Economic Development (CED) in 1976 produced a "Statement on National Policy" entitled *Nuclear Energy and National Security*. This statement was a proposal to transfer civilian nuclear fuel facilities in the West under the control of international auspices. Writing in 1976, the CED held that "for three decades, the Committee for Economic Development has had a respected influence on business and public policy. . . . Composed of two hundred leading business executives and educators, CED is devoted to these two objectives," first,

> to develop, through objective research and informed discussion, findings and recommendations for private and public policy which will contribute to preserving and strengthening our free society, achieving steady economic growth at high employment and reasonably stable prices, increasing productivity and living standards, providing greater and more equal opportunity for every citizen. . . . [Second,] to bring about increasing understanding by present and future leaders in business, government, and education and among concerned citizens of the importance of these objectives and the ways in which they can be achieved.[14]

On the CED Board of Trustees were chief executive officers (CEOs) from such firms as Exxon, Ford Motor Co., Atlantic Richfield (oil), IBM, Bethlehem Steel, Bechtel (engineering and construction), General Motors, Chase Manhattan Bank, Goodyear Tire & Rubber, Goldman Sachs (a leading investment firm), Texas Instruments, and Standard Oil of California (later Chevron).[15]

Directly responsible for the CED's *Nuclear Energy and National Security* statement/report was its Subcommittee on Nuclear Energy and National Security. On this subcommittee was an executive from Westinghouse Electric, one of two leading global firms at the time in the nuclear industry. (The other being General Electric, who had an executive on the CED Research and Policy Committee—which oversaw the formulation of the *Nuclear Energy* report.) Also on the subcommittee

was the president of the CBS Broadcast Group, the CEO of Tenneco (oil), and the president of the Northrop Corporation (military contractor).[16]
The authors of *Nuclear Energy and National Security* noted:

> The purpose of this statement is to explore ways to prepare or at least to slow the spread of individual national capabilities to produce nuclear explosives while still meeting the world's needs for energy. The spread of nuclear technology may be inevitable, but a multitude of national facilities for enriching uranium or extracting plutonium is not. There is still time, we believe, for the United States and other concerned countries to restrain and safeguard the nuclear power industry through export controls, improved inspection, and *multinational control of dangerous nuclear materials.*[17]

The CED cast its "multinational control" idea as a way to limit the proliferation of infrastructure that could produce nuclear weapons–grade material: "We believe that placing facilities for uranium enrichment and plutonium extraction under the control of several nations might prevent such facilities from being developed independently by individual nations."[18]

In a section titled "International Nuclear Fuel Facilities," the CED was more explicit in its reasoning on the future global development of nuclear power:

> An important possibility in minimizing the dangers of plutonium reprocessing and uranium enrichment is the development of multinationally owned and operated nuclear fuel cycle facilities. Placing chemical-reprocessing facilities or uranium-enrichment facilities under the control of several nations might prevent individual nations from developing such facilities independently. The main purpose could be the renunciation by individual nations of national physical control over a potential nuclear weapons mobilization base on condition that other nations be bound by similar restraints.

The CED added:

> Such an arrangement would also make it possible to pool resources and take advantage of economies of scale, shared risks, and common methods of waste disposal. Another

purpose might be to adopt unified security measures and safeguards for storage and transport of dangerous materials.

According to the CED, the IAEA (International Atomic Energy Agency) was "examining a proposal for internationally owned and managed nuclear fuel centers." Therefore, the CED's internationalization of the nuclear fuel cycle advocacy was a means to forward civilian nuclear power globally—and minimize the risk of nuclear weapons proliferation.[19]

The CED also advised that to make a multinational approach to the nuclear fuel cycle politically feasible the U.S. would have to forego the policy of seeking to establish monopolies/control over nuclear technology:

> Clearly, the United States cannot simultaneously take the initiative in promoting multinational fuel cycle facilities and unilaterally attempt to suppress the export of its technology. Unless other major potential exporters could be induced to participate, the United States could have only a modest short-term effect through a policy of export denial, and even that effort would appear offensively discriminatory unless it was coupled with alternative arrangements to assure fuel supplies and perhaps even to let the rest of the world participate in the planning and decision making where their crucial fuel supplies are concerned.

The CED specifically held that "the United States should be prepared to consider contributing to the success of multi-lateral arrangements, possibly by making its own enrichment facilities available to participants in such an international program."[20]

The nuclear science community in the late 1970s came out in support of the internationalization of the nuclear energy cycle (including plutonium production). It did so through the IAEA's International Nuclear Fuel Cycle Evaluation.

The International Nuclear Fuel Cycle Evaluation

As the Carter administration was conducting its policy review of plutonium in the aftermath of the Germany/Brazil nuclear trade deal, the IAEA in 1977 convened a Washington, DC, conference "in which 40 countries and four international organizations were represented."[21] The

Washington conference "laid down the organization, terms of reference, procedures and methodology for" the International Nuclear Fuel Cycle Evaluation (INFCE). The authors of the 1980 INFCE summary report explained that the nuclear fuel cycle evaluation work was conducted by "Working Groups," and the "22 co-chairmen were constituted as a Technical Co-ordinating Committee (TCC) to co-ordinate the work of the working groups from the technical point of view." The chair of the TCC was the American professor Abram Chayes. As noted in the INFCE report:

> In all, the eight working groups held 61 meetings on 174 days, in which a total of 519 experts, representing 46 countries and five international organizations, participated and produced more than 20,000 pages of documents. The TCC has met nine times. A first Plenary Conference was also held in Vienna from 27 to 29 November 1978, which decided on the procedures for preparing this report and the Working Group final reports.[22]

INFCE Working Group 4 was charged with identifying the means "of minimizing the risk of proliferation in relation to the reprocessing and recycle of nuclear fuels."[23] Working Group 4 (substantively titled Reprocessing, Plutonium Handling, Recycle), under the sub-heading "Proliferation Risk," noted that "plutonium is inevitably produced when operating nuclear power plants."[24] Thus, the working group "concluded that safeguards and institutional measures are more important than technical measures" in preventing nuclear weapons proliferation. "In all cases the principal deterrent" to countries adopting nuclear weapons "is the likely reaction of the international community."[25]

Under the heading "Institutional Arrangements, the Reprocessing, Plutonium Handling, Recycle," Working Group 4 explained:

> International confidence in the security and reliability of fuel cycle services is essential. This is likely to be enhanced by having several possible sources of supply, giving the customer a choice. Security of supply may also be better assured by multinational or international arrangements, which at the same time offer economic advantages (from economies of scale) and may help to reduce the risk of proliferation. . . . *It seems desirable that the evolution of institutional arrange-*

ments should be towards such multinational ventures and could eventually result in the development of regional nuclear fuel cycle centers.

The INFCE Working Group 4 held that "a scheme for the international storage of plutonium . . . could have important non-proliferation and assurance of supply advantages."[26]

If the CED's and INFCE's proposals had been successfully implemented, not only would the U.S. lose whatever dominance it still might have had over nuclear energy, but the political value of America's hegemony over the world's fossil fuel supplies would have been greatly diminished. The U.S. has the largest domestic supply of coal in the world.[27] Moreover, through naval deployments and a series of political alliances, the U.S. exercises hegemonic control over the oil rich Persian Gulf. This was especially the case before the fall of the Shah of Iran in 1979.[28] Therefore, a successful transition to an international system of plutonium production for civilian use along the lines proposed by the CED and the INFCE would have undermined the U.S. as the preeminent political power in the global world system.

The Ford Foundation, however, explicitly argued against the internationalization of the nuclear/plutonium fuel cycle. This position came to predominate the Carter administration, as a number of the individuals that formulated the Ford Foundation position on civilian plutonium came to hold various foreign policy positions in the administration.

The Ford Foundation/MITRE Report

The Carter administration's plutonium policy was based on a 1977 report sponsored by the Ford Foundation, titled *Nuclear Power Issues and Choices*. The report was "administered" by the MITRE Corporation, a think tank that manages research for the Defense Department and other government agencies. The Ford Foundation is among the wealthiest and most visible private foundations.[29] Established by Henry Ford in 1936, with assets in the tens of billions, the Ford Foundation finances studies in numerous fields, many having foreign policy implications.[30] Edward H. Berman in his history of the role the Carnegie, Ford, and Rockefeller foundations in American foreign policy explains that

> Ford Foundation personnel have been closely identified with United States foreign-policy establishment . . . . Trustees or

officers of the Ford Foundation who have figured prominently in American foreign policy since 1945 include Paul Hoffman, onetime president of the Studebaker Corporation and director of the Marshall Plan and of the first United States aid agency; John J. McCloy, assistant secretary of war, first high commissioner to Germany after World War II, president of the World Bank, chairman of the Rockefeller family's Chase Manhattan Bank, and a trustee of the Rockefeller Foundation; McGeorge Bundy, scion of a Boston family, dean of Harvard College, and national security advisor to President Kennedy and, briefly, to President Lyndon Johnson; Robert S. McNamara, onetime president of the Ford Motor Company, secretary of defense under presidents Kennedy and Johnson, and president of the World Bank.[31]

Berman adds that "the Ford Foundation's links to and support of the Council on Foreign Relations' research endeavors were significant. . . . In 1954, for example, the foundation made a grant of $1.5 million to the council for research projects; this was followed by many others in subsequent years."[32]

The group that composed the *Nuclear Power Issues and Choices* report was the Nuclear Energy Policy Study Group. This group was chaired by Spurgeon M. Keeny Jr., of the MITRE Corporation. Also part of this group were Richard Garwin from IBM and Albert Carnesale of Harvard University. Both Garwin and Carnesale were advisers to the CED's Subcommittee on Nuclear Energy and National Security, which wrote *Nuclear Energy and National Security*, described earlier. Additionally, on the Nuclear Energy Policy Study Group were individuals from the Brookings Institution and Resources for the Future (RFF).[33] Both Brookings and RFF have historically received much of their financing from the Ford Foundation.[34]

Political scientist Michael J. Brenner, in his exhaustive treatment of the formulation of the Carter administration's plutonium policy, explains that "the Ford/Mitre study entitled *Nuclear Power Issues and Choices* has often been cited as the administration's 'Bible' on all matters nuclear." Brenner goes on to point out:

Numbered among members of the study group that prepared the report were several persons who would take up important posts in the administration: Joseph S. Nye, who, as special deputy to the undersecretary for security assistance, science, and technology, headed the office that had primary direction of the early attempt to design the U.S. [plutonium] strategy, and who represented that strategy diplomatically; Spurgeon M. Keeny, Jr., appointed as deputy director of ACDA [Arms Control and Disarmament Agency]; Harold Brown, secretary of defense; Albert Carnesale, U.S. representative to the Technical Coordinating Committee of the International Fuel Cycle Evaluation; and Philip J. Farley, chief deputy to Ambassador Gerald Smith (Smith, as the president's special representative for non-proliferation affairs, had overall responsibility for conducting the delicate diplomacy needed to gain foreign government support for the International Fuel Cycle Evaluation launched in late 1977, and later for the legislatively decreed revision of agreements of cooperation).

Given the number of influential foreign policy positions within the Carter administration held by the authors of the Ford Foundation's report (*Nuclear Power Issues and Choices*), Brenner acknowledges that "it would be odd if its influence had not been pronounced."[35]

In its report the Ford Foundation/MITRE Nuclear Energy Policy Study Group outlined what would become the key elements of the Carter administration plutonium policy. The group argued that the "*U.S. policy should seek to encourage a broad consensus against the development of a plutonium economy.*" The study group went on to explain:

> Any U.S. proposal for international reexamination of the fuel cycle could hardly be credible if the United States were foraging ahead with its own plans for reprocessing fuel for LWRs [light water reactors] and with its program for early commercialization of the breeder reactor. The recommendations in this study for deferral and slowdown of these programs take on added significance in the context of export policy. Other countries may not follow the U.S. lead but most would at least reassess their own plans in the face of U.S. restraint. . . . In context of clear U.S. restraint . . . a more formal agreement embargoing exports to those countries— hopefully few—that did not voluntarily renounce national reprocessing and enrichment could be pursued with some prospects for success.

The Nuclear Energy Policy Study Group openly inveighed against the internationalization of plutonium production: "*it would be a mistake to encourage commercial reprocessing facilities in any form, national or multinational.*" This is because "such facilities would result in an international commerce in plutonium and would develop international experience in the separation and handling of plutonium."[36]

In its 2012 report, the Blue Ribbon Commission on America's Nuclear Future replicated the Ford Foundation late-1970s caution against plutonium energy. The commission did strike an internationalist (and even a pro-civilian plutonium) tone by arguing that "the United States should support the use of multi-national fuel-cycle facilities, under comprehensive access to the benefits of nuclear power while simultaneously reducing proliferation risks." The authors of the commission report noted that "the term 'multi-national fuel cycle facility' is commonly understood to encompass facilities associated with all aspects of the nuclear fuel cycle." Contrary to this internationalist posture, however, the report authors explain:

> The Commission wishes to stress that our support for multi-national management of such facilities should not be interpreted as support for additional countries becoming involved in enrichment or reprocessing facilities, but rather reflects our view that if these capabilities were to spread it would be far preferable—from a security and non-proliferation standpoint—if they did so under multi-national ownership, management, safeguards, and controls.[37]

Seemingly, the most important aspect of the 2012 blue ribbon commission report was its position that the U.S. government should not engage in the recycling of nuclear fuel (i.e., extracting plutonium from nuclear waste for civilian use). The commission made specific reference to breeder reactors (i.e., the kind developed by the U.S. in the 1970s at Clinch River, otherwise known as a Fast-Spectrum Reactor with Closed Fuel Cycle): "previously built reactors (mostly prototype/demo) were often unreliable and not economic." Moreover, the commission pointed to "significant capital cost for recycle facilities." Thus, research "is needed to provide a basis for design, licensing, and evaluating long-term economic viability."[38] The commission was rather pessimistic with regard to any current nuclear fuel recycling technology: "the timeframes involved in developing and deploying either breakthrough reactor and fuel-cycle technologies . . . are long: on the order of multiple decades even in a best-case scenario." It specifically argued against the U.S. deploying any nuclear fuel recycling technology/infrastructure:

> *As a group we concluded that it is premature at this point for the United States to commit irreversibly to any particular fuel cycle as a matter of government policy given the large uncertainties that exist about the merits and commercial viability of different fuel cycles and technology options. Rather, in the face of an uncertain future, there is a benefit to preserving and developing options so that the nuclear waste management program and the larger nuclear energy system can adapt effectively to changing conditions.*[39]

While the commission did call for more research into plutonium-based energy technology, it did not make "a specific recommendation with respect to [research] funding levels in future years, recognizing that this is a decision that will have to be made in the context of larger energy policy considerations and increasingly difficult federal budget constraints."[40]

As noted in chapter 2, corporate executives from the utility industry were represented on the commission. Also indicating that the commission is part of an economic elite policy-planning network, on the commission was the president of Resources for the Future (Phil Sharp), also a board member of Duke Energy. In addition, former U.S. Senator and future secretary of defense Chuck Hagel served on the commission. According to the commission's 2012 website:

> [Hagel] is Co-Chairman of the President's Intelligence Advisory Board; Chairman of The Atlantic Council; a member of the Secretary of Defense's Policy Board . . . and is a member of the Public Broadcasting Service (PBS) board of directors. He also serves on the Board of Directors of Chevron Corporation; the Advisory Boards of Deutsche Bank Americas; Corsair Capital; M.I.C. Industries; is a Director of the Zurich Holding Company of America; and is a Senior Advisor to McCarthy Capital Corporation.

Finally, on the commission was Albert Carnesale, who in the 1970s helped oversee both the Ford Foundation and CED reports on nuclear fuel recycling. Presently, Carnesale "is a member of the National Academy of Engineering, of the Council on Foreign Relations."[41]

Conclusion

Even as fossil fuels are possibly/seemingly running low and their massive burning is threatening to undermine the global ecosystem through climate change, humanity finds itself dependent on scarce/finite and perilous fossil fuels. This predicament was not necessarily inevitable. Under the auspices of economic elites (the Rockefeller Foundation, Lewis Strauss, and the report *Peaceful Uses of Atomic Energy*), the United States was leading the way on nuclear energy (chapter 5). Going into the 1970s there was an international governmental commitment to developing a plutonium economy, with the U.S. actively participating. The U.S. was seeking to perfect civilian plutonium production from the recycling of nuclear waste and the breeder reactor, which generates more plutonium than it consumes. Once, however, it became evident that the U.S.'s nuclear lead had been greatly diminished, and, in particular, other countries were intent on making nuclear fuel reprocessing available through international trade, the U.S. essentially turned against nuclear power—especially plutonium.

In the mid- to late 1970s the U.S. position on plutonium was discussed and debated within the economic elite policy-planning network. The Committee for Economic Development, through its Research and Policy Committee, posited a proposal to develop and propagate plutonium through multilateral processes. (This proposal was echoed by the nuclear scientific community through the INFCE.) The Ford Foundation adopted a different stance, arguing that the U.S. should undertake an international effort to suppress plutonium production/utilization—including embargoing those countries that did not comply and ending the U.S.'s own efforts to perfect nuclear fuel recycling and the breeder reactor.

The Ford Foundation position on plutonium became official U.S. policy—with numerous individuals that composed the Ford Foundation/MITRE report taking up key foreign policy posts within the Carter administration. This served to preserve the dominant U.S. position over the world's energy—composed almost entirely of fossil fuels. In creating an international political environment hostile to plutonium and unwilling to contribute to developing plutonium as a viable energy source, the

U.S. sought to place the world economy on an unsustainable economic and environmental track—one almost wholly dependent on fossil fuels. Despite the acceleration of global warming and the 2010 declaration by the International Energy Agency that world oil production reached its peak, the U.S. government's Blue Ribbon Commission on America's Nuclear Future (composed in significant part of economic elites) in 2012 argued against deploying nuclear recycling infrastructure—even in an effort to forward/perfect this technology.

What is ostensibly one of the world's great ironies (perhaps tragedies) is that the U.S. sought to globally suppress the civilian use of plutonium, while it pursued policies promoting the profligate use of energy. The U.S. embraced energy-profligate urban sprawl beginning in the 1920s. Its promoting of urban sprawl went into high gear in the 1930s (i.e., during the Great Depression). As shown in chapter 6, the U.S. government's political commitment to urban sprawl was maintained even after the oil shocks of the 1970s.

Conclusion

Energy and the Global Order

At the very beginning of this volume (the theoretical overview), I noted that in the most abstract, minimalist sense, the modern state is a result of energy (wind, coal, oil)—as energy allows for the relatively inexpensive projection of political power. Moreover, I explained that a prime function of the modern state is garnering access to energy to reliably power, grow the economy. This has brought states into acute conflict over energy sources. In the theoretical overview I also raise the point that to meaningfully understand any specific state in the modern era, we must grasp the precise energy politics confronting that state. This is because the modern state and energy have a dialectical and coterminous relationship that can only be comprehended within specific contexts. Economic elites have had an outsized role in shaping this relationship (chapter 2).

The modern state was founded on energy (wind power and heat to produce cannons for navies in the sixteenth century). This energy, military revolution served as the basis of the British empire. The shift to coal in the nineteenth century brought forward a new tension to global politics, where the German state challenged the status quo. The advanced German economy, powered by coal, created a political circumstance in which it needed reliable access to the international system—something Great Britain was determined to prevent (i.e., World War I) (chapter 1).

The twentieth century witnessed a new global politics—one based on oil. The oil economy shifted the center of Capitalism to the U.S., which was the leading producer of oil in the early twentieth century. The other major centers of industry and science (northwestern Europe and Japan) lack domestic oil. This set of circumstances propelled the U.S. to the top of the world system by the 1920s due to its virtual monopoly of what can be deemed the Third Industrial Revolution (alternatively known as the consumer durables revolution, the automobile revolution, Fordism, the age of oil). During the 1920s and 1930s the U.S. was unwilling to share the massive wealth based on the Third Industrial Revolution. This resulted in a politically unstable world system and world war again—this time in the Pacific as well as in Europe (chapters 3 and 4).

With the advent of the Cold War, the U.S. relied on the Third Industrial Revolution in its competition with the Soviet Union. Urban sprawl in the U.S. was utilized by the American government as a carrot (allowing access to its massive domestic market to its allies) and as a stick (denying access to its enemies). The oil shocks of the 1970s brought U.S. Cold War grand strategy into question. As a result American foreign policy became centered on the Persian Gulf—the region of the world with the largest reserves of conventional petroleum. This culminated with the 2003 invasion of Iraq. Additionally, the U.S. government has sponsored the unconventional fossil fuels revolution, for example, the Canadian oil sands (chapter 6).

Focusing on American energy policies brings the dialectical relationship between energy and the state into sharp relief. The American state, as noted, has politically sponsored, fostered the unconventional fossil fuels revolution, and this revolution enhances the power of the American state.[1] Conversely, the U.S. has not pursued solar power precisely because it would not enhance its global authority.

In the 1950s the U.S. government sought to bring about a nuclear energy revolution. It did so for geopolitical reasons, that is, to dominate the energy systems of other countries (chapter 5). Once nuclear energy in the late 1970s no longer served American hegemonic designs, the U.S. turned away from this energy source and undertook internationally a hostile tack toward it. This hostility is evident with the Nuclear Nonproliferation Act of 1978—by which the U.S. government sought to punish those countries, allies that continued to pursue plutonium (the next generation of nuclear energy). The U.S. also ended its own efforts to perfect plutonium as a source of energy. While American plutonium policy was ostensibly predicated on nuclear weapons proliferation concerns, it is noteworthy that the International Nuclear Fuel Cycle Evaluation (conducted by nuclear scientists drawn from all over the world) in 1980 correctly observed that plutonium production for civilian use did not pose a unique nuclear weapons dissemination risk. Put differently, nuclear weapons proliferation could take place in the absence of a plutonium economy, and, in fact, the international nuclear weapons club has expanded in the absence of energy derived from civilian plutonium. The International Nuclear Fuel Cycle Evaluation aptly noted that the most significant factor determining nuclear weapons proliferation is political. Namely, those countries that have the political will to obtain nuclear weapons can do so. The internationalization of the nuclear fuel cycle could have served to create the global political framework to put the world on a sustainable energy path (with minimal climate change emissions[2]) and been used as a basis to deter countries' nuclear weapons ambitions (chapter 7).

By rejecting solar and plutonium power, the U.S. in a proximate sense is defending its hegemonic, superpower status. More broadly, the U.S. is defending the current global state system—with all its instabilities and profoundly dangerous liabilities (war, nuclear conflagration, global warming, biodiversity destruction). Following from a theory that political authority in the modern era is a function of energy, solar holds the promise of a diffusion of energy production and political authority; plutonium represents the potential centralization of power generation and the corresponding formation of world government.

Notes

Preface

1. George A. Gonzalez, *Urban Sprawl, Global Warming, and the Empire of Capital* (Albany: State University of New York Press, 2009), *Energy and Empire: The Politics of Nuclear and Solar Power in the United States* (Albany: State University of New York Press, 2012), *Energy and the Politics of the North Atlantic* (Albany: State University of New York Press, 2013), and *American Empire and the Canadian Oil Sands* (New York: Palgrave Macmillan, 2016).

2. Justin Gillis, "For Third Year, the Earth in 2016 Set Heat Record," *New York Times*, January 19, 2017, A1; Russell Goldman, "No Icebreaker Needed: Thaw Lets Tanker Traverse Arctic," *New York Times*, August 27, 2017, A4; Hiroko Tabuchi, "Tree-Killing Visitors, Lured by Milder Winters," *New York Times*, August 29, 2017, A17, and "Japan Is Spending Billions to Prepare for Floods 'Beyond Anything We've Seen,'" *New York Times*, October 7, 2017, A5; David Leonhardt, "Irma, and the Rise of Extreme Rain," *New York Times*, September 12, 2017. Web; "Hunger Haunts the U.N. Festivities," *New York Times*, September 22, 2017, A26; Nadja Popovich, Henry Fountain and Adam Pearch, "We Charted Arctic Sea Ice for Nearly Every Day Since 1979. You'll See a Trend," *New York Times*, September 22, 2017. Web; Javier C. Hernández, " 'We Don't Exist': Life Inside Mongolia's Swelling Slums," *New York Times*, October 3, 2017, A11; Karen Weintraub, "A Less Hospitable Home," *New York Times*, October 3, 2017, D1; Somini Sengupta, "How Climate Change Disrupts Olive Industry," *New York Times*, October 25, 2017, A4; Lisa Friedman, "Auditor Issues Warning On Climate Change Costs," *New York Times*, October 24, 2017, A17; Jugal K. Patel, "In Antarctica, Two Crucial Glaciers Accelerate Toward the Sea," *New York Times*, October 26, 2017. Web; Lisa Friedman and Glenn Thrush, "Climate Report By U.S. Agencies Counters Trump," *New York Times*, November 4, 2017, A1; Radley Horton, Katharine Hayhoe, Robert Kopp and Sarah Doherty, "The Climate Risks We Face," *New York Times*, November 6, 2017. Web; Noah S. Diffenbaugh, "How We Know It Was Climate Change," *New York Times*, December 31, 2017, SR10; Kendra Pierre-Louis and Brad Plumer, "Global Warming Takes A Toll on Coral Reefs," *New York Times*, January 5, 2018, A9.

Chapter One

1. David Harvey, *The New Imperialism* (New York: Oxford University Press, 2003); Todd Emmanuel, *After the Empire: The Breakdown of the American Order*, trans. C. Jon Delogu (New York: Columbia University Press, 2003); Jan Nederveen Pieterse, *Globalization or Empire?* (New York: Routledge, 2004); Daniel H. Nexon and Thomas Wright, "What's at Stake in the American Empire Debate," *American Political Science Review* 101, no. 2 (2007): 253–271; Francis Shor, *Dying Empire: U.S. Imperialism and Global Resistance* (New York: Routledge, 2010); Sam Gindin and Leo Panitch, *The Making of Global Capitalism: The Political Economy of American Empire* (New York: Verso, 2012); Emanuele Saccarelli and Latha Varadarajan, *Imperialism Past and Present* (New York: Oxford University Press, 2015).

2. Edwin S. Hunt and James M. Murray, *A History of Business in Medieval Europe, 1200–1550* (New York: Cambridge University Press, 1999).

3. Charles Tilly, *Coercion, Capital, and European States, AD 990–1992* (Cambridge: Blackwell, 1992).

4. Geert H. Janssen, *Princely Power in the Dutch Republic* (New York: Manchester University Press, 2008).

5. Carlo M. Cipolla, *Guns, Sails, and Empires: Technological Innovations and the Early Phases of European Expansion 1400–1700* (New York: Pantheon, 1966), 81–89.

6. Maarten Prak, *The Dutch Republic in the Seventeenth Century: The Golden Age*, trans. Diane Webb (New York: Cambridge University Press), 62.

7. Christopher Haigh, *English Reformations: Religion, Politics, and Society under the Tudors* (New York: Oxford University Press, 1993)

8. Prak, *The Dutch Republic in the Seventeenth Century*, 64.

9. Michael Scott, *Ancient Worlds: A Global History of Antiquity* (New York: Basic Books, 2016).

10. Ralph Davis, *The Rise of the Atlantic Economies* (Ithaca: Cornell University Press, 1973); Roger Crowley, *Conquerors: How Portugal Forged the First Global Empire* (New York: Random House, 2015).

11. Roger Hainsworth and Christine Churches, *The Anglo-Dutch Naval Wars 1652–1674* (London: Sutton, 1998).

12. Paul M. Kennedy, *The Rise and Fall of British Naval Mastery*, 2nd ed. (New York: Humanity Books, 2006); Jeremy Black, *Naval Power: A History of Warfare and the Sea from 1500 Onwards* (New York: Palgrave Macmillan, 2009).

13. Zachary Callen, *Railroads and American Political Development: Infrastructure, Federalism, and State Building* (Lawrence: University Press of Kansas, 2016).

14. Historian Carlo M. Cipolla in *Guns, Sails, and Empires* observed:

> Exchanging oarsmen for sails and warriors for guns meant essentially the exchange of human energy for inanimate power. By turning wholeheartedly to the gun-carrying sailing ship, the Atlantic peoples

broke down the bottleneck inherent in the use of human energy and harnessed, to their advantage, larger quantities of power. It was then that European sails appeared aggressively on the most distant seas. (81)

15. Stig Förster, Wolfgang J. Mommsen, and Ronald Robinson, *Bismarck, Europe, and Africa: The Berlin Africa Conference 1884–1885 and the Onset of Partition* (New York: Oxford University Press, 1988); H. L. Wesseling, *Divide and Rule: The Partition of Africa, 1880–1914* (Westport: Praeger, 1996); Richard Price, *Making Empire: Colonial Encounters and the Creation of Imperial Rule in Nineteenth-Century Africa* (New York: Cambridge University Press, 2008); Muriel Evelyn Chamberlain, *The Scramble for Africa* (New York: Longman, 2010); G. A. Dominy, *Last Outpost on the Zulu Frontier: Fort Napier and the British Imperial Garrison* (Urbana: University of Illinois Press, 2016).

16. David Ormrod, *The Rise of Commercial Empires: England and the Netherlands in the Age of Mercantilism, 1650–1770* (New York: Cambridge University Press, 2008); Philip J. Stern and Carl Wennerlind, eds., *Mercantilism Reimagined: Political Economy in Early Modern Britain and Its Empire* (New York: Oxford University Press, 2013); Lars Magnusson, *Mercantilism: The Shaping of an Economic Language* (New York: Routledge, 2015); Krishan Kumar, *Visions of Empire* (Princeton: Princeton University Press, 2017).

17. Ellen Meiksins Wood, *The Origin of Capitalism* (New York: Monthly Review Press, 1999), and *Empire of Capital* (New York: Verso, 2003); Robert S. Duplessis, *Transitions to Capitalism in Early Modern Europe* (New York: Cambridge University Press, 1997); Steven G. Marks, *The Information Nexus: Global Capitalism from the Renaissance to the Present* (New York: Cambridge University Press, 2016); Abhishek Chatterjee, *Rulers and Capital in Historical Perspective: State Formation and Financial Development in India and the United States* (Philadelphia: Temple University Press, 2017).

18. Robert Greenhalgh Albion, *Forests and Sea Power: The Timber Problem of the Royal Navy, 1652–1862* (Cambridge: Harvard University Press, 1926 [1999]).

19. The Nazis invaded Norway to secure access to iron ore in Sweden. Kathleen Stokker, *Folklore Fights the Nazis: Humor in Occupied Norway, 1940–1945* (Detroit: Wayne State University Press, 1997).

20. Richard Martin, *Coal Wars: The Future of Energy and the Fate of the Planet* (New York: St. Martin's Press, 2015); Javier C. Hernández, "Windmills Stand Idle in China as Even More Are Being Constructed," *New York Times*, January 16, 2017, A8; Michael Forsythe, "China Halts Plan to Build Power Plants Fired by Coal," *New York Times*, January 19, 2017, A8.

21. John Hatcher, *The History of the British Coal Industry: Volume 1: Before 1700: Towards the Age of Coal* (New York: Oxford University Press, 1993).

22. Roger Morriss, *The Foundations of British Maritime Ascendancy: Resources, Logistics and the State, 1755–1815* (New York: Cambridge University Press, 2011).

23. Eric Grove, *The Royal Navy since 1815: A New Short History* (New York: Palgrave Macmillan, 2005).

24. Adria K. Lawrence, *Imperial Rule and the Politics of Nationalism: Anti-Colonial Protest in the French Empire* (New York: Cambridge University Press, 2013).

25. Ashley Jackson, *The British Empire: A Very Short Introduction* (New York: Oxford University Press, 2013).

26. John Gillingham, *Coal, Steel, and the Rebirth of Europe, 1945–1955: The Germans and French from Ruhr Conflict to Economic Community* (New York: Cambridge University Press, 2005).

27. Brendan Simms, *Europe: The Struggle for Supremacy, from 1453 to the Present* (New York: Basic Books, 2014); Peter H. Wilson, *Heart of Europe: A History of the Holy Roman Empire* (Cambridge: Belknap, 2016).

28. John Lesch, ed., *The German Chemical Industry in the Twentieth Century* (New York: Springer, 2000); Peter Watson, *The German Genius: Europe's Third Renaissance, the Second Scientific Revolution, and the Twentieth Century* (New York: Harper, 2011); William H. Brock, *The History of Chemistry: A Very Short Introduction* (New York: Oxford University Press, 2016).

29. William Bynum, *A Little History of Science* (New Haven: Yale University Press, 2013).

30. For a synopsis of the myriad arguments surrounding the causes of World War I, see William Mulligan, *The Origins of the First World War* (New York: Cambridge University Press, 2010); David M. Edelstein, *Over the Horizon: Time, Uncertainty, and the Rise of Great Powers* (Ithaca: Cornell University Press, 2017); Azar Gat, *The Causes of War and the Spread of Peace* (New York: Oxford University Press, 2017); Xu Qiyu, *Fragile Rise: Grand Strategy and the Fate of Imperial Germany, 1871–1914*, trans. Joshua Hill (Cambridge: MIT Press, 2017).

31. Shelley Baranowski, *Nazi Empire: German Colonialism and Imperialism from Bismarck to Hitler* (New York: Cambridge University Press, 2011), 9; see also Wolfgang J. Mommsen, *Imperial Germany, 1867–1918*, trans. Richard Deveson (New York: Arnold, 1995); and Dietrich Orlow, *A History of Modern Germany, 1871 to Present*, 6th ed. (Upper Saddle River: Prentice Hall, 2008), 61–65.

32. Mark Hewitson, *Germany and the Causes of the First World War* (New York: Berg, 2004), 25–26.

33. Robert K. Massie, *Dreadnought: Britain, Germany, and the Coming of the Great War* (New York: Random House, 1991).

34. Francis Torrance Williamson, *Germany and Morocco before 1905* (Baltimore: Johns Hopkins University Press, 1937); Jeffrey W. Taliaferro, *Balancing Risks: Great Power Intervention in the Periphery* (Ithaca: Cornell University Press, 2004).

35. Count Max Montgelas, *The Case for the Central Powers: An Impeachment of the Versailles Verdict*, trans. Constance Vesey (Westport: Greenwood, 1975 [1925]); Andreas Rose, *Between Empire and Continent: British Foreign Policy before the First World War*, trans. Rona Johnston (New York: Berghahn, 2017).

36. Grove, *The Royal Navy since 1815*.

37. Ronald W. Ferrier, *The History of the British Petroleum Company, Vol. 1: The Developing Years, 1901–1932* (New York: Cambridge University Press, 1982).

38. Ivo Nikolai Lambi, *The Navy and German Power Politics, 1862–1914* (London: Allen & Unwin, 1984).

39. Daniel Walker Howe, *What Hath God Wrought: The Transformation of America, 1815–1848* (New York: Oxford University Press, 2009).

40. William W. Freehling, *Prelude to Civil War: The Nullification Controversy in South Carolina, 1816–1836* (New York: Oxford University Press, 1992).

41. Alfred E. Eckes, *Opening America's Market: U.S. Foreign Trade Policy since 1776* (Chapel Hill: University of North Carolina Press, 1995).

42. Richard H. Vietor, *Environmental Politics and the Coal Coalition* (College Station: Texas A&M University Press, 1980), and *Energy Policy in America since 1945* (New York: Cambridge University Press, 1984); David Davis, *Energy Politics* (New York: St. Martin's Press, 1993); Barbara Freese, *Coal: A Human History*, 4th ed. (New York: Penguin, 2004); Marc Humphries, ed., *U.S. Coal: A Primer on the Major Issues* (Hauppauge: Novinka Books, 2004); Jeff Goodell, *Big Coal: The Dirty Secret behind America's Energy Future* (New York: Mariner, 2007); Brenda Shaffer, *Energy Politics* (Philadelphia: University of Pennsylvania Press, 2009); Christopher F. Jones, "A Landscape of Energy Abundance: Anthracite Coal Canals and the Roots of American Fossil Fuel Dependence, 1820–1860," *Environmental History* 15, no. 3 (2010): 449–484; Harvey Blatt, *America's Environmental Report Card*, 2nd ed. (Cambridge: MIT Press, 2011), 158.

43. Daniel Yergin, *The Prize: The Epic Quest for Oil, Money, and Power* (New York: Simon & Schuster, 1991), and *The Quest: Energy, Security, and the Remaking of the Modern World* (New York: Penguin, 2011); Torleif Haugland, Helge Ole Bergensen, and Kjell Roland, *Energy Structures and Environmental Futures* (New York: Oxford University Press, 1998).

44. Patrick M. Malone, *Waterpower in Lowell: Engineering and Industry in Nineteenth-Century America* (Baltimore: Johns Hopkins University Press, 2009).

45. Paul E. Johnson, *The Early American Republic, 1789–1829* (New York: Oxford University Press, 2006); Lawrence A. Peskin, *Manufacturing Revolution: The Intellectual Origins of Early American Industry* (Baltimore: Johns Hopkins University Press, 2007).

46. Alfred Chandler Jr., "Anthracite Coal and the Beginnings of the Industrial Revolution in the United States," *Business History Review* 46, no. 2 (1972): 141–181.

47. David Hounshell, *From the American System to Mass Production, 1800–1932: The Development of Manufacturing Technology in the United States* (Baltimore: Johns Hopkins University Press, 1985).

48. Yergin, *The Prize*, and *The Quest*; David Goodstein, *Out of Gas: The End of the Age of Oil* (New York: Norton, 2004).

49. Bernard P. Bellon, *Mercedes in Peace and War: German Automobile Workers, 1903–1945* (New York: Columbia University Press, 1992).

50. William Stivers, *Supremacy and Oil: Iraq, Turkey, and the Anglo-American World Order, 1918–1930* (Ithaca: Cornell University Press, 1982).

51. Robert Paul Thomas, *An Analysis of the Pattern of Growth of the Automobile Industry, 1895–1929* (New York: Arno, 1977); Jean-Pierre Bardou, Jean-Jacques Chanaron, Patrick Fridenson, and James M. Laux, *The Automobile Revolution: The Impact of an Industry* (Chapel Hill: University of North Carolina Press, 1982); T. C. Barker, "The International History of Motor Transport," *Journal of Contemporary History* 20, no. 1 (1985): 3–19; David J. St. Clair, *The Motorization of American Cities* (New York: Praeger, 1986).

52. Robert D. Atkinson, *The Past and Future of America's Economy: Long Waves of Innovation That Power Cycles of Growth* (Northampton: Edward Elgar, 2004); Alexander J. Field, "Technological Change and U.S. Productivity Growth in the Interwar Years," *Journal of Economic History* 66, no. 1 (2006): 203–234; Michael H. Hunt, *The American Ascendancy: How the United States Gained and Wielded Global Dominance* (Chapel Hill: University of North Carolina Press, 2007); Joan Hoff, *A Faustian Foreign Policy: From Woodrow Wilson to George W. Bush* (New York: Cambridge University Press, 2008); Stanley Buder, *Capitalizing on Change: A Social History of American Business* (Chapel Hill: University of North Carolina Press, 2009); Charles J. Shindo, *1927 and the Rise of Modern America* (Lawrence: University Press of Kansas, 2010).

53. Peter Fearon, *War, Prosperity, and Depression: The U.S. Economy 1917–45* (Lawrence: University Press of Kansas, 1987), 48.

54. Ann Markusen, *Profit Cycles, Oligopoly, and Regional Development* (Cambridge: MIT Press, 1985); Atkinson, *The Past and Future of America's Economy*.

55. Field, "Technological Change and U.S. Productivity Growth in the Interwar Years," 206.

56. Gonzalez, *Energy and the Politics of the North Atlantic.*

57. Christopher W. Wells, *Car Country: An Environmental History* (Seattle: University of Washington Press, 2014).

58. Jonathan G. Utley, *Going to War with Japan, 1937–1941* (New York: Fordham University Press, 2005).

59. Victor Madej, ed., *German War Economy: The Motorization Myth* (Allentown: Game, 1984), 3; R. L. DiNardo, *Mechanized Juggernaut or Military Anachronism? Horses and the German Army of World War II* (Mechanicsburg: Stackpole Books, 2008).

60. Neil H. Jacoby, *Multinational Oil: A Study in Industrial Dynamics* (New York: Macmillan, 1974), 37.

61. Arthur Jay Klinghoffer, *The Soviet Union & International Oil Politics* (New York: Columbia University Press, 1977); Douglas Rogers, *The Depths of Russia: Oil, Power, and Culture after Socialism* (Ithaca: Cornell University Press, 2015).

62. Bruce W. Jentleson, *Pipeline Politics: The Complex Political Economy of East-West Energy Trade* (Ithaca: Cornell University Press, 1986).

63. Andrew Scott Cooper, *The Oil Kings: How the U.S., Iran, and Saudi Arabia Changed the Balance of Power in the Middle East* (New York: Simon & Schuster, 2011).

64. Rachel Bronson, *Thicker than Oil: America's Uneasy Partnership with Saudi Arabia* (New York: Oxford University Press, 2006).

65. Chris Miller, *The Struggle to Save the Soviet Economy: Mikhail Gorbachev and the Collapse of the USSR* (Chapel Hill: University of North Carolina Press, 2016).

66. William S. Borden, *The Pacific Alliance: United States Foreign Economic Policy and Japanese Trade Recovery, 1947–1955* (Madison: University of Wisconsin Press, 1984); Michael Schaller, *Altered States: The United States and Japan since the Occupation* (New York: Oxford University Press, 1997); Gary Herrigel, *Industrial Constructions: The Sources of German Industrial Power* (New York: Cambridge University Press, 2000); Horst Siebert, *The German Economy: Beyond the Social Market* (Princeton: Princeton University Press, 2005); John Swenson-Wright, *Unequal Allies? United States Security and Alliance Policy toward Japan, 1945–1960* (Stanford: Stanford University Press, 2005); Belay Seyoum, *Export-Import Theory, Practices, and Procedures*, 2nd ed. (New York: Routledge, 2008); Ian Talley and Jeffrey Sparshott, "U.S. Blasts Germany's Economic Policies," *Wall Street Journal*, October 31, 2013. Web.

67. Gonzalez, *Energy and the Politics of the North Atlantic*, chap. 1.

68. Martin Sixsmith, *Putin's Oil: The Yukos Affair and the Struggle for Russia* (New York: Bloomsbury Academic, 2010); Thane Gustafson, *Wheel of Fortune: The Battle for Oil and Power in Russia* (Cambridge: Harvard University Press, 2012); Rogers, *The Depths of Russia*; James Kanter, "Europe Seeks Alternatives to Russian Gas Imports," *New York Times*, February 17, 2016, B2; Andrew E. Kramer, "Will Russia Actually Curb Oil Output?," *New York Times*, May 29, 2017, A6; Clifford Krauss, "Russia's Reliance On Oil Diplomacy Opens It to Risk," *New York Times*, October 30, 2017, A1.

69. Brad Plumer, "Looking for Trump's Climate Policy? Try the Energy Department," *New York Times*, May 25, 2017. Web.

70. Diane Cardwell, "Buffeted by Energy Politics," *New York Times*, May 31, 2017, B1.

71. Gonzalez, *Energy and Empire*; Frank N. Laird, *Solar Energy, Technology Policy, and Institutional Values* (New York: Cambridge University Press, 2001).

72. Donald Beattie, ed., *History and Overview of Solar Heat Technologies* (Cambridge: MIT Press, 1997).

73. Jacques Leslie, "Nevada's Solar Bait-and-Switch," *New York Times*, February 1, 2016, A21.

74. Blatt, *America's Environmental Report Card*, 2nd ed., 180–181; "The End of Clean Energy Subsidies?," *New York Times*, May 6, 2012, SR12.

75. Rachel Weiner, "Solyndra, Explained," *Washington Post*, June 1, 2012. Web.

76. Hiroko Tabuchi, "As U.S. Pulls Back on Climate, Others Step Up at Davos," *New York Times*, January 22, 2017, A9; Lisa Friedman, "E.P.A. Scrubs a Climate Website of 'Climate Change,' an Analysis Finds," *New York Times*, October 21, 2017, A10, "E.P.A. Bars 3 of Its Scientists From a Conference to Discuss Climate Change," *New York Times*, October 23, 2017, A16, "Pruitt Ousts Scientists From Panels At the E.P.A.," *New York Times*, November 1, 2017, A9, and "Trump Moves To Open Coasts For Oil Drilling," *New York Times*, January 5, 2018, A1.

77. The White House, *An America First Energy Plan*, https://www. whitehouse.gov/america-first-energy (accessed January 22, 2017). See also Lisa Friedman, "Trump Nominates a Coal Lobbyist to Be No. 2 at E.P.A.," *New York Times*, October, 5, 2017. Web, "For Climate Conference, a Sales Pitch on Fossil Fuels," *New York Times*, November 3, 2017, A12, and "How a Coal Baron's Wish List Became Trump's To-Do List," *New York Times*, January 10, 2018, B1; Jody Freeman and Joseph Goffman, "Rick Perry's Anti-Market Plan to Help Coal," *New York Times*, October, 25, 2017. Web.

78. Gonzalez, *American Empire and the Canadian Oil Sands*; Peter Baker and Coral Davenport, "President Revives Two Oil Pipelines Thwarted Under Obama," *New York Times*, January 25, 2017, A1.

79. Michael D. Shear, "Trump Abandoning Global Climate Accord," *New York Times*, June 2, 2017, A1.

80. Geeta Anand, "Until Recently a Coal Goliath, India Is Rapidly Turning Green," *New York Times*, June 3, 2017, A1; Keith Bradsher, "China Turns Economic Engine Toward Clean-Energy Leadership," *New York Times*, June 6, 2017, A1.

81. Gonzalez, *Energy and Empire*.

82. In 1954, the Atomic Energy Commission reported the following to the Congressional Joint Committee on Atomic Energy:

The United States could offer to export either heavy-water or light-water reactors under the Atoms-for-Peace program. Heavy-water reactors might be more attractive to European nations because they could probably obtain supplies of heavy water and natural uranium without depending on the United States. If, however, the United States selected light-water reactors for export, the [Atomic Energy] Commission would have to supply the slightly enriched uranium fuel because no European countries were likely to make the heavy financial commitment necessary to build an enrichment plant. One advantage, then, of using light-water reactors for export . . . was that the United States could control both the supply of uranium fuel elements and also reprocessing of spent fuel.

Richard G. Hewlett and Jack M. Holl, *Atoms for Peace and War 1953–1961: Eisenhower and the Atomic Energy Commission*, vol. 3 (Berkeley: University of

California Press, 1989), 197–198. See also Joseph A. Camilleri, *The State and Nuclear Power: Conflict and Control in the Western World* (Seattle: University of Washington Press, 1984), 193.

Michael T. Hatch writes that "past German dependence on American enriched uranium has given the United States great potential leverage." Michael T. Hatch, *Politics and Nuclear Power: Energy Policy in Western Europe* (Lexington: University Press of Kentucky, 1986), 133. Joseph A. Camilleri writes in more general terms when he explains that through the provision of nuclear fuel the United States sought to "impose a highly visible form of extraterritorial control over [its allies'] economic and foreign policies. If nothing else it called into question the independence of their national [nuclear] programs." *The State and Nuclear Power*, 256.

83. Michael J. Brenner, *Nuclear Power and Non-Proliferation: The Remaking of U.S. Policy* (New York: Cambridge University Press, 1981); Mark Hertsgaard, *Nuclear Inc.: The Men and Money Behind Nuclear Energy* (New York: Pantheon, 1983), 75–79; Camilleri describes the 1973 change in U.S. enriched nuclear fuel policy in the following:

> Whereas previously customers could obtain through "requirement contracts" as much enriched fuel as they needed with less than one year's advance notice, they were now expected to sign "fixed commitment" contracts at least eight years in advance of delivery of the first core. In addition, they had to agree to purchase specified amounts of enriched uranium over a moving ten-year period and to deliver the required uranium supplies regardless of their actual need for enriched fuel. . . . The net effect of the new contract system was to shift the risks to the user. *The State and Nuclear Power*, 195.

84. Matthew L. Wald, "Atomic Goal: 800 Years of Power from Waste," *New York Times*, September 25, 2013, B1; Diane Cardwell and Jonathan Soble, "Bankruptcy Rocks Nuclear Industry," *New York Times*, March 30, 2017, B1.

85. James H. Lebovic, *Flawed Logics: Strategic Nuclear Arms Control from Truman to Obama* (Baltimore: Johns Hopkins University Press, 2013); Michael D. Cohen, *When Proliferation Causes Peace: The Psychology of Nuclear Crises* (Washington, D.C.: Georgetown University Press, 2017); "One Finger on the Button Is Too Few," *New York Times*, October 12, 2017, A22.

86. Frederick Williams, "The Nuclear Non-Proliferation Act of 1978," *International Security* 3, no. 2 (1978): 45–50.

87. Brenner, *Nuclear Power and Non-Proliferation*, 191–199; "Shall We Call It the 'Bronze Standard'?," *New York Times*, February 6, 2012, A22; Choe Sang-Hun, "South Korea and U.S. Fail to Reach Deal on Nuclear Energy," *New York Times*, April 25, 2013, A4.

Japan is the only country without a nuclear weapons program that currently has a nuclear fuel recycling program. The *Wall Street Journal* reported that Japan is pursuing its nuclear fuel recycling program (i.e., plutonium production) "over the objections of the Obama administration." Jay Solomon and Miho Inada, "Japan's Nuclear Plan Unsettles U.S.," *Wall Street Journal*, May 2, 2013, A9. See also Frank N. von Hippel and Masafumi Takubo, "Japan's Nuclear Mistake," *New York Times*, November 29, 2012, A31; Hiroko Tabuchi, "Japanese Reactor Is Said to Stand on a Fault Line," *New York Times*, May 16, 2013, A8.

88. Wald, "Atomic Goal."

89. J. Michael Martinez, "The Carter Administration and the Evolution of American Nuclear Nonproliferation Policy, 1977–1981," *Journal of Policy History* 14, no. 3 (2002): 261–292.

90. Lewis A. Dunn, *Controlling the Bomb: Nuclear Proliferation in the 1980s* (New Haven: Yale University Press, 1982); Council on Foreign Relations, *Blocking the Spread of Nuclear Weapons* (New York: Council on Foreign Relations, 1986); William J. Broad, John Markoff, and David E. Sanger, "Israeli Test on Worm Called Crucial in Iran Nuclear Delay," *New York Times*, January 16, 2011, A1.

91. Rajiv Nayan, *The Nuclear Non-Proliferation Treaty and India* (New York: Routledge, 2011).

92. Olav Njølstad, *Nuclear Proliferation and International Order: Challenges to the Non-Proliferation Treaty* (New York: Routledge, 2010).

93. Mark Mazzetti, "U.S. Intelligence Finding Says Iran Halted Its Nuclear Arms Effort in 2003," *New York Times*, December 4, 2007, A1; Dana Allin and Steven Simon, *The Sixth Crisis: Iran, Israel, America, and the Rumors of War* (New York: Oxford University Press, 2010); Julie Hirschfeld Davis, "In Risky Game, Trump Taunts a Touchy Dictator," *New York Times*, September 25, 2017, A1; Sung Chull Kim and Michael D. Cohen, eds., *North Korea and Nuclear Weapons: Entering the New Era of Deterrence* (Washington, D.C.: Georgetown University Press, 2017).

94. Shuja Nawaz, *Crossed Swords: Pakistan, Its Army, and the Wars Within* (New York: Oxford University Press, 2008); Daniel S. Markey, *No Exit from Pakistan: America's Tortured Relationship with Islamabad* (New York: Cambridge University Press, 2013).

95. Salman Masood and Chris Buckley, "Pakistan Breaks Ground on Nuclear Power Plant Project with China," *New York Times*, November 26, 2013. Web.

96. Edward F. Wonder, *Nuclear Fuel and American Foreign Policy: Multilateralization for Uranium Enrichment* (Boulder: Westview, 1977).

97. Kenneth S. Deffeyes, *Hubbert's Peak: The Impending World Oil Shortage* (Princeton: Princeton University Press, 2001); David Goodstein, *Out of Gas: The End of the Age of Oil* (New York: Norton, 2004); Clifford Krauss, "Tapping a Trickle in West Texas," *New York Times*, November 2, 2007, C1; Stanley Reed, "Are the Days of Low Oil Prices Receding?," *New York Times*, October 16, 2017. Web.

98. Catherine Gautier and Jean-Louis Fellous, eds., *Facing Climate Change Together* (New York: Cambridge University Press, 2008); Mark Maslin, *Global Warming: A Very Short Introduction* (New York: Oxford University Press,

2009); James Lawrence Powell, *The Inquisition of Climate Science* (New York: Columbia University Press, 2011); Justin Gillis, "U.N. Says Lag in Confronting Climate Woes Will Be Costly," *New York Times*, January 17, 2014, A8; John Houghton, *Global Warming: The Complete Briefing*, 5th ed. (New York: Cambridge University Press, 2015); Eduardo Porter, "Why Slashing Nuclear Power May Backfire," *New York Times*, November 8, 2017, B1.

99. The 2011 Fukushima nuclear disaster greatly highlights the need for stronger safety and risk management efforts for nuclear power. Henry Fountain, "A Look at the Mechanics of a Partial Meltdown," *New York Times*, March 14, 2011, A9. See also Keith Bradsher, "Nuclear Power Expansion in China Stirs Concerns," *New York Times*, December 16, 2009, A1; David Lochbaum, *The NRC and Nuclear Power Plant Safety in 2010: A Brighter Spotlight Needed* (Cambridge: Union of Concerned Scientists, 2011); and Kate Brown, *Plutopia: Nuclear Families, Atomic Cities, and the Great Soviet and American Plutonium Disasters* (New York: Oxford University Press, 2013).

100. Mark Mazower, *Governing the World: The History of an Idea* (New York: Penguin, 2012); George A. Gonzalez, *The Politics of Star Trek: Justice, War, and the Future* (New York: Palgrave Macmillan, 2015), "*Justice League Unlimited* and the Politics of Globalization," *Foundation: The International Review of Science Fiction* 45, no. 123 (2016): 5–13, *The Absolute and Star Trek* (New York: Palgrave Macmillan, 2017), and "Star Trek: Nationalism as Pathology and Internationalism as Rationalism," *Foundation: The International Review of Science Fiction* (forthcoming 2018).

101. Brad Plumer, "U.S. Nuclear Comeback Stalls as 2 South Carolina Reactors Are Abandoned," *New York Times*, August 1, 2017, Page B6.

102. Rachel Pannett, "How Energy-Rich Australia Exported Its Way into an Energy Crisis," *Wall Street Journal*, July 10, 2017. Web; Clifford Krauss, "U.S. Boom in Natural Gas Could Ripple From the Arctic to Africa," *New York Times*, October 18, 2017, B3.

103. Matthew L. Wald, "Loan Program for Reactors Is Fizzling," *New York Times*, February 19, 2014, B3.

104. Eduardo Porter, "Innovation Sputters in Battle Against Carbon," *New York Times*, July 22, 2015, B1; Diane Cardwell and Julie Creswell, "Looking for Silver Linings," *New York Times*, February 11, 2016, B1; Dieter Helm, *Burn Out: The Endgame for Fossil Fuels* (New Haven, CT: Yale University Press, 2017).

105. Stanley Reed, "High Energy Costs Plaguing Europe," *International Herald Tribune*, December 27, 2012. Web; Nelson D. Schwartz, "Boom in Energy Spurs Industry in the Rust Belt," *New York Times*, September 9, 2014, A1.

106. Stanley Reed, "Eni Is Said to Abandon Polish Shale Aspirations," *New York Times*, January 15, 2014, B3; see also Eduardo Porter, "Behind Drop in Oil Prices, a Federal Role," *New York Times*, January 21, 2015, B1.

107. Tim Wallace, "Oceans Are Absorbing Almost All of the Globe's Excess Heat," *New York Times*, September 12, 2016. Web.

108. Coral Davenport, "Governments Await Obama's Move on Carbon to Gauge U.S. Climate Efforts," *New York Times*, May 27, 2014, A11, and

"Obama Pursuing Climate Accord in lieu of Treaty," *New York Times*, August 27, 2014, A1.

109. The 2015 COP produced a voluntary agreement on global warming emissions and not a binding treaty. Moreover, the targeted reductions will not prevent devastating global warming. Coral Davenport, "A Climate Accord Based on Global Peer Pressure," *New York Times*, December 15, 2014, A3; Justin Gillis and Somini Sengupta, "Progress Seen on Warming, with a Caveat," *New York Times*, September 28, 2015, A1; Steven E. Koonin, "Tough Realities of the Climate Talks," *New York Times*, November 4, 2015, A31; Stanley Reed, "Global Shift to Lower-Carbon Energy Is Too Slow," *New York Times*, November 10, 2015, B2; Coral Davenport, "Senate Rejects Obama Plan to Cut Emissions at Coal-Burning Plants," *New York Times*, November 18, 2015, A19, "Climate Deal Has Backing Needed to Enter Force, U.N. Signals," *New York Times*, September 21, 2016, A10, and "Nations Target a Powerful Gas in Climate Pact," *New York Times*, October 15, 2016, A1; Brad Plumer and Nadia Popovich, "Here's How Far the World Is From Meeting Its Climate Goals," *New York Times*, November 6, 2017. Web.

110. Paul Chastko, *Developing Alberta's Oil Sands: From Karl Clark to Kyoto* (Calgary: University of Calgary Press, 2004); Gonzalez, *American Empire and the Canadian Oil Sands*.

111. Coral Davenport and Steven Erlanger, "U.S. Hopes Boom in Natural Gas Can Curb Putin," *New York Times*, March 6, 2014, A1. See also "Natural Gas as a Diplomatic Tool," *New York Times*, March 7, 2014, A24; Clifford Krauss, "U.S. Gas Tantalizes Europe, but It's Not a Quick Fix," *New York Times*, April 8, 2014, B1; Stanley Reed and James Kanter, "For a European Energy Chief, a Difficult Alliance," *New York Times*, April 28, 2014, B1; Rick Gladstone, "Russia and Iran Reported in Talks on Energy Deal Worth Billions," *New York Times*, April 29, 2014, A12; Jim Yardley and Jo Becker, "How Putin Forged a Pipeline Deal That Derailed," *New York Times*, December 31, 2014, A1; Meghan L. O'Sullivan, "Trump Can Harness the Energy Boom," *New York Times*, September 15, 2017, A27, and *Windfall: How the New Energy Abundance Upends Global Politics and Strengthens American Power* (New York: Simon & Schuster, 2017). The 2017 sanctions leveled against Russia by the U.S. are viewed as an effort to shift European energy consumption from Russia to the U.S.—as the sanctions target the energy pipelines connecting Russia to Central Europe. The idea being that if Europe could not import natural gas from Russia via pipeline, the continent would switch to liquified natural gas imports from the U.S. David E. Sanger, "Seeking to End Sanctions, Trump and Putin Achieve the Opposite," *New York Times*, July 24, 2017, A5.

112. Yergin, *The Prize*; Norman Rich, *Hitler's War Aims: Ideology, the Nazi State, and the Course of Expansion* (New York: W. W. Norton, 1992); Victor Rothwell, *War Aims in the Second World War: The War Aims of the Major Belligerents, 1939–45* (Edinburgh: Edinburgh University Press, 2005); Adam Tooze, *The Wages of Destruction: The Making and Breaking of the Nazi Economy* (New

York: Viking, 2007); Andrew Roberts, *The Storm of War: A New History of the Second World War* (New York: Harper, 2011); David Stahel, *Kiev 1941: Hitler's Battle for Supremacy in the East* (New York: Cambridge University Press, 2012). 113.

Table 1.1 Automobile Ownership and Use in Cities*

Region	Per Capita Automobile Ownership (per 1,000 people)	Per Capita Automobile Use (km)	Ratio of Per Capita U.S. Automobile Use Compared to Other Urban Areas
U.S. cities	587	18,155	— — —
Australian/ NZ cities	575	11,387	1.60
Canadian cities	530	8,645	2.10
W. European cities	414	6,202	2.93
High-Income Asian cities	210	3,614	5.02

Source: Jeffrey R. Kenworthy, "Energy Use and CO_2 Production in the Urban Passenger Transport Systems of 84 International Cities: Findings and Policy Implications," in *Urban Energy Transition from Fossil Fuels to Renewable Power*, ed. Peter Droege (Amsterdam: Elsevier, 2008), 211–236.

*Figures for most recent year available: 1995.

U.S. cities: Atlanta, Chicago, Denver, Houston, Los Angeles, New York, Phoenix, San Diego, San Francisco.

Australian/New Zealand cities: Brisbane, Melbourne, Perth, Sydney, Wellington.

Canadian cities: Calgary, Montreal, Ottawa, Toronto, Vancouver.

Western European cities: Graz, Vienna, Brussels, Copenhagen, Helsinki, Lyon, Nantes, Paris, Marseilles, Berlin, Frankfurt, Hamburg, Dusseldorf, Munich, Ruhr, Stuttgart, Athens, Milan, Bologna, Rome, Amsterdam, Oslo, Barcelona, Madrid, Stockholm, Bern, Geneva, Zurich, London, Manchester, Newcastle, Glasgow.

High-Income Asian cities: Osaka, Sapporo, Tokyo, Hong Kong, Singapore, Taipei.

Chapter Two

1. Robert A. Dahl and Charles E. Lindblom, *Politics, Economics, and Welfare* (New Haven: Yale University Press, 1953); Robert A. Dahl, *A Preface to Democratic Theory* (Chicago: University of Chicago Press, 1956); Robert A.

Dahl, *Who Governs? Democracy and Power in an American City* (New Haven: Yale University Press, 1961 [2005]); Sheldon Kamieniecki, *Corporate America and Environmental Policy: How Often Does Business Get Its Way?* (Palo Alto: Stanford University Press, 2006); Frank R. Baumgartner, Jeffrey M. Berry, Marie Hojnacki, David C. Kimball, and Beth L. Leech, *Lobbying and Policy Change: Who Wins, Who Loses, and Why* (Chicago: University of Chicago Press, 2009).

2. David B. Truman, *The Governmental Process: Political Interests and Public Opinion* (New York: Knopf, 1951).

3. Theodore J. Lowi, *The End of Liberalism: The Second Republic of the United States* (New York: Norton, 1979).

4. Grant McConnell, *Private Power and American Democracy* (New York: Knopf, 1966).

5. Dahl and Lindblom, "Preface," in *Politics, Economics, and Welfare*, xxxvii.

6. Arthur Selwyn Miller, *The Modern Corporate State: Private Governments and the American Constitution* (Westport: Greenwood, 1976). See also Brink Lindsey and Steven Teles, *The Captured Economy: How the Powerful Enrich Themselves, Slow Down Growth, and Increase Inequality* (New York: Oxford University Press, 2017).

7. Marc Weiss, *The Rise of the Community Builders: The American Real Estate Industry and Urban Land Planning* (New York: Columbia University Press, 1987); Gonzalez, *Urban Sprawl, Global Warming, and the Empire of Capital*, chap. 4.

8. Weiss, *The Rise of the Community Builders*; Gonzalez, *Urban Sprawl, Global Warming, and the Empire of Capital*; Vishaan Chakrabarti, "America's Urban Future," *New York Times*, April 17, 2014, A23.

9. Joan Hoff Wilson, *American Business and Foreign Policy, 1920–1933* (Lexington: University Press of Kentucky, 1971), chap. 7.

10. E.g., Robert J. Duffy, *Nuclear Politics in America: A History and Theory of Government Regulation* (Lawrence: University of Kansas Press, 1997); Frank N. von Hippel, "It Could Happen Here," *New York Times*, March 24, 2011, A31; Eric Lichtblau, "Lobbyists' Long Effort to Revive Nuclear Industry Faces New Test," *New York Times*, March 25, 2011, A1.

11. Hertsgaard, *Nuclear Inc.*

12. Ibid., 177.

13. Frank G. Dawson, *Nuclear Power: Development and Management of a Technology* (Seattle: University of Washington Press, 1976).

14. Robert Vandenbosch and Susanne E. Vandenbosch, *Nuclear Waste Stalemate: Political and Scientific Controversies* (Salt Lake City: University of Utah Press, 2007); Max S. Power, *America's Nuclear Wastelands: Politics, Accountability, and Cleanup* (Pullman: Washington State University Press, 2008); J. Samuel Walker, *The Road to Yucca Mountain: The Development of Radioactive Waste Policy in the United States* (Berkeley: University of California Press, 2009); Matthew L. Wald, "Report Urges Storing Spent Nuclear Fuel, Not Reprocessing It," *New York Times*, April 26, 2011, A16; John M. Broder and

Matthew L. Wald, "Report Blasts Management Style of Nuclear Regulatory Commission Chairman," *New York Times*, June 11, 2011, A13.

15. Rick Eckstein, *Nuclear Power and Social Power* (Philadelphia: Temple University Press, 1997).

16. John R. Logan and Harvey L. Molotch, *Urban Fortunes: The Political Economy of Place* (Berkeley: University of California Press, 1987 [2007]); George A. Gonzalez, *The Politics of Air Pollution: Urban Growth, Ecological Modernization, and Symbolic Inclusion* (Albany: State University of New York Press, 2005), and "The U.S. Politics of Water Pollution Policy: Urban Growth, Ecological Modernization, and the Vending of Technology," *Capitalism Nature Socialism* 24, no. 4 (2013): 105-21; Brad Plumer, "Why Hurricane Irma Could Hurt a Lot," *New York Times*, September 8, 2017, A17; Lizette Alvarez, "Waters Rise and Hurricanes Roar, but Florida Keeps On Building," *New York Times*, September 19, 2017, A1; Nellie Bowles, "Nothing Is Too Strange for Cities Wooing Amazon to Build There," *New York Times*, September 25, 2017. Web; James B. Stewart, "Following Amazon In the Hunt For a Home," *New York Times*, October 27, 2017, B1.

17. Matthew L. Wald, "U.S. Supports New Nuclear Reactors in Georgia," *New York Times*, February 17, 2010, B1, and "Nuclear Power's Death Somewhat Exaggerated," *New York Times*, April 11, 2012, F4.

18. David A. Kirsch, *The Electric Vehicle and the Burden of History* (New Brunswick: Rutgers University Press, 2000); Joseph J. Romm, *The Hype about Hydrogen: Fact and Fiction in the Race to Save the Climate* (Washington, DC: Island Press, 2004); William J. Mitchell, Christopher E. Borroni-Bird, and Lawrence D. Burns, *Reinventing the Automobile: Personal Urban Mobility for the 21st Century* (Cambridge: MIT Press, 2010); Neal E. Boudette, "Fuel Cells Gain a Following, with a Push from California," *New York Times*, July 22, 2016, B4; Farhad Manjoo, "Upstart Car, Unexpectedly, from an Old-Line Carmaker," *New York Times*, September 15, 2016, B1; Brad Plummer, "Electric Cars' Breakout Could Be Near," *New York Times*, July 10, 2017, B3; Bill Vlasic, "Tesla Delivers a Mass-Market Car. Can It Upend an Industry?," *New York Times*, July 30, 2017, A1; Bill Vlasic and Neal E. Boudette, "U.S. Auto Giants Stake a Claim To a Future With Less Gasoline," *New York Times*, October 3, 2017, A1; Keith Bradsher, "China Hastens A Global Move To Electric Cars," *New York Times*, October 10, 2017, A1; Jack Ewing, "Diesel Scandal Could Slow Volkswagen's Electric Push," *New York Times*, October 28, 2017, B2.

19. Panel on the Impact of the Peaceful Uses of Atomic Energy, *Peaceful Uses of Atomic Energy*, vol. 1 (Washington, DC: Government Printing Office, 1956), xi.

20. Panel on the Impact of the Peaceful Uses of Atomic Energy, *Peaceful Uses of Atomic Energy*, vol. 2 (Washington, DC: Government Printing Office, 1956), xiii–xviii.

21. Panel on the Impact of the Peaceful Uses of Atomic Energy, *Peaceful Uses of Atomic Energy*, vol. 1, 2.

22. I offer a full description this of model elsewhere (George A. Gonzalez, *Corporate Power and the Environment: The Political Economy of U.S. Environmental Policy* [Lanham: Rowman & Littlefield, 2001], 10–13), so here I will only provide its central features.

23. Theda Skocpol, *States and Social Revolutions* (Cambridge: Cambridge University Press, 1979); Eric A. Nordlinger, *On the Autonomy of the Democratic State* (Cambridge: Harvard University Press, 1981); Stephen Skowronek, *Building a New American State: The Expansion of National Administrative Capacities, 1877–1920* (Cambridge: Cambridge University Press, 1982); Theda Skocpol, "Bringing the State Back In: Strategies of Analysis in Current Research," in Peter Evans, Dietrich Rueschemeyer, and Theda Skocpol, eds., *Bringing the State Back In* (Cambridge: Cambridge University Press, 1985); Daniel Carpenter, *The Forging of Bureaucratic Autonomy: Reputations, Networks, and Policy Innovations in Executive Agencies, 1862–1928* (Princeton: Princeton University Press, 2001).

24. See also Christopher Sellars, *Crabgrass Crucible: Suburban Nature and the Rise of Environmentalism in Twentieth-Century America* (Chapel Hill: University of North Carolina Press, 2012).

25. Adam Rome, *The Bulldozer in the Countryside: Suburban Sprawl and the Rise of American Environmentalism* (Cambridge: Cambridge University Press, 2001), chap. 1; see also Gail Radford, *Modern Housing for America: Policy Struggles in the New Deal Era* (Chicago: University of Chicago Press, 1996).

26. Stephen Krasner, *Defending the National Interest: Raw Materials Investments and U.S. Foreign Policy* (Princeton: Princeton University Press, 1978); see also John G. Ikenberry, *Reasons of State: Oil Politics and the Capacities of American Government* (Ithaca: Cornell University Press, 1988), and *Liberal Leviathan: The Origins, Crisis, and Transformation of the American World Order* (Princeton: Princeton University Press, 2012).

27. Theda Skocpol, *Protecting Soldiers and Mothers: The Political Origins of Social Policy in the United States* (Cambridge: Harvard University Press, 1992); Theda Skocpol, Marshall Ganz, and Ziad Munson, "A Nation of Organizers: The Institutional Origins of Civic Voluntarism in the United States," *American Political Science Review* 94, no. 3 (2000): 527–546.

28. Patrick McGrath, *Scientists, Business, and the State, 1890–1960* (Chapel Hill: University of North Carolina Press, 2002); Andrew Rich, *Think Tanks, Public Policy, and the Politics of Expertise* (New York: Cambridge University Press, 2004); Judith A. Layzer, "Deep Freeze: How Business Has Shaped the Global Warming Debate in Congress," in Michael E. Kraft and Sheldon Kamieniecki, eds., *Business and Environmental Policy* (Cambridge: MIT Press, 2007); Hiroko Tabuchi, "U.S. Climate Change Policy: Made in California," *New York Times*, September 27, 2017, A1.

29. Theda Skocpol, "A Brief Response [to G. William Domhoff]," *Politics and Society* 15, no. 3 (1986/87): 332.

30. Seth Shulman, *Undermining Science: Suppression and Distortion in the Bush Administration* (Berkeley: University of California Press, 2006); Catherine Gautier, *Oil, Water, and Climate: An Introduction* (New York: Cambridge University Press, 2008); Judith A. Layzer, *Open for Business: Conservatives'*

Opposition to Environmental Regulation (Cambridge: MIT Press, 2012); George A. Gonzalez, "Is Obama's 2014 Greenhouse Gas Reduction Plan Symbolic? The Creation of the U.S. EPA and a Reliance on the States," *Capitalism Nature Socialism* 26, no. 2 (2015): 92–104; "The Court Enters the Climate Wars," *New York Times*, February 11, 2016, A30; Micheel D. Shear and Brad Plumer, "Trump Has Choice to Make Between Science and His Base," *New York Times*, August 9, 2017, A14; Christine Todd Whitman, "How Not To Run The E.P.A.," *New York Times*, September 8, 2017, A27; Henry Fountain, "News Article On Climate Research Ruled Faulty," *New York Times*, September 17, 2017, A8; Lisa Friedman, "As Trump Takes Aim at Obama's Clean Power Plan, a Legal Battle Looms," *New York Times*, September 29, 2017, A15; Lisa Friedman and Brad Plumer, "E.P.A. Announces Bid to Roll Back Emissions Policy," *New York Times*, October 10, 2017, A1; "Nailing the Coffin on Climate Relief," *New York Times*, October 11, 2017, A22; Lisa Friedman, "Carbon Dioxide Is Harmless, Says Trump Pick for Environmental Adviser," *New York Times*, October 14, 2017, A9, "For U.S., Climate Talks Are Awkward Moment," *New York Times*, October 19, 2017, A10, and "Syria Joins Paris Climate Accord, Leaving Only the U.S. Opposed," *New York Times*, November 8, 2017, A8; "Mr. Trump's Conflicted Regulators," *New York Times*, October 18, 2017, A26; Brad Plumer, "A Climate Report That Changes Minds? Don't Bet on It," *New York Times*, November 5, 2017, A22; "Alone and Adrift in a Warming World," *New York Times*, November 10, 2017, A26.

31. Powell, *The Inquisition of Climate Science*; Justin Gillis, "Ending Its Summer Melt, Arctic Sea Ice Sets a New Low That Leads to Warnings," *New York Times*, September 20, 2012, A8; Brad Plumer and Coral Davenport, "E.P.A. Chief Is Planning A Test of Climate Science," *New York Times*, July 1, 2017, A12.

32. Gautier and Fellous, *Facing Climate Change Together*; Houghton, *Global Warming*.

33. John M. Broder and Elisabeth Rosenthal, "Obama Has Goal to Wrest a Deal in Climate Talks," *New York Times*, December 18, 2009, A1; John M. Broder, "Director of Policy on Climate Will Leave, Her Goal Unmet," *New York Times*, January 25, 2011, A15, and "House Panel Votes to Strip E.P.A. of Power to Regulate Greenhouse Gases," *New York Times*, March 11, 2011, A18.

34. John F. Manley, "Neo-pluralism: A Class Analysis of Pluralism I and Pluralism II," *American Political Science Review* 77, no. 2 (1983): 368–383.

35. Ralph Miliband, *The State in Capitalist Society* (New York: Basic Books, 1969); Colin Hay, Michael Lister, and David Marsh, eds., *The State: Theories and Issues* (New York: Palgrave Macmillan, 2006), chap. 2; Fred Block, "Understanding the Diverging Trajectories of the United States and Western Europe: A Neo-Polanyian Analysis," *Politics & Society* 35, no. 1, 2007: 3–33; Paul Wetherly, Clyde W. Barrow, and Peter Burnham, eds., *Class, Power and the State in Capitalist Society: Essays on Ralph Miliband* (New York: Palgrave Macmillan, 2008); Clyde W. Barrow, *Toward a Critical Theory of States: The Poulantzas-Miliband Debate after Globalization* (Albany: State University of New York Press, 2016).

36. Clyde W. Barrow, *Critical Theories of the State* (Madison: University of Wisconsin Press, 1993), 17; Barrow explains that "corporations emerged as

the dominant economic institutions in capitalist societies by the end of the nineteenth century." He goes on to note that as early as the late 1920s "the bulk of U.S. economic activity, whether measured in terms of assets, profits, employment, investment, market shares, or research and development, was concentrated in the fifty largest financial institutions and five hundred largest nonfinancial corporations." See also, Thomas Piketty, *Capital in the Twenty-First Century*, trans. Arthur Goldhammer (Cambridge: Belknap Press, 2014); Patricia Cohen, "Study Finds Global Wealth Is Flowing to the Richest," *New York Times*, January 19, 2015, B6; Gerry Mullany, "World's 8 Richest Have as Much Wealth as Bottom Half, Oxfam Says," *New York Times*, January 16, 2017. Web.

Political scientists Jeffrey A. Winters and Benjamin I. Page, writing in 2009, hold that "it is now appropriate to . . . think about the possibility of *extreme* political inequality, involving great political influence by a very small number of extremely wealthy individuals." They go on to add that "we argue that it is useful to think about the U.S. political system in terms of oligarchy." Jeffrey A. Winters and Benjamin I. Page, "Oligarchy in the United States," *Perspectives on Politics* 7, no. 4 (2009), 744, emphasis in original; see also Paul Krugman, "Oligarchy, American Style," *New York Times*, November 4, 2011, A31, and "The Undeserving Rich," *New York Times*, January 20, 2014, A17; Jeffrey A. Winters, *Oligarchy* (New York: Cambridge University Press, 2011); Shaila Dewan and Robert Gebeloff, "One Percent, Many Variations," *New York Times*, January 15, 2012, A1; David Leonhardt, "All for the 1%, 1% for All," *New York Times*, May 4, 2014, MM23; Nicholas Kristof, "An Idiot's Guide to Inequality," *New York Times*, July 24, 2014, A27; Anna Bernasek, "The Typical Household, Now Worth a Third Less," *New York Times*, July 27, 2014, BU6; Neil Irwin, "Economic Expansion for Everyone? Not Anymore," *New York Times*, September 27, 2014, B1; Robert Frank, "Another Widening Gap: The Haves vs. the Have-Mores," *New York Times*, November 16, 2014, BU4.

37. Paul Krugman, "Paranoia of the Plutocrats," *New York Times*, January 27, 2014, A19.

38. Nicholas Confessore, "Big-Money Donors Demand Larger Say in Party Strategy," *New York Times*, March 2, 2014, A1.

39. Carl Hulse and Ashley Parker, "Koch Group, Spending Freely, Hones Attack on Government," *New York Times*, March 21, 2014, A1.

40. Gail Collins, "Billion Dollar Babies," *New York Times*, March 6, 2014, A29.

41. Nicholas Confessore, "New Rules Would Rein in Nonprofits' Political Role," *New York Times*, November 27, 2013, A1; "The Koch Party," *New York Times*, January 26, 2014, SR14; Carl Hulse, "With Senate at Stake, Koch Groups Start Endorsing by Name," *New York Times*," October 7, 2016, A16; Gordon Lafer, *The One Percent Solution: How Corporations Are Remaking America One State at a Time* (Ithaca: Cornell University Press, 2017); Kenneth P. Vogel and Jeremy W. Peters, "In Alabama Win, Model of New Bannon Alliance," *New York Times*, September 29, 2017, Page A1.

42. Timothy Kuhner, *Capitalism v. Democracy: Money in Politics and the Free Market Constitution* (Palo Alto: Stanford University Press, 2014); Robert E. Mutch, *Buying the Vote: A History of Campaign Finance Reform* (New York: Oxford University Press, 2014); Eric Lichtblau, "Paralyzed F.E.C. Can't Do Its Job, Chairwoman Says," *New York Times*, May 3, 2015, A1; Nicholas Confessore, Sarah Cohen, and Karen Yourish, "A Wealthy Few Lead in Giving to Campaigns," *New York Times*, August 2, 2015, A1; Nicholas Confessore, "How Deep Pockets of One Family Helped Shake Up Trump Campaign," *New York Times*, August 19, 2016, A15; Amy Chozick and Jonathan Martin, "Clinton Uses Access to Woo the Ultrarich," *New York Times*, September 4, 2016, A1; Nicholas Confessore and Rachel Shorey, "Outside Money Favors Clinton at a 2-to-1," *New York Times*, October 23, 2016, A1; Kenneth P. Vogel and Rachel Shorey, "Wooing Donors, Democrats Start 2020 Race Early," *New York Times*, September 3, 2017, A1; Celestine Bohlen, "American Democracy Is Drowning in Money," *International New York Times*, September 21, 2017, S4; Carl Hulse, "Face to Face With Failure, and the Donors Aren't Happy," *New York Times*, September 23, 2017, A12; Kenneth P. Vogel, "Battling Trump, Liberals Descend Into Tug of War," *New York Times*, October 8, 2017, A1.

43. "When 'Super PACs' Become Lobbyists," *New York Times*, November 27, 2012, A30; Eric Lipton and Ben Protess, "Law Doesn't End Revolving Door on Capitol Hill," *New York Times*, February 2, 2014, A1; "The Capitol's Spinning Door Accelerates," *New York Times*, February 3, 2014, A22; Nicholas Confessore, "Financier Plans Big Ad Campaign on Environment," *New York Times*, February 18, 2014, A1; Eric Lipton and Jonathan Weisman, "Lobbyists Who Once Cheered Tax Overhaul Now Work to Kill It," *New York Times*, April 2, 2014, B1; Paul Krugman, "Charlatans, Cranks and Kansas," *New York Times*, June 30, 2014, A19; Ashley Parker, "Outside Money Drives a Deluge of Political Ads," *New York Times*, July 28, 2014, A1; Jonathan Weisman, "G.O.P. Error Reveals Donors and the Price of Access," *New York Times*, September 25, 2014, A15; Eric Lipton, "Lobbyists, Bearing Gifts, Pursue Attorneys General," *New York Times*, October 29, 2014, A1; Zephyr Teachout, *Corruption in America: From Benjamin Franklin's Snuff Box to Citizens United* (Cambridge: Harvard University Press, 2014); Eric Lichtblau, "I.R.S. Expected to Stand Aside as Nonprofits Increase Role in 2016 Race," *New York Times*, July 6, 2015, A13; Eric Lichtblau and Nicholas Confessore, "What Campaign Filings Won't Show: Super PACs' Growing Sway," *New York Times*, July 15, 2015. Web; Alan Rappeport and Thomas Kaplan, "A Battle to Protect Proposed Tax Breaks," *New York Times*, September 29, 2017, A16.

44. Eric Lipton, "(Legal) Sprees with Lobbyists," *New York Times*, January 20, 2014, A1; Nicholas Confessore and Eric Lipton, "Seeking to Ban Online Betting, G.O.P. Donor Tests Influence," *New York Times*, March 28, 2014, A1; Jonathan Weisman, "G.O.P. Error Reveals Donors and the Price of Access," *New York Times*, September 25, 2014, A15; Tara Siegel Bernard, "A Citizen's Guide to Buying Political Access," *New York Times*, November 19, 2014, F7; Eric Lipton,

"Energy and Regulators on One Team," *New York Times*, December 7, 2014, A1; Ashley Parker, " 'Koch Primary' Tests Hopefuls in the G.O.P.," *New York Times*, January 21, 2015, A1; Eric Lipton, "Leader on Environment Gets Support of Industry," *New York Times*, March 7, 2015, A12; Carl Hulse, "Is the Supreme Court Naïve About Corruption? Ask Jack Abramoff," *New York Times*, July 6, 2016, A15; Amy Chozick, "Republicans Pounce as Clinton Denigrates Many of Trump's Backers," September 11, 2016, A18; Jonathan Martin, Alexander Burns, and Maggie Haberman, "Cut Ties to Trump, Big Donors Tell R.N.C.," *New York Times*, October 14, 2016, A14.

45. Joshua Barkan, *Corporate Sovereignty: Law and Government under Capitalism* (Minneapolis: University of Minnesota Press, 2013); Eric L. Lewis, "Who Are 'We the People'?" *New York Times*, October 5, 2014, SR1.

46. Barrow, *Critical Theories of the State*, 16; Nicholas Confessore, "Public Goals, Private Interests in Debt Campaign," *New York Times*, January 10, 2013, A1; Eric Lipton, "Fight Over Wage Illustrates Web of Industry Ties," *New York Times*, February 10, 2014, A1; Eric Lipton, Nicholas Confessore, and Brooke Williams, "Top Scholars or Lobbyists? Often It's Both," *New York Times*, August 9, 2016, A1.

47. William Appleman Williams, *The Roots of the Modern American Empire* (New York: Random House, 1969), 98.

48. Ibid.

49. G. William Domhoff, *The Bohemian Grove and Other Retreats* (New York: Harper and Row, 1974).

50. Michael Useem, *The Inner Circle: Large Corporations and the Rise of Business Political Activity in the U.S. and U.K.* (Oxford: Oxford University Press, 1984); see also Beth Mintz and Michael Schwartz, *The Power Structure of American Business* (Chicago: University of Chicago Press, 1985).

51. G. William Domhoff, *Who Rules America?*, 7th ed. (New York: McGraw-Hill, 2013), chap. 4; David Gelles, "Soros Gives Billions to His Charity, Now the Second Biggest in the U.S.," *New York Times*, October 18, 2017, B1; Scott Shane, Spencer Woodman and Michael Forsythe, "Being Famously Wealthy, as Quietly as Possible," *New York Times*, November 8, 2017, A1.

52. G. William Domhoff, *The Powers That Be* (New York: Random House, 1978), 61.

53. James Weinstein, *The Corporate Ideal in the Liberal State: 1900–1918* (Boston: Beacon Press, 1968); David Eakins, "Business Planners and America's Postwar Expansion," in David Horowitz, ed., *Corporations and the Cold War* (New York: Monthly Review Press, 1969); David Eakins, "Policy-Planning for the Establishment," in Ronald Radosh and Murray N. Rothbard, eds., *A New History of Leviathan* (New York: E. P. Dutton & Co., 1972); Gabriel Kolko, *The Triumph of Conservatism: A Reinterpretation of American History, 1900–1916* (New York: Free Press, 1977 [1963]); Domhoff, *The Powers That Be*; Domhoff, *Who Rules America?*, chap. 4.

54. Fred Bunyan Joyner, *David Ames Wells: Champion of Free Trade* (Cedar Rapids: Torch Press, 1939); Walter Lafeber, *The New Empire: An*

Interpretation of American Expansion, 1860–1898 (Ithaca: Cornell University Press, 1963); Williams, *Roots of the Modern American Empire*; Richard W. Turk, *The Ambiguous Relationship: Theodore Roosevelt and Alfred Thayer Mahan* (New York: Greenwood, 1987); Warren Zimmermann, *First Great Triumph: How Five Americans Made Their Country a World Power* (New York: Farrar, Straus and Giroux, 2002).

55. Weinstein, *Corporate Ideal in the Liberal State*; Eakins, "Business Planners and America's Postwar Expansion"; Domhoff, *The Powers That Be*; G. William Domhoff, *The Power Elite and the State* (New York: Aldine de Gruyter, 1990); G. William Domhoff, *State Autonomy or Class Dominance?* (New York: Aldine de Gruyter, 1996); Domhoff, *Who Rules America?*; Edward H. Berman, *The Ideology of Philanthropy: The Influence of the Carnegie, Ford, and Rockefeller Foundations on American Foreign Policy* (Albany: State University of New York Press, 1983); Clyde W. Barrow, *Universities and the Capitalist State: Corporate Liberalism and the Reconstruction of American Higher Education, 1894–1928* (Madison: University of Wisconsin Press, 1990); Clyde W. Barrow, "Corporate Liberalism, Finance Hegemony, and Central State Intervention in the Reconstruction of American Higher Education," *Studies in American Political Development* 6 (Fall 1992): 420–444; Barrow, *Critical Theories of the State*, chap. 1, and *Toward a Critical Theory of States*, chap. 3; Mark Dowie, *American Foundations: An Investigative History* (Cambridge: MIT Press, 2001); Christopher J. Cyphers, *The National Civic Federation and the Making of New Liberalism, 1900–1915* (Westport: Praeger, 2002); Inderjeet Parmar, "American Foundations and the Development of International Knowledge Networks," *Global Networks* 2, no. 1 (2002): 13–30; Joan Roelofs, *Foundations and Public Policy: The Mask of Pluralism* (Albany: State University of New York Press, 2003); Jane Mayer, "How Right-Wing Billionaires Infiltrated Higher Education," *Chronicle of Higher Education*, February 12, 2016. Web.

56. Domhoff, *The Powers That Be*, 63; see also Eric Lipton and Brooke Williams, "Scholarship or Business? Think Tanks Blur the Line," *New York Times*, August 8, 2016, A1; Eric Bonds, "Beyond Denialism: Think Tank Approaches to Climate Change," *Sociology Compass* 10, no. 4 (2016): 306–317; Kenneth P. Vogel, "Think Tank, Funded by Google, Is Stung By Backlash After Firing a Google Critic," *New York Times*, September 2, 2017, A13.

57. Eakins, "Policy-Planning for the Establishment"; Domhoff, *The Powers That Be*, 61–87; Domhoff, *Who Rules America?*, chap. 4; Barrow, *Critical Theories of the State*, chap. 1, and *Toward a Critical Theory of States*, chap. 3; Gonzalez, *American Empire and the Canadian Oil Sands*, chap. 6; Sheila Kaplan and Eric Lipton, "Chemical Industry Ally Vies for Top E.P.A. Post," *New York Times*, September 20, 2017, A16. The economic elite–led policy-planning network has two groupings—one that is characterized as "moderate" or "corporate liberal" and the other as "conservative." While these two groups will frequently compromise on issues, they sometimes cannot. When they cannot find common ground, their struggles will usually spill over into government, where each will utilize its political strength to try and get its

way. Weinstein, *Corporate Ideal in the Liberal State*; Eakins, "Business Planners and America's Postwar Expansion"; Eakins, "Policy-Planning for the Establishment"; Domhoff, *The Powers That Be*, chap. 3; Domhoff, *The Power Elite and the State*, 38–39; Barrow, *Critical Theories of the State*, chap. 1, and *Toward a Critical Theory of States*.

58. Mark Dowie, *Losing Ground: American Environmentalism at the Close of the Twentieth Century* (Cambridge: MIT Press, 1995), 58–59; Dowie, *American Foundations*; Roelofs, *Foundations and Public Policy*.

59. Susan R. Schrepfer, *The Fight to Save the Redwoods: A History of Environmental Reform, 1917–1978* (Madison: University of Wisconsin Press, 1983), 10; see also Holway R. Jones, *John Muir and the Sierra Club: The Battle for Yosemite* (San Francisco: Sierra Club, 1965); and Richard J. Orsi, " 'Wilderness Saint' and 'Robber Baron': The Anomalous Partnership of John Muir and the Southern Pacific Company for Preservation of Yosemite National Park," *Pacific Historian* 29 (Summer–Fall 1985): 136–152.

60. Schrepfer, *Fight to Save the Redwoods*, 171–173; see also Michael Cohen, *The History of the Sierra Club, 1892–1970* (San Francisco: Sierra Club Books, 1988).

61. Schrepfer, *Fight to Save the Redwoods*, 113; see also George A. Gonzalez, "The Wilderness Act of 1964 and the Wilderness Preservation Policy Network," *Capitalism Nature Socialism* 20, no. 4 (2009): 31–52.

62. Gonzalez, *Corporate Power and the Environment*; George A. Gonzalez, "Ideas and State Capacity, or Business Dominance? A Historical Analysis of Grazing on the Public Grasslands," *Studies in American Political Development* 15 (Fall 2001): 234–244; Gonzalez, *The Politics of Air Pollution*; George A. Gonzalez, "The Comprehensive Everglades Restoration Plan: Economic or Environmental Sustainability?," *Polity* 37, no. 4 (2005): 466–490; Owen Temby, "Trouble in Smogville: The Politics of Toronto's Air Pollution during the 1950s," *Journal of Urban History* 39, no. 4 (2013): 669–689; Owen Temby and Ryan O'Connor, "Property, Technology, and Environmental Policy: The Politics of Acid Rain in Ontario, 1978–1985," *Journal of Policy History* 27, no. 4 (2015): 636–669; Owen Temby and Joshua MacFadyen, "Urban Elites, Energy, and Smoke Policy in Montreal during the Interwar Period," *Urban History Review* 45, no. 1 (2016): 37–49.

63. Felicity Barringer, "A Coalition for Firm Limit on Emissions," *New York Times*, January 19, 2007, C1.

64. Blue Ribbon Commission on America's Nuclear Future, Commission Members, http://cybercemetery.unt.edu/archive/brc/20120620215412/http://brc.gov/index.php?q=commission-members (viewed on October 18, 2012).

65. Samuel Hays, "The Politics of Reform in Municipal Government in the Progressive Era," *Pacific Northwest Quarterly* 55, no. 4 (1964): 157–169; G. William Domhoff, *Who Really Rules? New Haven and Community Power Reexamined* (Santa Monica: Goodyear, 1978).

66. Logan and Molotch, *Urban Fortunes*, 152.

67. Barrow, *Critical Theories of the State*, chap. 2, and *Toward a Critical Theory of States*, chap. 5; John S. Dryzek, *Democracy in Capitalist Times* (New

York: Oxford University Press, 1996); Stanley Aronowitz and Peter Bratsis, eds., *Paradigm Lost: State Theory Reconsidered* (Minneapolis: University of Minnesota Press, 2002); Paul Wetherly, *Marxism and the State: An Analytical Approach* (New York: Palgrave Macmillan, 2005).

68. Harvey Molotch, "The City as a Growth Machine: Towards a Political Economy of Place," *American Journal of Sociology* 82, no. 2 (1976): 309–322; Harvey Molotch, "Capital and Neighborhood in the United States," *Urban Affairs Quarterly* 14, no. 3 (1979): 289–312; Logan and Molotch, *Urban Fortunes*.

69. Weiss, *The Rise of the Community Builders*; Gonzalez, *Urban Sprawl, Global Warming, and the Empire of Capital*, chap. 3.

Chapter Three

1. Klaus Fischer, *Hitler and America* (Philadelphia: University of Pennsylvania Press, 2011).

2. Robert Fishman, *Bourgeois Utopias: The Rise and Fall of Suburbia* (New York: Basic Books, 1987); Robert M. Fogelson, *Bourgeois Nightmares: Suburbia, 1870–1930* (New Haven: Yale University Press, 2005); Paul L. Knox, *Metroburbia, USA* (Piscataway: Rutgers University Press, 2008); Jed Kolko, "Return to Cities an Urban Legend, Mostly," *New York Times*, May 24, 2017, A18.

3. *Report of the President's Conference on Unemployment* (Washington, DC: Government Printing Office, 1921), 7–14.

4. Ibid., 20.

5. Ibid., 9, 14, and 89.

6. Ibid., 96, emphasis added.

7. Frederic L. Paxson, "The American Highway Movement, 1916–1935," *American Historical Review* 51, no. 2 (1946): 239–241.

8. American Road Congress, *Papers, Addresses, and Resolutions before the American Road Congress, Richmond, Virginia, November 20–23, 1911* (Baltimore: Waverly Press, 1911).

9. Hugh Chalmers, "Relation of the Automobile Industry to the Good Roads Movement, in American Road Congress," in *Papers, Addresses, and Resolutions before the American Road Congress, Richmond, Virginia, November 20–23, 1911* (Baltimore: Waverly Press, 1911), 142–143.

10. Ibid., 149.

11. *President's Conference on Unemployment*, 21.

12. Ibid., 118.

13. Weiss, *The Rise of the Community Builders*, 67.

14. Adam Rome, *The Bulldozer in the Countryside: Suburban Sprawl and the Rise of American Environmentalism* (Cambridge: Cambridge University Press, 2001), chap. 1; see also Gail Radford, *Modern Housing for America: Policy Struggles in the New Deal Era* (Chicago: University of Chicago Press, 1996).

15. Rome, *Bulldozer in the Countryside*, 22–23.

16. *President's Conference on Unemployment*, 118.

17. Greg Hise, *Magnetic Los Angeles: Planning the Twentieth-Century Metropolis* (Baltimore: Johns Hopkins University Press, 1997), 38.

18. Weiss, *The Rise of the Community Builders*, 29.

19. Christine M. Rosen, *The Limits of Power: Great Fires and the Process of City Growth in America* (Cambridge: Cambridge University Press, 1986); Stanley K. Schultz, *Constructing Urban Culture: American Cities and City Planning, 1800–1920* (Philadelphia: Temple University Press, 1989); Robert M. Fogelson, *Downtown: Its Rise and Fall, 1880–1950* (New Haven: Yale University Press, 2001); Mark Tebeau, *Eating Smoke: Fire in Urban America, 1800—1950* (Baltimore: Johns Hopkins University Press, 2003); Robert A. Beauregard, *When America Became Suburban* (Minneapolis: University of Minnesota Press, 2006); Dorceta E. Taylor, *The Environment and the People in American Cities: 1600s—1900s* (Durham: Duke University Press, 2009).

20. Donald N. Dewees, "The Decline of the American Street Railways," *Traffic Regulation* 24 (1970): 563–581; Mark S. Foster, *From Streetcar to Superhighway: American City Planners and Urban Transportation, 1900–1940* (Philadelphia: Temple University Press, 1981); Clay McShane, *Down the Asphalt Path: The Automobile and the American City* (New York: Columbia University Press, 1994); Jane Holtz Kay, *Asphalt Nation: How the Automobile Took Over America and How We Can Take It Back* (Berkeley: University of California Press, 1998), chap. 8.

21. James Flink, *The Car Culture* (Cambridge: MIT Press, 1975), and *The Automobile Age* (Cambridge: MIT Press, 1990); John A. Jakle and Keith A. Sculle, *Motoring: The Highway Experience in America* (Athens: University of Georgia Press, 2008).

22. Donald F. Davis, *Conspicuous Production: Automobiles and Elites in Detroit, 1899–1933* (Philadelphia: Temple University Press, 1988).

23. Kenneth T. Jackson, *Crabgrass Frontier: The Suburbanization of the United States* (New York: Oxford University Press, 1985); Robert Fishman, *Bourgeois Utopias: The Rise and Fall of Suburbia* (New York: Basic Books, 1987); Fogelson, *Bourgeois Nightmares*; Robert Bruegmann, *Sprawl: A Compact History* (Chicago: University of Chicago Press, 2005); Kevin M. Kruse and Thomas J. Sugrue, eds., *The New Suburban History* (Chicago: University of Chicago Press, 2006).

24. Flink, *The Car Culture*, and *The Automobile Age*; Davis, *Conspicuous Production*.

25. As quoted in Davis, *Conspicuous Production*, 117, ellipsis in original.

26. Ibid., 121.

27. Mark S. Foster, "The Model-T, the Hard Sell, and Los Angeles's Urban Growth: The Decentralization of Los Angeles during the 1920s," *Pacific Historical Review* 44 (November 1975), 483.

28. For example, Robert M. Fogelson, *The Fragmented Metropolis, Los Angeles, 1850–1930* (Cambridge: Harvard University Press, 1967); Foster, "The Model-T, the Hard Sell, and Los Angeles's Urban Growth"; Scott Bottles, *Los*

Angeles and the Automobile: The Making of the Modern City (Los Angeles: University of California Press, 1987).

29. Fogelson, *The Fragmented Metropolis*, and *Downtown*; Foster, "The Model-T, the Hard Sell, and Los Angeles's Urban Growth"; Martin Wachs, "Autos, Transit, and the Sprawl of Los Angeles: The 1920s," *Journal of the American Planning Association* 50, no. 3 (1984): 297–310; B. Marchand, *The Emergence of Los Angeles: Population and Housing in the City of Dreams, 1940–1970* (London: Pion, 1986); Hise, *Magnetic Los Angeles*; Greg Hise, "'Nature's Workshop' Industry and Urban Expansion in Southern California, 1900–1950," *Journal of Historical Geography* 27, no. 1 (2001): 74–92; William B. Fulton, *The Reluctant Metropolis: The Politics of Urban Growth in Los Angeles* (Baltimore: Johns Hopkins University Press, 2001).

30. Martha L. Olney, *Buy Now, Pay Later: Advertising, Credit, and Consumer Durables in the 1920s* (Chapel Hill: University of North Carolina Press, 1991), 9, parentheses in original.

31. Peter O. Muller, *Contemporary Suburban America* (Englewood Cliffs: Prentice-Hall, 1981); Lizabeth Cohen, "Is There an Urban History of Consumption?," *Journal of Urban History* 29, no. 2 (2003): 87–106; Matthew D. Lassiter, *The Silent Majority: Suburban Politics in the Sunbelt South* (Princeton: Princeton University Press, 2005); Beauregard, *When America Became Suburban*.

32. Olney, *Buy Now, Pay Later*, 9.

33. Ibid.

34. Ibid., 22, emphasis added.

35. Ibid.

36. Roger Miller, "Selling Mrs. Consumer: Advertising and the Creation of Suburban Socio-Spatial Relations, 1910–1930," *Antipode* 23, no. 3 (1991): 263–306; Victor J. Visor, "Winning the Peace: American Planning for a Profitable Postwar World," *Journal of American Studies* 35, no. 1 (2001): 111–126.

37. Rosa-Maria Gelpi and François Julien-Labruyère, *The History of Consumer Credit: Doctrines and Practices* (New York: St. Martin's Press, 2000), chap. 8; Rowena Olegario, *A Culture of Credit: Embedding Trust and Transparency in American Business* (Cambridge: Harvard University Press, 2006).

38. Most automobiles in the 1920s were purchased through credit. Nonetheless, as consumer credit historian Lendol Caldwell explains, "throughout the 1920s 25 to 40 percent of Americans in any given year continued to buy cars for cash." Lendol Calder, *Financing the American Dream: A Cultural History of Consumer Credit* (Princeton: Princeton University Press, 1999), 194. The terms of retail automotive credit were rather stringent during the 1920s. Loan terms required one-third of the purchase price upon signing, and the amortization period on automobile loans was from six to twelve months. Moreover, economic historian Martha Olney reports that the "effective annual interest rate exceeded 30 percent" on automobiles purchased through credit in the 1920s. Martha L. Olney, "Credit as a Production-Smoothing Device: The Case of Automobiles, 1913–1938," *Journal of Economic History* 49, no. 2

(1989), 381. In the 1930s automotive credit terms were substantially liberalized. A general liberalization occurred in the 1930s on terms of credit with regard to the purchase of consumer durables. Calder, *Financing the American Dream*, 275.

39. Hounshell, *From the American System to Mass Production*, chaps. 6, 7, and 8; Abrams, *America Transformed*.

40. Fearon, *War, Prosperity, and Depression*, 48.

41. Markusen, *Profit Cycles, Oligopoly, and Regional Development*; Atkinson, *The Past and Future of America's Economy*.

42. Field, "Technological Change and U.S. Productivity Growth in the Interwar Years," 206.

43. Fearon, *War, Prosperity, and Depression*, 55.

Historian T. C. Barker in the following reports automobile ownership during the 1930s among the leading economies of the world at the time:

> There were then [1939] only 2,000,000 cars of all makes registered in the whole country [of Great Britain] (and 460,000 motor cycles), while the United States, with less than three times the population, possessed 30,000,000 cars. And Britain was well ahead of the other Europeans. France, for instance, had only 1,600,000 cars in 1938 and Germany, still at an earlier stage of market growth, had fewer: 1,100,000 cars (and 1,300,000 motor cycles).

Barker, "The International History of Motor Transport," 6.

44. Fearon, *War, Prosperity, and Depression*, 55.

45. Ibid., 58; see also Jean-Pierre Bardou, Jean-Jacques Chanaron, Patrick Fridenson, and James M. Laux, *The Automobile Revolution: The Impact of an Industry* (Chapel Hill: University of North Carolina Press, 1982); David J. St. Clair, *The Motorization of American Cities* (New York: Praeger, 1986); Matthew Paterson, *Automobile Politics* (New York: Cambridge University Press, 2007).

46. Elliot Rosen, *Roosevelt, the Great Depression, and the Economics of Recovery* (Charlottesville: University of Virginia Press, 2005), 118.

47. Maury Klein, *The Genesis of Industrial America, 1870–1920* (New York: Cambridge University Press, 2007), 181.

48. Richard B. Du Boff, *Accumulation and Power: An Economic History of the United States* (Armonk: M. E. Sharpe, 1989), 83.

49. Josephine Young Case, *Owen D. Young and American Enterprise: A Biography* (Boston: David R. Godine, 1982); David Nye, *Image Worlds: Corporate Identities at General Electric, 1890–1930* (Cambridge: MIT Press, 1985).

50. Report of the Committee on Recent Economic Changes, of the President's Conference on Unemployment, *Recent Economic Changes in the United States*, vols. 1–2 (New York: McGraw-Hill, 1929), v.

51. Ibid.

52. Ibid., 236.

53. Ibid., 254.

54. Ibid., 422.

55. Tooze, *The Wages of Destruction*, 27; Stephen A. Schuker, *American Reparations to Germany, 1919–33: Implications for the Third World Debt Crisis* (Princeton: Princeton Studies in International Finance, 1988).

56. Tooze, *The Wages of Destruction*, 691–692, fn. 39; see also Frank Costigliola, *Awkward Dominion: American Political, Economic, and Cultural Relations with Europe, 1919–1933* (Ithaca: Cornell University Press, 1984); E. H. Carr, *The Twenty Years Crisis, 1919–1930* (London: Macmillan, 1939); Charles Kindleberger, *The World in Depression 1929–1939* (Berkeley: University of California Press, 1986); and Patrick O. Cohrs, *The Unfinished Peace after World War I: America, Britain, and the Stabilisation of Europe, 1919–1932* (New York: Cambridge University Press, 2006).

57. E. J. Feuchtwanger, *From Weimar to Hitler* (New York: St. Martin's Press, 1993), 209.

58. Joan Hoff, *A Faustian Foreign Policy: From Woodrow Wilson to George W. Bush* (New York: Cambridge University Press, 2008), 69.

59. Tooze, *The Wages of Destruction*, 28.

60. William S. Borden, *The Pacific Alliance: United States Foreign Economic Policy and Japanese Trade Recovery, 1947–1955* (Madison: University of Wisconsin Press, 1984); Michael Schaller, *Altered States: The United States and Japan since the Occupation* (New York: Oxford University Press, 1997); Gary Herrigel, *Industrial Constructions: The Sources of German Industrial Power* (New York: Cambridge University Press, 2000); Horst Siebert, *The German Economy: Beyond the Social Market* (Princeton: Princeton University Press, 2005); John Swenson-Wright, *Unequal Allies? United States Security and Alliance Policy toward Japan, 1945–1960* (Stanford: Stanford University Press, 2005); Belay Seyoum, *Export-Import Theory, Practices, and Procedures*, 2nd edition (New York: Routledge, 2008).

61. Tooze, *The Wages of Destruction*, 25.

62. Feuchtwanger, *From Weimar to Hitler*, 172; Jonathan Wright, *Gustav Stresemann: Weimar's Greatest Statesman* (New York: Oxford University Press, 2002).

63. Feuchtwanger, *From Weimar to Hitler*, 209.

64. Tooze, *The Wages of Destruction*, 25.

65. Ibid., 28; see also Hans Mommsen, "National Socialism: Continuity and Change," in Hans Mommsen, ed., *From Weimar to Auschwitz: Essays on German History* (Princeton: Princeton University Press), 141–163; and Herman Beck, *The Fateful Alliance: German Conservatives and Nazis in 1933* (New York: Berghahn, 2008).

66. Tooze, *The Wages of Destruction*, 14; E. E. Schattschneider, *Politics, Pressures and the Tariff: A Study of Free Private Enterprise in Pressure Politics,*

as Shown in the 1929–1930 Revision of the Tariff (New York: Prentice-Hill, 1935 [1963]).

67. Wilson, *American Business and Foreign Policy*, 11.

68. Alfred E. Eckes Jr., *Opening America's Market: U.S. Foreign Trade Policy since 1776* (Chapel Hill: University of North Carolina Press, 1995), 49; Hoff, *A Faustian Foreign Policy*, 73.

69. Melvyn Leffler, *The Elusive Quest: America's Pursuit of European Stability and French Security, 1919–1933* (Chapel Hill: University of North Carolina Press, 1979).

70. Richard J. Evans, *The Coming of the Third Reich* (New York: Penguin, 2004), 252.

71. Tooze, *The Wages of Destruction*, 14. The terms of the Young Plan would have had Germany liquidating its debt until 1988, at a total payout of $28 billion. Historian Feuchtwanger holds that "whatever immediate advantages Germany gained from the Young Plan they were overshadowed by the psychological incubus of a debt that was to continue for another sixty years. This was exploited to the full by the nationalist opposition" within Germany. Feuchtwanger, *From Weimar to Hitler*, 209. See also Gordon Alexander Craig, *Germany, 1866–1945* (New York: Oxford University Press, 1978); and Eberhard Kolb, *The Weimar Republic* (New York: Routledge, 2005).

72. Steve Isser, *The Economics and Politics of the United States Oil Industry, 1920–1990: Profits, Populism, and Petroleum* (New York: Routledge, 1996); Roger M. Olien and Diana Davids Olien, *Oil and Ideology: The Cultural Creation of the American Petroleum Industry* (Chapel Hill: University of North Carolina Press, 2000); Diana Davids Olien and Roger M. Olien, *Oil in Texas: The Gusher Age, 1895–1945* (Austin: University of Texas Press, 2002).

Chapter Four

1. Robert Dallek, *Franklin D. Roosevelt and American Foreign Policy, 1932–1945* (New York: Oxford University Press, 1995).

2. Ibid., 24.

3. Ibid., 30. Roosevelt was inaugurated as president on March 4, 1933.

4. Ibid., 31.

5. Ibid., 37.

6. Ibid., 38.

7. Ibid., 40.

8. Keith J. Volanto, *Texas, Cotton, and the New Deal* (College Station: Texas A&M University-Commerce, 2004).

9. The National Industrial Recovery Act was not successfully implemented, and, ultimately, vacated by the Supreme Court. Michael A. Bernstein, *The Great Depression: Delayed Recovery and Economic Change in America, 1929–1939* (New York: Cambridge University Press, 1987); Colin Gordon, *New Deals: Business, Labor, and Politics in America, 1920–1935* (New York: Cam-

bridge University Press, 1994); Kenneth Finegold and Theda Skocpol, *State and Party in America's New Deal* (Madison: University of Wisconsin Press, 1995); Domhoff, *State Autonomy or Class Dominance?*; Michael D. Bordo, Claudia Goldin, and Eugene N. White, eds., *The Defining Moment: The Great Depression and the American Economy in the Twentieth Century* (Chicago: University of Chicago Press, 1998); William H. Becker and William M. McClenahan Jr., *The Market, the State, and the Export-Import Bank of the United States, 1934–2000* (Cambridge: Cambridge University Press, 2003).

10. Dallek, *Franklin D. Roosevelt*, 92.

11. Hoff, *A Faustian Foreign Policy*, 73.

12. Dallek, *Franklin D. Roosevelt*, 93.

U.S. trade policy under Roosevelt during the 1930s was less nationalistic than other countries. Power Chu, "A History of the Hull Trade Program, 1934–1939" (PhD dissertation, Columbia University, 1957); Eckes, *Opening America's Market*.

13. Michael E. Stone, "The Housing Problem in the United States: Origins and Prospects," *Socialist Review* 52, no. 4 (1980), 80.

14. Fearon, *War, Prosperity, and Depression*, chap. 7.

15. Ibid., 119.

16. John M. Gries and James Ford, eds., *The President's Conference on Home Builders and Home Ownership: Home Finance and Taxation* (Washington, DC: National Capital Press, 1932), v.

17. Ibid., 22.

18. Ibid., 23.

19. Ibid., 25–26.

20. Ibid., 24.

21. Weiss, *The Rise of the Community Builders*, 146.

22. Gries and Ford, *The President's Conference on Home Builders*, 26.

23. Eugene Nelson White, *The Regulation and Reform of the American Banking System, 1900–1929* (Princeton: Princeton University Press, 1983).

24. Ibid., 163.

25. Julian H. Zimmerman, *The FHA Story in Summary, 1934–1959* (Washington, DC: U.S. Federal Housing Administration, 1959), 3.

26. Elmus Wicker, *The Banking Panics of the Great Depression* (New York: Cambridge University Press, 1996).

27. Gries and Ford, *The President's Conference on Home Builders*, 26.

28. Zimmerman, *The FHA Story in Summary*, 5; Weiss, *The Rise of the Community Builders*, 146.

29. Markusen, *Profit Cycles, Oligopoly, and Regional Development*; Atkinson, *The Past and Future of America's Economy*; Field, "Technological Change and U.S. Productivity Growth in the Interwar Years," 203–236.

30. Fearon, *War, Prosperity, and Depression*, 58; see also Robert Paul Thomas, *An Analysis of the Pattern of Growth of the Automobile Industry, 1895–1929* (New York: Arno, 1977); Bardou, Chanaron, Fridenson, and Laux, *The Automobile Revolution*, chap. 6.

31. Fearon, *War, Prosperity, and Depression*, 58.

32. Ibid., 91.

33. Kay, *Asphalt Nation*, 196; see also Markusen, *Profit Cycles*, 165.

34. Robert Brenner, *The Boom and the Bubble: The U.S. in the World Economy* (New York: Verso, 2002); Robert A. Beauregard, *When America Became Suburban* (Minneapolis: University of Minnesota Press, 2006).

35. Sidney Hyman, *Marriner S. Eccles: Private Entrepreneur and Public Servant* (Stanford: Stanford University Graduate School of Business, 1976), 144.

36. Hyman, *Marriner S. Eccles*, 142; see also Rudy Abramson, *Spanning the Century: The Life of W. Averell Harriman, 1891–1986* (New York: W. Morrow, 1992).

37. Hyman, *Marriner S. Eccles*, 142.

38. Ibid. This board headed up the Federal Home Loan Bank System, created in 1932. It was made up of eleven regionally based home loan banks that served as a central credit agency similar to of the Federal Reserve System.

39. Paxson, "The American Highway Movement, 1916–1935," 242; see also Gonzalez, *The Politics of Air Pollution*, chap. 4; Tammy Ingram, *Dixie Highway: Road Building and the Making of the Modern South, 1900–1930* (Chapel Hill: University of North Carolina Press, 2014); Martin T. Olliff, *Getting Out of the Mud: The Alabama Good Roads Movement and Highway Administration, 1898–1928* (Tuscaloosa: The University of Alabama Press, 2017).

40. James Dunn, *Driving Forces: The Automobile, Its Enemies, and the Politics of Mobility* (Washington, DC: Brookings Institution Press, 1998).

41. Kay, *Asphalt Nation*, 205.

42. Paxson, "The American Highway Movement," 250.

43. Stan Luger, "Review of *Sloan Rules: Alfred Sloan and the Triumph of General Motors*," *American Historical Review* 110, no. 1, (2005), 174; see also Kay, *Asphalt Nation*, 218–219; Stan Luger, *Corporate Power, American Democracy, and the Automobile Industry* (New York: Cambridge University Press, 2000).

44. Bradford Snell, *American Ground Transport* (Washington, DC: U.S. Government Printing Office, 1974); Glenn Yago, *The Decline of Transit: Urban Transportation in German and U.S. Cities, 1900–1970* (New York: Cambridge University Press, 1984); Scott Bottles, *Los Angeles and the Automobile: The Making of the Modern City* (Los Angeles: University of California Press, 1987).

45. Hyman, *Marriner S. Eccles*, 141.

46. Ibid., 143.

47. John Stilgoe, *Borderland: Origins of the American Suburb, 1820–1939* (New Haven: Yale University Press, 1988); Robert Fishman, *Bourgeois Utopias: The Rise and Fall of Suburbia* (New York: Basic Books, 1987); Weiss, *The Rise of the Community Builders*; Robert Bruegmann, *Sprawl: A Compact History* (Chicago: University of Chicago Press, 2005); Fogelson, *Bourgeois Nightmares*; Emily Badger, "More Rides to Hail May Mean More Traffic to Bear," *New York Times*, October 17, 2017, B4; Steven Kurutz, "Exit the Expressway," *New York*

Times, October 22, 2017, ST1; Conor Dougherty, "Getting to Yes on Nimby Street," *New York Times*, December 3, 2017, BU1.

48. Weiss, *The Rise of the Community Builders*, 146.

49. Zimmerman, *The FHA Story in Summary*, 7–8.

50. Jeffrey M. Hornstein, *A Nation of Realtors: A Cultural History of the Twentieth-Century American Middle Class* (Durham: Duke University Press, 2005), 150.

51. Weiss, *The Rise of the Community Builders*, 146; Binyamin Appelbaum, "Without Loan Giants, 30-Year Mortgage May Fade Away," *New York Times*, March 4, 2011, A1.

52. Weiss, *The Rise of the Community Builders*, 148.

53. Ibid., 147; see also Hornstein, *A Nation of Realtors*, 150–152.

54. Kay, *Asphalt Nation*, 201.

55. Muller, *Contemporary Suburban America*, 44.

56. Kay, *Asphalt Nation*, 201.

57. Jackson, *Crabgrass Frontier*, 206, 209.

By promoting low-density urban development and sprawl, the federal government eschewed a network of intellectuals advocating what was known as *social housing* during the 1920s and 1930s. Drawing from experiences in Europe, such thinkers argued that apartment complex housing that emphasized community living—wherein services like day care and schooling for children were provided as well as recreational facilities and activities—were economically and socially preferable to suburban tract housing. Historian Gail Radford points out that the few U.S. experiments in social housing proved to be successful. These projects built in the 1930s—in places like Philadelphia and Harlem—were well planned, affordable, aesthetically pleasing, and provided important amenities to their residents. Moreover, Radford finds that residents of U.S. social housing generally found living there to be agreeable and advantageous. While federal housing projects built in the post–World War II period only allowed the poor, the housing reformers' experiments were mostly occupied by white- and blue-collar workers. Gail Radford, *Modern Housing for America: Policy Struggles in the New Deal Era* (Chicago: University of Chicago Press, 1996); Nicholas Bloom, *Public Housing That Worked: New York in the Twentieth Century* (Philadelphia: University of Pennsylvania Press, 2008).

58. Olney, *Buy Now, Pay Later*.

59. Michael French, *U.S. Economic History since 1945* (Manchester: Manchester University Press, 1997); Brenner, *The Boom and the Bubble*; Robert Brenner, "New Boom or New Bubble: The Trajectory of the U.S. Economy," *New Left Review* 25 (January/February 2004): 57–102; Norman Frumkin, *Tracking America's Economy* (Armonk: M. E. Sharpe, 2004); Louis Uchitelle, "Goodbye, Production (and Maybe Innovation)," *New York Times*, December 24, 2006, sec. 3, 4.

60. Peter S. Goodman, "The Economy: Trying to Guess What Happens Next," *New York Times*, November 25, 2007, sec. 4, 1.

61. Martin Fackler, "Toyota Expects Decline in Annual Profit," *New York Times*, May 9, 2008, C3.

62. Keith Bradsher, *High and Mighty: SUVs: The World's Most Dangerous Vehicles and How They Got That Way* (New York: Public Affairs, 2002); John A. C. Conybeare, *Merging Traffic: The Consolidation of the International Automobile Industry* (Lanham: Rowman & Littlefield, 2004); Helmut Becker, *High Noon in the Automotive Industry* (New York: Springer, 2006), 12; Neal E. Boudette and Norihiko Shirouzu, "Car Makers' Boom Years Now Look Like a Bubble," *Wall Street Journal*, May 20, 2008, A1; Stacy C. Davis, Susan W. Diegel, and Robert G. Boundy, *Transportation Energy Data Book*, 35th ed. (Washington, DC: Department of Energy, 2016), table 3.11, chap. 3, 16; Hiroko Tabuchi, "Japan Seeks to Squelch Its Tiny Cars," *New York Times*, June 9, 2014, B1; Bill Vlasic, "Fuel Targets Threatened by Demand for Big Autos," *New York Times*, July 19, 2016, B2; Neal E. Boudette, "Unmatched 7-Year Rise In Auto Sales Comes to End," *New York Times*, January 4, 2018, B1.

63. Todd Zaun, "Honda Tries to Spruce Up a Stodgy Image," *New York Times* March 19, 2005, C3; Martin Fackler, "Toyota's Profit Soars, Helped by U.S. Sales," *New York Times*, August 5, 2006, C4; Hiroko Tabuchi, "Toyota Is Back on Top in Sales," *New York Times*, January 29, 2013, B7.

64. Nick Bunkley, "Toyota Ahead of G.M. in 2008 Sales," *New York Times*, January 22, 2009, B2.

65. R. J. Overy, "Cars, Roads, and Economic Recovery in Germany, 1932–8," *Economic History Review* 28, no. 3 (1975): 466–483.

66. Ibid., 474.

67. Neil Gregor, *Daimler-Benz in the Third Reich* (New Haven: Yale University Press, 1998), 37.

68. Overy, "Cars, Roads, and Economic Recovery in Germany," 475; see also Bernard Bellon, *Mercedes in Peace and War: German Automobile Workers, 1903–1945* (New York: Columbia University Press, 1990); Wolfgang Sachs, *For Love of the Automobile*, trans. Don Reneau (Los Angeles: University of California Press, 1992); Henry Ashby Turner Jr., *General Motors and the Nazis: The Struggle for Control of Opel, Europe's Biggest Carmaker* (New Haven: Yale University Press, 2005), chap. 1.

69. Yago, *The Decline of Transit*, 35–36.

70. Robert F. Freeland, *The Struggle for Control of the Modern Corporation: Organizational Change at General Motors, 1924–1970* (New York: Cambridge University Press, 2001).

71. Yago, *The Decline of Transit*, 31.

72. Turner, *General Motors and the Nazis*, 3.

73. Ibid., 7.

74. Yago, *The Decline of Transit*, 36.

75. Turner, *General Motors and the Nazis*, 9.

76. As quoted in ibid., 39.

77. Ibid., chap. 3.

78. Adolf Hitler, *Hitler's Second Book: The Unpublished Sequel to Mein Kampf*, ed. Gerhard L. Weinberg, trans. Krista Smith (New York: Enigma Books, 2003), 107.

79. Ibid., 112.

80. Ibid., 107.

81. T. Hughes, "Technological Momentum in History: Hydrogenation in Germany, 1989–1933," *Past and Present* 44 (August 1969): 106–132.

82. Ibid., 122.

83. Ibid., 120.

84. Hughes, "Technological Momentum in History," 122–123; Raymond G. Stokes, *Opting for Oil: The Political Economy of Technological Change in the West German Chemical Industry, 1945–1961* (New York: Cambridge University Press, 1994), 32–33; Tooze, *The Wages of Destruction*, 151.

85. Tooze, *The Wages of Destruction*, 151.

86. Yergin, *The Prize*; Norman Rich, *Hitler's War Aims: Ideology, the Nazi State, and the Course of Expansion* (New York: W.W. Norton, 1992); Victor Rothwell, *War Aims in the Second World War: The War Aims of the Major Belligerents, 1939–45* (Edinburgh: Edinburgh University Press, 2005).

87. Throughout World War II, 75 percent of Germany's army was horse-drawn. Madej, *German War Economy*, 3; R. L. DiNardo, *Mechanized Juggernaut or Military Anachronism? Horses and the German Army of World War II* (Mechanicsburg, PA: Stackpole Books, 2008).

88. Stokes, *Opting for Oil*; Haugland, Bergensen, and Roland, *Energy Structures and Environmental Futures*.

Chapter Five

1. *Rockefeller Foundation Annual Report, 1956* (New York: Rockefeller Foundation, 1957), 11–12.

2. Peter Collier and David Horowitz, *The Rockefellers: An American Dynasty* (New York: Holt, Rinehart, and Winston, 1976); Raymond B. Fosdick, *The Story of the Rockefeller Foundation* (New York: Transaction, 1988 [1952]); Peter J. Johnson and John Ensor Harr, *The Rockefeller Century: Three Generations of America's Greatest Family* (New York: Scribner, 1988).

3. Steven Palmer, *Launching Global Health: The Caribbean Odyssey of the Rockefeller Foundation* (Ann Arbor: University of Michigan Press, 2010); Nicolas Guilhot, ed., *The Invention of International Relations Theory: Realism, the Rockefeller Foundation, and the 1954 Conference on Theory* (New York: Columbia University Press, 2011).

4. Berman, *Influence of the Carnegie, Ford, and Rockefeller Foundations on American Foreign Policy*, 5.

5. Richard G. Hewlett and Oscar E. Anderson Jr., *The New World, 1939/1946: A History of the United States Atomic Energy Commission* (University

Park: Pennsylvania State University Press, 1962); Corbin Allardice and Edward R. Trapnell, *The Atomic Energy Commission* (New York: Praeger, 1974), 8 and 11; G. Pascal Zachary, *Endless Frontier: Vannevar Bush—Engineer of the American Century* (New York: Free Press, 1997).

　　6. Zachary, *Endless Frontier*, 82.

　　7. Ibid., 83–84.

　　8. Allardice and Trapnell, *The Atomic Energy Commission*, chap. 5.

　　9. Richard G. Hewlett and Francis Duncan, *Atomic Shield, 1947/1952: A History of the United States Atomic Energy Commission*, vol. 2 (University Park: Pennsylvania State University Press, 1969), 115–117.

　　10. Allardice and Trapnell, *The Atomic Energy Commission*, 62.

　　11. As quoted in Daniel Ford, *The Cult of the Atom: The Secret Papers of the Atomic Energy Commission* (New York: Simon & Schuster, 1982), 33. See also Allardice and Trapnell, *The Atomic Energy Commission*, 104, and Richard Pfau, *No Sacrifice Too Great: The Life of Lewis L. Strauss* (Charlottesville: University Press of Virginia, 1984), 99.

　　12. Pfau, *No Sacrifice Too Great*, 38.

　　13. Ibid., 84.

　　14. Ibid., 54.

　　15. Allardice and Trapnell, *The Atomic Energy Commission*, 33–34.

　　16. Pfau, *No Sacrifice Too Great*, 128.

　　17. Ibid., 185–186.

　　18. Ibid., 211.

　　19. Richard G. Hewlett and Jack M. Holl, *Atoms for Peace and War 1953–1961: Eisenhower and the Atomic Energy Commission* (Berkeley: University of California Press, 1989), 13.

　　20. Ibid., 194.

　　21. Panel on the Impact of the Peaceful Uses of Atomic Energy, *Peaceful Uses of Atomic Energy*, vol. 1, xi.

　　22. Panel on the Impact of the Peaceful Uses of Atomic Energy, *Peaceful Uses of Atomic Energy*, vol. 2, xiii–xviii.

　　23. Panel on the Impact of the Peaceful Uses of Atomic Energy, *Peaceful Uses of Atomic Energy*, vol. 1, 2, emphasis added.

　　24. Ibid., 95.

　　25. Ibid., 97.

　　26. Everett L. Hollis, "The United States Atomic Energy Act of 1954: A Brief Survey," in J. Guéron, J. A. Lane, I. R. Maxwell, and J. R. Menke, eds., *The Economics of Nuclear Power: Including Administration and Law* (New York: McGraw-Hill, 1957), 495–496.

　　27. Hertsgaard, *Nuclear Inc.*; David Nye, *Image Worlds: Corporate Identities at General Electric, 1890–1930* (Cambridge: MIT Press, 1985).

　　28. Frank T. Kryza, *The Power of Light: The Epic Story of Man's Quest to Harness the Sun* (New York: McGraw-Hill, 2003), 22.

　　29. Ibid., 73.

30. Ibid., 75. See also Adam Baidawi, "For Musk, an Energy Feat The Size of a Football Field," *New York Times*, December 1, 2017, B4.

31. Kryza, *The Power of Light*, 26–27.

32. Ibid., 27.

33. Ibid., 259.

34. *Proceedings of the World Symposium on Applied Solar Energy, Phoenix, AZ, Nov. 1–5, 1955* (San Francisco: Jorgenson & Co., 1956), 3.

35. Harvey Strum, "The Association for Applied Solar Energy/Solar Energy Society, 1954–1970," *Technology and Culture* 26, no. 3 (1985): 572.

36. *Proceedings of the World Symposium on Applied Solar Energy*, 15–16.

37. Ibid., 303.

38. Henry B. Sargent, "The Association for Applied Solar Energy," in *Proceedings of the World Symposium on Applied Solar Energy*, 18.

39. Harvey Strum and Fred Strum, "American Solar Energy Policy, 1952–1970," *Environmental Review* 7 (Summer 1983): 136; see also Frank N. Laird, *Solar Energy, Technology Policy, and Institutional Values* (New York: Cambridge University Press, 2001), 52–53.

40. Strum, "Association for Applied Solar Energy/Solar," 578.

41. Strum and Strum, "American Solar Energy Policy, 1952–1970," 147. See also William D. Metz and Allen L. Hammond, *Solar Energy in America* (Washington, DC: American Association for the Advancement of Science, 1978), and Laird, *Solar Energy, Technology Policy, and Institutional Values*, 166–167.

42. Strum and Strum, "American Solar Energy Policy, 1952–1970," 136.

43. Ibid., 141.

44. Ibid.

45. Ibid., 150.

46. Dawson, *Nuclear Power*, 77.

Chapter Six

1. Doug Stokes and Sam Raphael, *Global Energy Security and American Hegemony* (Baltimore: Johns Hopkins University Press, 2010).

2. Gonzalez, *Urban Sprawl, Global Warming, and the Empire of Capital*.

3. Francisco Parra, *Oil Politics: A Modern History of Petroleum* (New York: I. B. Tauris, 2004); Harvey Blatt, *America's Environmental Report Card: Are We Making the Grade?* (Cambridge: MIT Press, 2005), 100; Roy L. Nersesian, *Energy for the 21st Century* (Armonk: M. E. Sharpe, 2007), 205; John S. Duffield, *Over a Barrel: The Costs of U.S. Foreign Oil Dependence* (Stanford: Stanford University Press, 2008); Steffen Hertog, *Princes, Brokers, and Bureaucrats: Oil and the State in Saudi Arabia* (Ithaca: Cornell University Press, 2010).

4. Muller, *Contemporary Suburban America*; Robert A. Beauregard, *When America Became Suburban* (Minneapolis: University of Minnesota Press, 2006); Knox, *Metroburbia, USA*.

5. Foster, *From Streetcar to Superhighway*; Jeffrey R. Kenworthy and Felix B. Laube, with Peter Newman, Paul Barter, Tamim Raad, Chamlong Poboon, and Benedicto Guia Jr., *An International Sourcebook of Automobile Dependence in Cities 1960–1990* (Boulder: University Press of Colorado, 1999).

6. John M. Blair, *The Control of Oil* (New York: Pantheon, 1976); Ed Shaffer, *The United States and the Control of World Oil* (New York: St. Martin's Press, 1983); George Philip, *The Political Economy of International Oil* (Edinburgh: Edinburgh University Press, 1994).

7. American Petroleum Institute, *Petroleum Facts and Figures: Centennial Edition* (New York: American Petroleum Institute, 1959), 246–247.

8. Yergin, *The Prize*; Deffeyes, *Hubbert's Peak*.

9. John M. Blair, *The Control of Oil* (New York: Pantheon, 1976); Shaffer, *The United States and the Control of World Oil*; Richard H. Vietor, *Energy Policy in America since 1945* (New York: Cambridge University Press, 1984); Philip, *The Political Economy of International Oil*; Ian Rutledge, *Addicted to Oil: America's Relentless Drive for Energy Security* (New York: I. B. Tauris, 2005); Bronson, *Thicker than Oil*.

10. James A. Bill, *The Eagle and the Lion: The Tragedy of American-Iranian Relations* (New Haven: Yale University Press, 1988); Ikenberry, *Reasons of State*; Simon Bromley, *American Hegemony and World Oil: The Industry, the State System and the World Economy* (University Park: Pennsylvania State University Press, 1991); Steve A. Yetiv, *Crude Awakenings: Global Oil Security and American Foreign Policy* (Ithaca: Cornell University Press, 2004), and *Explaining Foreign Policy: U.S. Decision-Making in the Gulf Wars* (Baltimore: Johns Hopkins University Press, 2011); Robert J. Pauly Jr., *U.S. Foreign Policy and the Persian Gulf: Safeguarding American Interests through Selective Multilateralism* (Burlington: Ashgate, 2005); "America's Forever Wars," *New York Times*, October 23, 2017, A20.

11. E.g., Frederic Dewhurst and the Twentieth Century Fund, *America's Needs and Resources: A New Survey* (New York: Twentieth Century Fund, 1955); Thomas Reynolds Carskadon and George Henry Soule, *USA in New Dimensions: The Measure and Promise of America's Resources, A Twentieth Century Fund Survey* (New York: Macmillan, 1957); Arnold B. Barach and the Twentieth Century Fund, *USA and Its Economic Future: A Twentieth Century Fund Survey* (New York: Macmillan, 1964).

12. "As Oil Consultant, He's without Like or Equal," *New York Times*, July 27, 1969, sec. 3, 3; Shaffer, *The United States and the Control of World Oil*, 214–218. In a 1969 profile of Walter J. Levy, entitled "As Oil Consultant, He's without Like or Equal," the *New York Times* noted that "he is readily acknowledged as the 'dean of oil consultants' even by competitors." The profile went on to explain that "there are few, if any, major oil controversies in which Mr. Levy has not acted as a consultant," and that he "has been an advisor to most of the major oil companies, most of the important consuming countries and many of the large producing countries."

13. Walter L. Buenger, and Joseph A. Pratt, *But Also Good Business: Texas Commerce Banks and the Financing of Houston and Texas, 1886–1986* (College Station: Texas A&M University Press, 1986), 299.

14. Twentieth Century Fund Task Force on the International Oil Crisis, *Paying for Energy* (New York: McGraw-Hill, 1975), vii–viii; Twentieth Century Fund Task Force on United States Energy Policy, *Providing for Energy* (New York: McGraw-Hill, 1977), xi–xii; Robin W. Winks, *Laurence S. Rockefeller: Catalyst for Conservation* (Washington, DC: Island Press, 1997), 44 and 196.

15. Twentieth Century Fund Task Force on United States Energy Policy, *Providing for Energy*, 9.

16. Ibid., 9, emphasis in original.

17. Ibid., 5, emphasis in original.

18. Ibid., 5.

19. Jo Craven McGinty, "How Do Americans Spend Their Energy Savings? On More Energy," *Wall Street Journal*, December 12, 2014. Web.

20. Twentieth Century Fund Task Force on United States Energy Policy, *Providing for Energy*, 23, emphasis in original.

21. Ibid., 23–24.

22. Ibid., 24.

23. Twentieth Century Fund Task Force on the International Oil Crisis, *Paying for Energy*, 15.

24. Committee for Economic Development, *Achieving Energy Independence* (New York: Committee for Economic Development, 1974), 30.

25. Ibid., 6.

26. "Energy Efficiency Fails to Cut Consumption—Study," *Reuters*, November 27, 2007; Horace Herring and Steve Sorrell, eds., *Energy Efficiency and Sustainable Consumption: The Rebound Effect* (New York: Palgrave Macmillan, 2009); Coral Davenport, "Amid Pipeline and Climate Debate, Energy-Efficiency Bill Is Derailed," *New York Times*, May 13, 2014, A12; Michael Shellenberger and Ted Nordhaus, "The Problem with Energy Efficiency," *New York Times*, October 9, 2014, A35.

27. Winston Harrington and Virginia McConnell, *Resources for the Future Report: Motor Vehicles and the Environment* (Washington, DC: Resources for the Future, 2003), chaps. 6 and 7.

28. Energy Information Administration, *Annual Energy Review 2003* (Washington, DC: U.S. Department of Energy, 2004), 57; *Light-Duty Automotive Technology, Carbon Dioxide Emissions, and Fuel Economy Trends: 1975 through 2012* (Washington, DC: U.S. Environmental Protection Agency, 2013), iii.

29. Rutledge, *Addicted to Oil*, 10.

30. The U.S. Energy Department reports that in 2007, 8.9 million barrels of oil per day (mb/d) were used to power the U.S. automobile fleet (including light trucks and motorcycles). In a sluggish economy, the amount of oil used to power the US automotive fleet went from 8.7 mb/d in 2008 to 8.2 mb/d in 2014. Automotive, motorcycle, bus, and truck driving in the United States

consumed a total of 12.9 mb/d in 2014. Global petroleum production 2008 through 2014 ranged annually from 83 mb/d to 88 mb/d. Stacy C. Davis, Susan W. Diegel, and Robert G. Boundy, *Transportation Energy Data Book*, 35th ed. (Washington, DC: Department of Energy, 2016), table 1.3, chap. 1, 4; table 1.14, chap. 1, 19.

31. Duffield, *Over a Barrel*, chap. 2; Davis, Diegel, and Boundy, *Transportation Energy Data Book*, table 1.14 and table 1.15, chap. 1, 19–20.

32. While American oil consumption peaked around 20.7 million barrels per day (mb/d) from 2004 to 2007, the economic recession resulted in a decline of petroleum use in the United States to roughly 19 mb/d from 2008 to 2014. Davis, Diegel, and Boundy, *Transportation Energy Data Book*, table 1.4, chap. 1, 5.

By way of comparison, the International Energy Agency reported that oil consumption in the European Union in 2009 was 12.2 mb/d. European Union oil consumption in 2011 was 11.6 mb/d and 11.7 mb/d in 2015. The European Union in 2009 had a population of 500 million, whereas the United States had one of 300 million. China, with about 20 percent of the global population, in 2009 consumed 8.1 mb/d. Oil consumption in China in 2011 was 9 mb/d and 11 mb/d in 2015. International Energy Agency, *World Energy Outlook 2010* (Paris: International Energy Agency, 2010), 105; International Energy Agency, *World Energy Outlook 2012* (Paris: International Energy Agency, 2012), table 3.2, 85; International Energy Agency, *World Energy Outlook 2016* (Paris: International Energy Agency, 2016), table 3.2, 115. U.S. consumption of oil for 2009 was 22 barrels per capita, or per person. In China it was 2.4 barrels. Jad Mouawad, "China's Growth Shifts the Geopolitics of Oil," *New York Times*, March 19, 2010, B1.

33. Philip, *The Political Economy of International Oil*, 195; Paul Roberts, *The End of Oil: On the Edge of a Perilous New World* (New York: Houghton Mifflin, 2004); Rutledge, *Addicted to Oil*, chap. 1; Matthew L. Wald, "When It Comes to Replacing Oil Imports, Nuclear Is No Easy Option, Experts Say," *New York Times*, May 9, 2005, A14; Bruce Podobnik, *Global Energy Shifts: Fostering Sustainability in a Turbulent Age* (Philadelphia: Temple University Press, 2006), chaps. 5 and 6; Duffield, *Over a Barrel*, chap. 2.

34. Twentieth Century Fund Task Force on United States Energy Policy, *Providing for Energy*, 1977, 24–25, emphasis in original.

35. Committee for Economic Development, *Achieving Energy Independence*, 29.

36. Stanley Reed, "Prices Fall to 6-Year Low for U.S. Oil," *New York Times*, March 17, 2015, B1, and "Outlook for Oil Prices 'Only Getting Murkier,' Energy Agency Says," *New York Times*, April 15, 2015. Web.

37. Yergin, *The Prize*, and *The Quest*; Steve Coll, *Private Empire: Exxon-Mobil and American Power* (New York: Penguin, 2013).

38. Tim Weiner, "Man in the News: John Mark Deutch; Reluctant Helmsman for a Troubled Agency," *New York Times*, March 11, 1995. Web;

Mark Mazzetti, *The Way of the Knife: The CIA, a Secret Army, and a War at the Ends of the Earth* (New York: Penguin, 2013), 16.

39. Michael A. Levi, *The Canadian Oil Sands: Energy Security vs. Climate Change* (New York: Council on Foreign Relations, 2009), 45.

40. Richard N. Haass, "Foreword," in Michael A. Levi, *The Canadian Oil Sands: Energy Security vs. Climate Change* (New York: Council on Foreign Relations, 2009), vii.

41. Clifford Krauss, "Pipeline Plan Was Begun amid Dim U.S. Forecasts," *New York Times*, November 7, 2015, A12.

While the high-profile Keystone XL Pipeline project that would have connected the Canadian oil sands to Texas was rejected in 2015 by the Obama administration, the infrastructure to transport to the U.S. Canadian oil sands petroleum is nevertheless expanding. Clifford Krauss and Ian Austen, "Rocky Road for Canadian Oil," *New York Times*, May 13, 2014, B1; Clifford Krauss, "Looking for a Way Around Keystone XL, Canadian Oil Hits the Rails," *New York Times*, October 31, 2013, B1; Clifford Krauss, "Working Around Keystone XL, Suncor Energy Steps Up Oil Production in Canada," *New York Times*, November 22, 2013, B3; Jad Mouawad and Ian Austen, "To Make Shipping Oil Safer, Railroads Agree to 8 Measures," *New York Times*, February 22, 2014, B3; Coral Davenport, "Report Finds Higher Risks if Oil Line Is Not Built," *New York Times*, June 7, 2014, A13.

42. Laurence Shoup and William Minter, *Imperial Brain Trust: The Council on Foreign Relations and United States Foreign Policy* (New York: Monthly Review Press, 1977); Domhoff, *The Power Elite and the State*, chap. 5.

43. Laurence H. Shoup, "Shaping the National Interest: The Council on Foreign Relations, the Department of State, and the Origins of the Postwar World, 1939–1943" (PhD thesis, Northwestern University, 1974), 42.

44. Inderjeet Parmar, "The Issue of State Power: The Council on Foreign Relations as a Case Study," *Journal of American Studies* 29, no. 1 (1995): 73–95, " 'Mobilizing America for an Internationalist Foreign Policy': The Role of the Council on Foreign Relations," *Studies in American Political Development* 13 (Fall 1999): 337–373, and *Think Tanks and Power in Foreign Policy: A Comparative Study of the Role and Influence of the Council on Foreign Relations and the Royal Institute of International Affairs, 1939–1945* (New York: Palgrave Macmillan, 2004).

45. Parmar, "The Issue of State Power," 82.

46. Ibid.

47. Harly Notter, *Postwar Foreign Policy Preparation, 1939–1945* (Washington, DC: U.S. Government Printing Office, 1949 [1973]); Shoup, "Shaping the National Interest"; Shoup and Miner, *Imperial Brain Trust*; Robert D. Schulzinger, *The Wise Men of Foreign Affairs: The History of the Council on Foreign Relations* (New York: Columbia University Press, 1984); Domhoff, *The Power Elite and the State*, chap. 5; Parmar, "The Issue of State Power," " 'Mobilizing America for an Internationalist Foreign Policy,' " and *Think Tanks and Power*

in Foreign Policy; Neil Smith, *American Empire: Roosevelt's Geographer and the Prelude to Globalization* (Berkeley: University of California Press, 2003).

48. Kenworthy and Laube, *An International Sourcebook of Automobile Dependence in Cities 1960–1990*; Elisabeth Rosenthal, "Across Europe, Irking Drivers Is Urban Policy," *New York Times*, June 27, 2011, A1; David Jolly, "French Automakers' Biggest Problem? French Consumers," *New York Times*, January 30, 2013, B4; Vanessa Furmans, "Europe's Car Makers Spin Their Wheels," *Wall Street Journal*, October 1, 2013, A1; Dan Bilefsky, "A Plan to Limit Cars in Paris Collides with French Politics," *New York Times*, December 16, 2014, A11; Winne Hu, "Barcelona's Lesson on 'Superblocks,'" *New York Times*, October 2, 2016, MB1.

49. Louis Armand, *Some Aspects of the European Energy Problem: Suggestions for Collective Action* (Paris: Organisation for European Economic Co-operation, 1955).

50. Commission for Energy, *Europe's Growing Needs of Energy: How Can They Be Met?* (Paris: Organisation for European Economic Co-operation, 1956), 25.

51. Ibid., 73.

52. Ibid., 26.

53. Ibid., 73.

54. Ibid., 56.

55. Armand, *Some Aspects of the European Energy Problem*, 46.

56. Energy Advisory Commission, *Towards a New Energy Pattern in Europe* (Paris: Organisation for European Economic Co-operation, 1960), 13–14.

57. Ibid., 83.

58. Ibid., 61.

59. Ibid., 83–84.

60. Shaffer, *The United States and the Control of World Oil*, chap. 7; Haugland, Bergensen, and Roland, *Energy Structures and Environmental Futures*, 55.

61. Haugland, Bergensen, and Roland, *Energy Structures and Environmental Futures*, 33; James Dunn, *Miles to Go: European and American Transportation Policies* (Cambridge: MIT Press, 1981); Nigel Lucas, *Western European Energy Policies: A Comparative Study of the Influence of Institutional Structures on Technical Change* (Oxford: Clarendon, 1985).

62. Harvey Blatt, *America's Environmental Report Card: Are We Making the Grade?*, 2nd ed. (Cambridge: MIT Press, 2011), 142–143; see also Daniel C. Esty and Michael E. Porter, "Pain at the Pump? We Need More," *New York Times*, April 28, 2011, A25; Valerie J. Karplus, "The Case for a Higher Gasoline Tax," *New York Times*, February 22, 2013, A23; Joshua L. Schank, "America's Highways, Running on Empty," *New York Times*, June 2, 2014, A21; Jonathan Weisman, "Plan to Refill Highway Fund Stokes Conflict in Congress," *New York Times*, June 10, 2014, A15; Patricia Cohen, "Gasoline-Tax Increase Finds Little Support," *New York Times*, January 3, 2015, B1; "Raise the Gas Tax to Fix America's Roads," *New York Times*, January 11, 2015, SR10.

63. Simon Romero, "Oil-Rich Norwegians Take World's Highest Gasoline Prices in Stride," *New York Times*, April 30, 2005, C1; see also Molly O'Meara Sheehan, *City Limits: Putting the Brakes on Sprawl* (Washington, DC: Worldwatch Institute, 2001).

64. Laird, *Solar Energy, Technology Policy, and Institutional Values*; Travis Bradford, *Solar Revolution: The Economic Transformation of the Global Energy Industry* (Cambridge: MIT Press, 2006).

65. Dorothy Nelkin and Michael Pollak, *The Atom Besieged: Antinuclear Movements in France and Germany* (Cambridge: MIT Press, 1981).

66. Irvin C. Bupp and Jean-Claude Derian, *The Failed Promise of Nuclear Power: The Story of Light Water* (New York: Basic Books, 1978); Peter Stoett, "Toward Renewed Legitimacy? Nuclear Power, Global Warming, and Security," *Global Environmental Politics* 3, no. 1 (2003): 99–116; Jane Dawson and Robert Darst, "Meeting the Challenge of Permanent Nuclear Waste Disposal in an Expanding Europe: Transparency, Trust and Democracy," *Environmental Politics* 15, no. 4 (2006): 610–627; Vandenbosch and Vandenbosch, *Nuclear Waste Stalemate*; Power, *America's Nuclear Wastelands*; Matthew L. Wald, "As Nuclear Waste Languishes, Expense to U.S. Rises," *New York Times*, February 17, 2008, A22; Matthew L. Wald, "A Safer Nuclear Crypt," *New York Times*, July 6, 2011, B1; William M. Alley and Rosemarie Alley, *Too Hot to Touch: The Problem of High-Level Nuclear Waste* (New York: Cambridge University Press, 2013); Matthew L. Wald, "Texas Company, Alone in U.S., Cashes In on Nuclear Waste," *New York Times*, January 21, 2014, B1; Matthew L. Wald, "Nuclear Waste Solution Seen in Desert Salt Beds," *New York Times*, February 10, 2014, A9; Matthew L. Wald, "Nuclear Waste Is Allowed Above Ground Indefinitely," *New York Times*, August 30, 2014, A13.

67. Hatch, *Politics and Nuclear Power*.

68. James M. Jasper, *Nuclear Politics: Energy and the State in the United States, Sweden, and France* (Princeton: Princeton University Press, 1990); Steven Erlanger, "French Plans for Energy Reaffirm Nuclear Path," *New York Times*, August 17, 2008, A6; Gabrielle Hecht, *The Radiance of France: Nuclear Power and National Identity after World War II* (Cambridge: MIT Press, 2009).

69. Henry Nau, *National Politics and International Technology: Nuclear Reactor Development in Western Europe* (Baltimore: Johns Hopkins University Press, 1974); James Kanter, "German Chancellor Calls for Tests of Europe's Nuclear Reactors," *New York Times*, March 24, 2011, B3.

70. Between 1981 and 1986, U.S. daily consumption of petroleum increased by 120,000 barrels, whereas Western European consumption dropped 490,000 barrels. Philip, *The Political Economy of International Oil*, 195; see also Hatch, *Politics and Nuclear Power*; Peter Nijkamp, *Sustainable Cities in Europe: A Comparative Analysis of Urban Energy-Environmental Policies* (London: Earthscan, 1994); Frank J. Convery, ed., *A Guide to Policies for Energy Conservation: The European Experience* (Northampton: Edward Elgar,

1998); Haugland, Bergensen, and Roland, *Energy Structures and Environmental Futures*; Peter Newman, Timothy Beatley, and Heather Boyer, *Resilient Cities: Responding to Peak Oil and Climate Change* (Washington, DC: Island Press, 2009).

71. Dorothy Nelkin and Michael Pollak, *The Atom Besieged: Extraparliamentary Dissent in France and Germany* (Cambridge: MIT Press, 1981); Hecht, *The Radiance of France*; Blatt, *America's Environmental Report Card*, 2nd ed., 216.

72. "France Bets on Geothermal Energy," *New York Times*, September 17, 2014. Web.

73. Stanley Reed, "With Controls, Britain Allows Hydraulic Fracturing to Explore for Gas," *New York Times*, December 14, 2012, B3.

74. Mark Scott, "Europe Struggles in Shale Gas Race," *New York Times*, April 25, 2013, F7.

75. Ibid. Great Britain has recently taken political, regulatory steps toward allowing hydrofracking, as has Germany. Stanley Reed, "France Oil Giant Is Expected to Seek Shale Gas in Britain," *New York Times*, January 12, 2014, A11; Stanley Reed, "Britain Proposes Easier Access to Tap Shale Rock Energy," *New York Times*, May 23, 2014.Web; Melissa Eddy and Stanley Reed, "Germany Takes Step Toward Permitting Fracking," *New York Times*, June 6, 2014, B2; Stanley Reed, "Britain to Expand Land Available for Oil and Gas Drilling," *New York Times*, July 28, 2014, B2.

76. Stanley Reed, "Eni Is Said to Abandon Polish Shale Aspirations," *New York Times*, January 15, 2014, B3.

77. Mark Landler, "With Its Gas Prices Already High, Europe Is Less Rattled by Jump," *New York Times*, June 1, 2004, C1; Jad Mouawad and Heather Timmons, "Trading Frenzy Adds to Jump in Price of Oil," *New York Times*, April 29, 2006, A1.

78. Andrew Jordan, Dave Huitema, Harro van Asselt, Tim Rayner, and Frans Berkhout, eds., *Climate Change Policy in the European Union: Confronting the Dilemmas of Mitigation and Adaptation?* (New York: Cambridge University Press, 2010).

79. Stephen Castle, "European Union Proposes Easing of Climate Rules," *New York Times*, January 23, 2014, A1.

80. Nicholas Kulish, "German City Wonders How Green Is Too Green," *New York Times*, August 7, 2008, A8; Kate Galbraith, "Europe's Way of Encouraging Solar Power Arrives in the U.S.," *New York Times*, March 13, 2009, B1.

81. James Kanter, "A Solar and Wind Revolution from a Land of Oil," *New York Times*, March 13, 2011. Web.

82. James Kanter, "Energy Efficiency Proves Unattractive for Policy Makers in Europe," *New York Times*, January 16, 2011. Web.

83. David Buchan, *Energy and Climate Change: Europe at the Crossroads* (New York: Oxford University Press, 2009); Caterina De Lucia, *Environmental Policies for Air Pollution and Climate Change in the New Europe* (New York: Routledge, 2010); Antonio Marquina, ed., *Global Warming and Climate Change: Prospects and Policies in Asia and Europe* (New York: Palgrave Macmillan, 2010); Castle, "European Union Proposes Easing of Climate Rules."

84. Curt Gasteyger, ed., *The Future for European Energy Security* (New York: St. Martin's Press, 1985); George W. Hoffman, *The European Energy Challenge: East and West* (Durham: Duke University Press, 1985); Elisabeth Rosenthal, "Germany Dims Nuclear Plants, but Hopes to Keep Lights On," *New York Times*, August 30, 2011, A1.

85. Melissa Eddy and Stanley Reed, "Germany's Effort at Clean Energy Proves Complex," *New York Times*, September 19, 2013, A6; Melissa Eddy, "German Energy Official Sounds a Warning," *New York Times*, January 21, 2014. Web; Melissa Eddy, "German Energy Push Runs into Problems," *New York Times*, March 19, 2014. Web; Justin Gillis, "Sun and Wind Transforming Global Landscape," *New York Times*, September 14, 2014, A1; Melissa Eddy, "Missing Its Own Goals, Germany Renews Effort to Cut Carbon Emissions," *New York Times*, December 4, 2014, A6; Melissa Eddy, "Germans Balk at Plan for Wind Power Lines," *New York Times*, December 25, 2014, A6; Stanley Reed, "$222 Billion Shift Hits a Snag," *New York Times*, October 7, 2017, B1, and "Power Prices Go Negative in Germany, a Positive for Consumers," *New York Times*, December 26, 2017, B3.

86. Stanley Reed and Mark Scott, "In Europe, Paid Permits for Pollution Are Fizzling," *New York Times*, April 22, 2013, B1.

87. Stanley Reed, "European Lawmakers Support Carbon Trading System," *New York Times*, December 11, 2013, B11, and "A Bid to Revive Carbon Credits in Europe," *New York Times*, February 7, 2014, B7.

88. Duffield, *Over a Barrel*; Michael J. Graetz, *The End of Energy: The Unmaking of America's Environment, Security, and Independence* (Cambridge: MIT Press, 2011); International Energy Agency, CO_2 *Emissions from Fuel Combustion: Highlights*, 2016 ed. (Paris: International Energy Agency, 2016).

Table 6.1 Carbon Dioxide (CO_2) Per Capita: Emissions of Selected Countries*

Countries	Per Capita CO_2 Emissions (in tons)
United States	16.2
Russia	11.9
Japan	9.6
Germany	8.9
United Kingdom	6.5
China	7.5
France	4.7
India	1.7

*All selected countries have populations over forty million.

Source: Justin Gillis and Nadja Popovich, "The U.S. Is the Biggest Carbon Polluter in History. It Just Walked Away from the Paris Climate Deal," *New York Times*, June 1, 2017. Web. See also International Energy Agency, CO_2 *Emissions from Fuel Combustion*.

Table 6.2 Energy Consumption Per Capita of Selected Countries*

Countries	Energy Consumption Per Capita (Ton of Oil Equivalent)
United States	7.8
Russia	4.7
France	4.4
Japan	4.1
European Union (27)	3.7
China	1.4
India	0.5

*All selected countries have populations over forty million.

Source: Christian de Perthuis, *Economic Choices in a Warming World* (New York: Cambridge University Press, 2011), 238–239.

Chapter Seven

1. Stephen Kurczy, "International Energy Agency Says 'Peak Oil' Has Hit," *The Christian Science Monitor*, November 11, 2010. Web.

2. John M. Broder and Clifford Krauss, "Shell Gets Tentative Approval to Drill in Arctic," *New York Times*, August 5, 2011, A1; Earl Boebert and James M. Blossom, *Deepwater Horizon: A Systems Analysis of the Macondo Disaster* (Cambridge, MA: Harvard University Press, 2016); Coral Davenport, "U.S. Reveals Latest Safety Rules on Arctic Drilling," *New York Times*, July 8, 2016, A12; Lisa Friedman, "Interior Dept. Proposes Drilling Within Arctic Refuge, Angering Environmentalists," *New York Times*, September 17, 2017, A21; Anne-Marie Brady, *China as a Polar Great Power* (New York: Cambridge University Press, 2017); Christina Caron, "How a 672,000-Gallon Oil Spill Was Nearly Invisible," *New York Times*, October 29, 2017. Web.

3. Robbie Brown and Ian Urbina, "Panel Seeks Stiffer Rules for Drilling of Gas Wells," *New York Times*, August 11, 2011, A13; John Hurdle, "Pennsylvania Report Left Out Data on Poisons in Water Near Gas Site," *New York Times*, November 3, 2012, A14; Tom Wilber, *Under the Surface: Fracking, Fortunes, and the Fate of the Marcellus Shale* (Ithaca: Cornell University Press, 2012); Terrence Henry and Kate Galbraith, "As Fracking Proliferates, So Do Wastewater Wells," *New York Times*, March 29, 2013, A21.

4. Goodell, *Big Coal*; Patrick Reis, "Study: World's 'Peak Coal' Moment Has Arrived," *New York Times*, September 29, 2010. Web; John M. Broder, "Court Reverses E.P.A. on Big Mining Project," *New York Times*, March 24, 2012, A10.

5. Mark Maslin, *Global Warming: A Very Short Introduction* (New York: Oxford University Press, 2009); Powell, *The Inquisition of Climate Science*; Houghton, *Global Warming*.

6. "Tar Sands and the Carbon Numbers," *New York Times*, August 22, 2011, A18; Gonzalez, *American Empire and the Canadian Oil Sands*.

7. Tom Zeller Jr. "Studies Say Natural Gas Has Its Own Environmental Problems," *New York Times*, April 20, 2011, B1; "EPA Methane Report Further Divides Fracking Camps," *Associated Press*, April 28, 2013; Michael Wines, "Colorado Governor Proposes Strict Limits on Greenhouse Gas Leaks from Drilling," *New York Times*, November 19, 2013, A12; Coral Davenport, "Study Finds Methane Leaks Negate Benefits of Natural Gas as a Fuel for Vehicles," *New York Times*, February 14, 2014, A14.

8. Michael Wines, "Emissions of Methane Exceed Estimates," *New York Times*, November 26, 2013, A14; Clifford Krauss, "Exxon Tries to Cut Methane Leaks, a Culprit in Warming," *New York Times*, September 26, 2017, B6.

9. Justin Gillis and David Jolly, "Slowdown in Carbon Emissions Worldwide, but Coal Burning Continues to Grow," *New York Times*, November 19, 2013, A7; Coral Davenport, "E.P.A. Staff Struggling to Create Pollution Rule," *New York Times*, February 5, 2014, A12; Eric Lipton and Barry Meier, "Trump Unravels Coal Mine Limits On Federal Land," *New York Times*, August 7, 2017, A1; "Using the E.P.A. to Prop Up Big Coal," *New York Times*, September 18, 2017, A22; Jacqueline Williams, "Question Roiling Australia: Does Planet Need More Coal?," *New York Times*, October 15, 2017, A6; Keith Bradsher, "China to Take A Harder Line On Pollution," *New York Times*, October 24, 2017, B1; Keith Bradsher and Lisa Friedman, "China Plans Huge Market for Trading Pollution Credits," *New York Times*, December 20, 2017, B1.

10. Elizabeth Kolbert, *The Sixth Extinction: An Unnatural History* (New York: Henry Holt, 2014); Naomi Oreskes and Erik M. Conway, *The Collapse of Western Civilization: A View from the Future* (New York: Columbia University Press, 2014); Anthony D. Barnosky, *Dodging Extinction: Power, Food, Money, and the Future of Life on Earth* (Berkeley: University of California Press, 2016); Jeff Goodell, *The Water Will Come: Rising Seas, Sinking Cities, and the Remaking of the Civilized World* (New York: Little, Brown, 2017); Justin Gillis, "Scientists Sound Alarm on Climate," *New York Times*, March 18, 2014, D1, and "Study Warns of a Perilous Climate Shift within Decades," *New York Times*, March 23, 2016, A11; William B. Gail, "A New Dark Age Looms," *New York Times*, April 19, 2016, A27; John Schwartz, "400," *New York Times*, October 4, 2016, D3; Jugal K. Patel and Justin Gillis, "An Iceberg the Size of Delaware Just Broke Away from Antarctica," *New York Times*, July 12, 2017. Web; Tatiana Schlossberg, " 'Biological Annihilation' Said to Be Underway," *New York Times*, July 12, 2017, A5; Lisa Friedman, "Greenhouse Gases Increase, but Scientists at NOAA Say 'It's Complicated," *New York Times*, July 14, 2017, A10; Peter Brannen, "When Life on Earth Nearly Vanished," *New York Times*, July 30, 2017, SR2; Mike Ives, "Climate Change Lands at the Airport," *New York Times*, October 1, 2017, BU6; Nicholas Casey, "Living Off a Glacier, While It Lasts," *New York Times*, November 26, 2017, A1; Jim Robbins, "Widespread Tree Die-Offs Feared," *New York Times*, December 12, 2017, D4.

11. Intergovernmental Panel on Climate Change (IPCC), *Special Report on Renewable Energy Sources and Climate Change Mitigation* (Geneva: Intergovernmental Panel on Climate Change, 2011).

12. Theodore A. Parish, Vyacheslav V. Khromov, and Igor Carron, eds., *Safety Issues Associated with Plutonium Involvement in the Nuclear Fuel Cycle* (New York: Springer, 1999); Jeremy Bernstein, *Plutonium: A History of the World's Most Dangerous Element* (Ithaca: Cornell University Press, 2009); James Mahaffey, *Atomic Awakening: A New Look at the History and Future of Nuclear Power* (New York: Pegasus, 2010).

13. William O. Lowrance, "Nuclear Futures for Sale: To Brazil from West Germany, 1975," *International Security* 1, no. 2 (1976): 147–166.

14. Research and Policy Committee of the Committee for Economic Development, *Nuclear Energy and National Security* (New York: Committee for Economic Development, 1976), 80.

15. Ibid., 81–84.

16. Ibid., 4–6.

17. Ibid., 8, emphasis added.

18. Ibid., 9.

19. Ibid., 58–59.

20. Ibid.

21. *International Nuclear Fuel Cycle Evaluation (INFCE): Summary Volume* (Vienna: International Atomic Energy Agency, 1980), 1.

22. Ibid., 2–3.

23. Ibid., 137.

24. Ibid., 147.

25. Ibid., 148–149; see also John Mueller, *Atomic Obsession* (New York: Oxford University Press, 2010); William J. Broad, "For Iran, Enriching Uranium Only Gets Easier," *New York Times*, March 8, 2010, D1; Jeffrey W. Knopf, ed., *Security Assurances and Nuclear Nonproliferation* (Palo Alto: Stanford University Press, 2012).

26. *International Nuclear Fuel Cycle Evaluation (INFCE): Summary Volume*, 154–155, emphasis added.

27. Goodell, *Big Coal*.

28. David Harvey, *The New Imperialism* (New York: Oxford University Press, 2003); see also Willian J. Broad, "In Taking Crimea, Putin Gains a Sea of Fuel Reserves," *New York Times*, May 18, 2014, A1.

29. Mark Dowie, *American Foundations: An Investigative History* (Cambridge: MIT Press, 2001); Roelofs, *Foundations and Public Policy*.

30. Richard Magat, *The Ford Foundation at Work: Philanthropic Choices, Methods, and Styles* (New York: Plenum, 1979); Inderjeet Parmar, *Foundations of the American Century: The Ford, Carnegie, and Rockefeller Foundations in the Rise of American Power* (New York: Columbia University Press, 2011); Karen Ferguson, *Top Down: The Ford Foundation, Black Power, and the Reinvention of Racial Liberalism* (Philadelphia: University of Pennsylvania Press, 2013).

31. Berman, *Influence of the Carnegie, Ford, and Rockefeller Foundations on American Foreign Policy*, 63.

32. Ibid., 153.

33. Nuclear Energy Policy Study Group, *Nuclear Power Issues and Choices* (New York: Ford Foundation/MITRE, 1977), 417–418; Research and Policy Committee of the Committee for Economic Development, *Nuclear Energy and National Security*, 6.

34. Magat, *The Ford Foundation at Work*, 165 and 172.

35. Berman, *Influence of the Carnegie, Ford, and Rockefeller Foundations on American Foreign Policy*, 118–119.

36. Nuclear Energy Policy Study Group, *Nuclear Power Issues and Choice*, 380–381, emphasis added.

37. Blue Ribbon Commission on America's Nuclear Future, *Report to the Secretary of Energy* (Washington, DC: Author, 2012), xiv–xv.

38. Ibid., 105, parentheses in original.

39. Ibid., 101, emphasis in original.

40. Ibid., 107.

41. Blue Ribbon Commission on America's Nuclear Future, Commission Members, archived 20 June 2012: http://brc.gov/index.php?q=commission-members (viewed April 17, 2013).

Conclusion

1. Coral Davenport and Steven Erlanger, "U.S. Hopes Boom in Natural Gas Can Curb Putin," *New York Times*, March 6, 2014, A1. See also "Natural Gas as a Diplomatic Tool," *New York Times*, March 7, 2014, A24; Clifford Krauss, "U.S. Gas Tantalizes Europe, but It's Not a Quick Fix," *New York Times*, April 8, 2014, B1; Stanley Reed and James Kanter, "For a European Energy Chief, a Difficult Alliance," *New York Times*, April 28, 2014, B1; Rick Gladstone, "Russia and Iran Reported in Talks on Energy Deal Worth Billions," *New York Times*, April 29, 2014, A12; Jim Yardley and Jo Becker, "How Putin Forged a Pipeline Deal That Derailed," *New York Times*, December 31, 2014, A1; O'Sullivan, "Trump Can Harness the Energy Boom," and *Windfall*.

2. Michael Shellenberger, "How Not to Deal with Climate Change," *New York Times*, June 30, 2016, A27.

Selected Bibliography

Abrams, Richard M. *America Transformed: Sixty Years of Revolutionary Change, 1941–2001.* New York: Cambridge University Press, 2006.

Allardice, Corbin, and Edward R. Trapnell. *The Atomic Energy Commission.* New York: Praeger, 1974.

Alley, William M., and Rosemarie Alley. *Too Hot to Touch: The Problem of High-Level Nuclear Waste.* New York: Cambridge University Press, 2013.

Alvarez, Lizette. "Waters Rise and Hurricanes Roar, but Florida Keeps On Building." *New York Times,* September 19, 2017, A1.

Armand, Louis. *Some Aspects of the European Energy Problem: Suggestions for Collective Action.* Paris: Organisation for European Economic Co-operation, 1955.

Aronowitz, Stanley. *Taking It Big: C. Wright Mills and the Making of Political Intellectuals.* New York: Columbia University Press, 2012.

Aronowitz, Stanley, and Peter Bratsis, eds. *Paradigm Lost: State Theory Reconsidered.* Minneapolis: University of Minnesota Press, 2002.

Atkinson, Robert D. *The Past and Future of America's Economy: Long Waves of Innovation That Power Cycles of Growth.* Northampton: Edward Elgar, 2004.

Balogh, Brian. *Chain Reaction: Expert Debate and Public Participation in American Commercial Nuclear Power, 1945–1975.* New York: Cambridge University Press, 1991.

Banks, Ferdinand E. *The Political Economy of Oil.* Lexington: Lexington Books, 1980.

Baranowski, Shelley. *Nazi Empire: German Colonialism and Imperialism from Bismarck to Hitler.* New York: Cambridge University Press, 2011.

Bardou, Jean-Pierre, Jean-Jacques Chanaron, Patrick Fridenson, and James M. Laux. *The Automobile Revolution: The Impact of an Industry.* Chapel Hill: University of North Carolina Press, 1982.

Barker, T. C. "The International History of Motor Transport." *Journal of Contemporary History* 20, no. 1 (1985): 3–19.

Barnosky, Anthony. *Dodging Extinction: Power, Food, Money, and the Future of Life on Earth.* Berkeley: University of California Press, 2016.

Barrett, Paul. *The Automobile and Urban Transit*. Philadelphia: Temple University Press, 1983.

Barrow, Clyde W. *Universities and the Capitalist State: Corporate Liberalism and the Reconstruction of American Higher Education, 1894–1928*. Madison: University of Wisconsin Press, 1990.

———. "Corporate Liberalism, Finance Hegemony, and Central State Intervention in the Reconstruction of American Higher Education." *Studies in American Political Development* 6 (Fall 1992): 420–444.

———. *Critical Theories of the State*. Madison: University of Wisconsin Press, 1993.

———. "The Return of the State: Globalization, State Theory, and the New Imperialism." *New Political Science* 27, no. 2 (2005): 123–145.

———. *Toward a Critical Theory of States: The Poulantzas-Miliband Debate after Globalization*. Albany: State University of New York Press, 2016.

Baumgartner, Frank R., Jeffrey M. Berry, Marie Hojnacki, David C. Kimball, and Beth L. Leech. *Lobbying and Policy Change: Who Wins, Who Loses, and Why*. Chicago: University of Chicago Press, 2009.

Beattie, Donald, ed. *History and Overview of Solar Heat Technologies*. Cambridge: MIT Press, 1997.

Beauregard, Robert A. *When America Became Suburban*. Minneapolis: University of Minnesota Press, 2006.

Bellon, Bernard P. *Mercedes in Peace and War: German Automobile Workers, 1903–1945*. New York: Columbia University Press, 1992.

Bento, Antonio, Maureen L. Cropper, Ahmed Mushfiq Mobarak, and Katja Vinha. "The Effects of Urban Spatial Structure on Travel Demand in the United States." *The Review of Economics and Statistics* 87, no. 3 (2005): 466–478.

Berman, Edward H. *Influence of the Carnegie, Ford, and Rockefeller Foundations on American Foreign Policy*. Albany: State University of New York Press, 1983.

"Beyond Denialism: Think Tank Approaches to Climate Change." *Sociology Compass* 10, no. 4 (2016): 306–317.

Bindas, Kenneth J. *Modernity and the Great Depression: The Transformation of American Society, 1930–1941*. Lawrence: University Press of Kansas, 2017.

Blair, John M. *The Control of Oil*. New York: Pantheon, 1976.

Blatt, Harvey. *America's Environmental Report Card: Are We Making the Grade?* Cambridge: MIT Press, 2005.

———. *America's Environmental Report Card: Are We Making the Grade?*, 2nd ed. Cambridge: MIT Press, 2011.

Block, Fred. "Understanding the Diverging Trajectories of the United States and Western Europe: A Neo-Polanyian Analysis." *Politics & Society* 35, no. 1 (2007): 3–33.

Blue Ribbon Commission on America's Nuclear Future. *Report to the Secretary of Energy*. Washington, DC: Author, 2012.

Bohlen, Celestine. "American Democracy Is Drowning in Money." *International New York Times*, September 21, 2017, S4.

Bonds, Eric. "Beyond Denialism: Think Tank Approaches to Climate Change." *Sociology Compass* 10, no. 4 (2016): 306–317.

Bradford, Travis. *Solar Revolution: The Economic Transformation of the Global Energy Industry*. Cambridge: MIT Press, 2006.

Bradsher, Keith. *High and Mighty: SUVs—The World's Most Dangerous Vehicles and How They Got That Way*. New York: Public Affairs, 2002.

Brady, Anne-Marie. *China as a Polar Great Power*. New York: Cambridge University Press, 2017.

Braudel, Fernand. *Civilization and Capitalism, 15th–18th Century*, vols. 1–3. New York: Harper & Row, 1982/1984.

Brenner, Michael J. *Nuclear Power and Non-Proliferation: The Remaking of U.S. Policy*. New York: Cambridge University Press, 1981.

Brenner, Robert. *The Boom and the Bubble: The U.S. in the World Economy*. New York: Verso, 2002.

Bronson, Rachel. *Thicker than Oil: America's Uneasy Partnership with Saudi Arabia*. New York: Oxford University Press, 2006.

Bromley, Simon. *American Hegemony and World Oil: The Industry, the State System and the World Economy*. University Park: Pennsylvania State University Press, 1991.

———. "The United States and the Control of Oil." *Government and Opposition* 40, no. 2 (2005): 225–255.

Buder, Stanley. *Capitalizing on Change: A Social History of American Business*. Chapel Hill: University of North Carolina Press, 2009.

Bupp, Irvin C., and Jean-Claude Derian. *The Failed Promise of Nuclear Power: The Story of Light Water*. New York: Basic Books, 1978.

Büthe, Tim. "Taking Temporality Seriously: Modeling History and the Use of Narratives as Evidence." *American Political Science Review* 96, no. 3 (2002): 481–493.

Callen, Zachary. *Railroads and American Political Development: Infrastructure, Federalism, and State Building*. Lawrence: University Press of Kansas, 2016.

Camilleri, Joseph A. *The State and Nuclear Power: Conflict and Control in the Western World*. Seattle: University of Washington Press, 1984.

Campbell, John L. *Nuclear Power and the Contradiction of U.S. Policy*. Ithaca: Cornell University Press, 1988.

Castle, Stephen. "European Union Proposes Easing of Climate Rules." *New York Times*, January 23, 2014, A1.

Chandler, Alfred, Jr. "Anthracite Coal and the Beginnings of the Industrial Revolution in the United States." *Business History Review* 46, no. 2 (1972): 141–181.

Chastko, Paul. *Developing Alberta's Oil Sands: From Karl Clark to Kyoto*. Calgary: University of Calgary Press, 2004.

Chatterjee, Abhishek. *Rulers and Capital in Historical Perspective: State Formation and Financial Development in India and the United States.* Philadelphia: Temple University Press, 2017.

Christoff, Peter. "Ecological Modernization, Ecological Modernities." *Environmental Politics* 5, no. 3 (1996): 476–500.

Cipolla, Carlo M. *Guns, Sails, and Empires: Technological Innovations and the Early Phases of European Expansion 1400–1700.* New York: Pantheon, 1966.

Cohen, Lizabeth. *A Consumers' Republic: The Politics of Mass Consumption in Postwar America.* New York: Alfred A. Knopf, 2003.

Coll, Steve. *Private Empire: ExxonMobil and American Power.* New York: Penguin, 2013.

Collier, Peter, and David Horowitz. *The Rockefellers: An American Dynasty.* New York: Holt, Rinehart, and Winston, 1976.

Commission for Energy. *Europe's Growing Needs of Energy: How Can They Be Met?* Paris: Organisation for European Economic Co-operation, 1956.

Conybeare, John A. C. *Merging Traffic: The Consolidation of the International Automobile Industry.* Lanham: Rowman & Littlefield, 2004.

Cyphers, Christopher, J. *The National Civic Federation and the Making of New Liberalism, 1900–1915.* Westport: Praeger, 2002.

Dahl, Robert A. *A Preface to Democratic Theory.* Chicago: University of Chicago Press, 1956.

———. *Who Governs? Democracy and Power in an American City.* New Haven: Yale University Press, 1961 [2005].

Dahl, Robert A., and Charles E. Lindblom. *Politics, Economics, and Welfare.* New Haven: Yale University Press, 1953.

———. "Preface." In *Politics, Economics, and Welfare.* New Haven: Yale University Press, 1976.

Dallek, Robert. *Franklin D. Roosevelt and American Foreign Policy, 1932–1945.* New York: Oxford University Press, 1995.

Davis, David. *Energy Politics.* New York: St. Martin's Press, 1993.

Deffeyes, Kenneth S. *Hubbert's Peak: The Impending World Oil Shortage.* Princeton: Princeton University Press, 2001.

Domhoff, G. William. *The Bohemian Grove and Other Retreats.* New York: Harper and Row, 1974.

———. *The Powers That Be.* New York: Random House, 1978.

———. *Who Really Rules? New Haven and Community Power Reexamined.* Santa Monica: Goodyear, 1978.

———. *The Power Elite and the State.* New York: Aldine de Gruyter, 1990.

———. *State Autonomy or Class Dominance?* New York: Aldine de Gruyter, 1996.

———. *Who Rules America?*, 7th ed. New York: McGraw-Hill, 2013.

Domhoff, G. William, and Michael J. Webber. *Class and Power in the New Deal.* Palo Alto: Stanford University Press, 2011.

Dowie, Mark. *Losing Ground: American Environmentalism at the Close of the Twentieth Century.* Cambridge: MIT Press, 1995.

———. *American Foundations: An Investigative History.* Cambridge: MIT Press, 2001.

Dryzek, John S. *Democracy in Capitalist Times.* New York: Oxford University Press, 1996.

Du Boff, Richard B. *Accumulation and Power: An Economic History of the United States.* Armonk: M. E. Sharpe, 1989.

Duffield, John S. *Over a Barrel: The Costs of U.S. Foreign Oil Dependence.* Stanford: Stanford University Press, 2008.

Duffy, Robert J. *Nuclear Politics in America: A History and Theory of Government Regulation.* Lawrence: University Press of Kansas, 1997.

Dunn, James. *Miles to Go: European and American Transportation Policies.* Cambridge: MIT Press, 1981.

———. *Driving Forces: The Automobile, Its Enemies, and the Politics of Mobility.* Washington, DC: Brookings Institution Press, 1998.

Duplessis, Robert S. *Transitions to Capitalism in Early Modern Europe.* New York: Cambridge University Press, 1997.

Eakins, David. "Business Planners and America's Postwar Expansion." In *Corporations and the Cold War,* ed. David Horowitz. New York: Monthly Review Press, 1969.

———. "Policy-Planning for the Establishment." In *A New History of Leviathan,* ed. Ronald Radosh and Murray N. Rothbard. New York: E. P. Dutton & Co., 1972.

Eckes, Alfred E. *Opening America's Market: U.S. Foreign Trade Policy since 1776.* Chapel Hill: University of North Carolina Press, 1995.

Eckstein, Rick. *Nuclear Power and Social Power.* Philadelphia: Temple University Press, 1997.

Edelstein, David M. *Over the Horizon: Time, Uncertainty, and the Rise of Great Powers.* Ithaca: Cornell University Press, 2017.

Energy Advisory Commission. *Towards a New Energy Pattern in Europe.* Paris: Organisation for European Economic Co-operation, 1960.

Fearon, Peter. *War, Prosperity, and Depression: The U.S. Economy 1917–45.* Lawrence: University Press of Kansas, 1987.

Feuchtwanger, E.J. *From Weimar to Hitler: Germany, 1918–33.* New York: St. Martin's Press, 1995.

Field, Alexander J. "Technological Change and U.S. Productivity Growth in the Interwar Years." *Journal of Economic History* 66, no. 1 (2006): 203–234.

Finegold, Kenneth, and Theda Skocpol. *State and Party in America's New Deal.* Madison: University of Wisconsin Press, 1995.

Fischer, Klaus. *Hitler and America.* Philadelphia: University of Pennsylvania Press, 2011.

Fishman, Robert. *Bourgeois Utopias: The Rise and Fall of Suburbia.* New York: Basic Books, 1987.

Flink, James. *The Car Culture.* Cambridge: MIT Press, 1975.

———. *The Automobile Age*. Cambridge: MIT Press, 1990.

Fogelson, Robert M. *Bourgeois Nightmares: Suburbia, 1870–1930*. New Haven: Yale University Press, 2005.

Fong, Benjamin Y. "The Climate Crisis? It's Capitalism, Stupid." *New York Times*, November 20, 2017. Web.

Foster, Mark S. *From Streetcar to Superhighway: American City Planners and Urban Transportation, 1900–1940*. Philadelphia: Temple University Press, 1981.

French, Michael. *U.S. Economic History since 1945*. Manchester: Manchester University Press, 1997.

Gat, Azar. *The Causes of War and the Spread of Peace*. New York: Oxford University Press, 2017.

Gautier, Catherine. *Oil, Water, and Climate: An Introduction*. New York: Cambridge University Press, 2008.

Gautier, Catherine, and Jean-Louis Fellous, eds. *Facing Climate Change Together*. New York: Cambridge University Press, 2008.

Gillis, Justin, and Nadja Popovich. "The U.S. Is the Biggest Carbon Polluter in History. It Just Walked Away from the Paris Climate Deal." *New York Times*, June 1, 2017. Web.

Gindin, Sam, and Leo Panitch. *The Making of Global Capitalism: The Political Economy of American Empire*. New York: Verso, 2012.

Gonzalez, George A. *Corporate Power and the Environment: The Political Economy of U.S. Environmental Policy*. Lanham: Rowman & Littlefield, 2001.

———. "Ideas and State Capacity, or Business Dominance? A Historical Analysis of Grazing on the Public Grasslands." *Studies in American Political Development* 15 (Fall 2001): 234–244.

———. "The Comprehensive Everglades Restoration Plan: Economic or Environmental Sustainability?" *Polity* 37, no. 4 (2005): 466–490.

———. *The Politics of Air Pollution: Urban Growth, Ecological Modernization, and Symbolic Inclusion*. Albany: State University of New York Press, 2005.

———. "The Wilderness Act of 1964 and the Wilderness Preservation Policy Network." *Capitalism Nature Socialism* 20, no. 4 (2009): 31–52.

———. *Urban Sprawl, Global Warming, and the Empire of Capital*. Albany: State University of New York Press, 2009.

———. *Energy and Empire: The Politics of Nuclear and Solar Power in the United States*. Albany: State University of New York Press, 2012.

———. *Energy and the Politics of the North Atlantic*. Albany: State University of New York Press, 2013.

———. "The U.S. Politics of Water Pollution Policy: Urban Growth, Ecological Modernization, and the Vending of Technology." *Capitalism Nature Socialism* 24, no. 4 (2013): 105-21.

———. "Is Obama's 2014 Greenhouse Gas Reduction Plan Symbolic? The Creation of the U.S. EPA and a Reliance on the States." *Capitalism Nature Socialism* 26, no. 2 (2015): 92–104.

———. *The Politics of Star Trek: Justice, War, and the Future*. New York: Palgrave Macmillan, 2015.

———. *American Empire and the Canadian Oil Sands*. New York: Palgrave Macmillan, 2016.

———. "*Justice League Unlimited* and the Politics of Globalization." *Foundation: The International Review of Science Fiction* 45, no. 123 (2016): 5–13.

———. *The Absolute and Star Trek*. New York: Palgrave Macmillan, 2017.

———. "Star Trek: Nationalism as Pathology and Internationalism as Rationalism." *Foundation: The International Review of Science Fiction* (forthcoming 2018).

Goodell, Jeff. *Big Coal: The Dirty Secret behind America's Energy Future*. New York: Mariner, 2007.

———. *The Water Will Come: Rising Seas, Sinking Cities, and the Remaking of the Civilized World*. New York: Little, Brown, 2017.

Goodstein, David. *Out of Gas: The End of the Age of Oil*. New York: Norton, 2004.

Graetz, Michael J. *The End of Energy: The Unmaking of America's Environment, Security, and Independence*. Cambridge: MIT Press, 2011.

Grossman, Peter Z. *U.S. Energy Policy and the Pursuit of Failure*. Cambridge: Cambridge University Press, 2013.

Harvey, David. *The New Imperialism*. New York: Oxford University Press, 2003.

Hatch, Michael T. *Politics and Nuclear Power: Energy Policy in Western Europe*. Lexington: University Press of Kentucky, 1986.

Haugland, Torleif, Helge Ole Bergensen, and Kjell Roland. *Energy Structures and Environmental Futures*. New York: Oxford University Press, 1998.

Hay, Colin, Michael Lister, and David Marsh, eds. *The State: Theories and Issues*. New York: Palgrave Macmillan, 2006.

Hays, Samuel. "The Politics of Reform in Municipal Government in the Progressive Era." *Pacific Northwest Quarterly* 55, no. 4 (1964): 157–169.

Hecht, Gabrielle. *The Radiance of France: Nuclear Power and National Identity after World War II*. Cambridge: MIT Press, 2009.

Heinberg, Richard. *The Party's Over: Oil, War, and the Fate of Industrial Societies*, 2nd ed. Gabriola Island: New Society Publishers, 2005.

Helm, Dieter. *Burn Out: The Endgame for Fossil Fuels*. New Haven: Yale University Press, 2017.

Herring, Horace, and Steve Sorrell, eds. *Energy Efficiency and Sustainable Consumption: The Rebound Effect*. New York: Palgrave Macmillan, 2009.

Hertog, Steffen. *Princes, Brokers, and Bureaucrats: Oil and the State in Saudi Arabia*. Ithaca: Cornell University Press, 2010.

Hertsgaard, Mark. *Nuclear Inc.: The Men and Money Behind Nuclear Energy*. New York: Pantheon, 1983.

Hewlett, Richard G., and Francis Duncan. *Atomic Shield, 1947/1952: A History of the United States Atomic Energy Commission*, vol. 2. University Park: Pennsylvania State University Press, 1969.

Hewlett, Richard G., and Jack M. Holl. *Atoms for Peace and War 1953–1961: Eisenhower and the Atomic Energy Commission*, vol. 3. Berkeley: University of California Press, 1989.

Hewlett, Richard G., and Oscar E. Anderson Jr. *The New World, 1939/1946: A History of the United States Atomic Energy Commission*, vol. 1. University Park: Pennsylvania State University Press, 1962.

Hoff, Joan. *A Faustian Foreign Policy: From Woodrow Wilson to George W. Bush*. New York: Cambridge University Press, 2008.

Hollis, Everett L. "The United States Atomic Energy Act of 1954: A Brief Survey." In *The Economics of Nuclear Power: Including Administration and Law*, ed. J. Guéron, J. A. Lane, I. R. Maxwell, and J. R. Menke. New York: McGraw-Hill, 1957.

Hornstein, Jeffrey M. *A Nation of Realtors: A Cultural History of the Twentieth-Century American Middle Class*. Durham: Duke University Press, 2005.

Houghton, John. *Global Warming: The Complete Briefing*, 5th ed. New York: Cambridge University Press, 2015.

Hounshell, David A. *From the American System to Mass Production, 1800–1932: The Development of Manufacturing Technology in the United States*. Baltimore: Johns Hopkins University Press, 1984.

Hulse, Carl. "Face to Face With Failure, and the Donors Aren't Happy." *New York Times*, September 23, 2017, A12.

"Hunger Haunts the U.N. Festivities." *New York Times*, September 22, 2017, A26.

Hunt, Edwin S., and James M. Murray. *A History of Business in Medieval Europe, 1200–1550*. New York: Cambridge University Press, 1999.

Hyman, Sidney. *Marriner S. Eccles: Private Entrepreneur and Public Servant*. Stanford: Stanford University Graduate School of Business, 1976.

Ikenberry, John G. *Reasons of State: Oil Politics and the Capacities of American Government*. Ithaca: Cornell University Press, 1988.

———. *Liberal Leviathan: The Origins, Crisis, and Transformation of the American World Order*. Princeton: Princeton University Press, 2012.

Ingram, Tammy. *Dixie Highway: Road Building and the Making of the Modern South, 1900–1930*. Chapel Hill: University of North Carolina Press, 2014.

International Atomic Energy Agency. *Fast Breeder Reactors: Experience and Trends*, vol. 2. Paris: International Atomic Energy Agency, 1986.

International Energy Agency, *CO_2 Emissions from Fuel Combustion: Highlights*, 2016 ed. Paris: International Energy Agency, 2016.

International Nuclear Fuel Cycle Evaluation (INFCE): Summary Volume. Vienna: International Atomic Energy Agency, 1980.

Jackson, Kenneth T. *Crabgrass Frontier: The Suburbanization of the United States*. New York: Oxford University Press, 1985.

Janssen, Geert H. *Princely Power in the Dutch Republic*. New York: Manchester University Press, 2008.

Jones, Christopher F. "A Landscape of Energy Abundance: Anthracite Coal Canals and the Roots of American Fossil Fuel Dependence, 1820–1860." *Environmental History* 15, no. 3 (2010): 449–484.

Kalicki, Jan H., and David L. Goldwyn, eds. *Energy and Security: Toward a New Foreign Policy Strategy.* Baltimore: Johns Hopkins University Press, 2005.

Kamieniecki, Sheldon. *Corporate America and Environmental Policy: How Often Does Business Get Its Way?* Palo Alto: Stanford University Press, 2006.

Kay, Jane Holtz. *Asphalt Nation: How the Automobile Took Over America and How We Can Take It Back.* Berkeley: University of California Press, 1998.

Kenworthy, Jeffrey R. "Energy Use and CO_2 Production in the Urban Passenger Transport Systems of 84 International Cities: Findings and Policy Implications." In *Urban Energy Transition from Fossil Fuels to Renewable Power*, ed. Peter Droege. Amsterdam: Elsevier, 2008.

Kenworthy, Jeffrey R., and Felix B. Laube, with Peter Newman, Paul Barter, Tamim Raad, Chamlong Poboon, and Benedicto Guia Jr. *An International Sourcebook of Automobile Dependence in Cities 1960–1990.* Boulder: University Press of Colorado, 1999.

Kim, Sung Chull and Michael D. Cohen, eds. *North Korea and Nuclear Weapons: Entering the New Era of Deterrence.* Washington, D.C.: Georgetown University Press, 2017.

Kirsch, David A. *The Electric Vehicle and the Burden of History.* New Brunswick: Rutgers University Press, 2000.

Klein, Maury. *The Genesis of Industrial America, 1870–1920.* New York: Cambridge University Press, 2007.

Knox, Paul L. *Metroburbia, USA.* Piscataway: Rutgers University Press, 2008.

Kolbert, Elizabeth. *The Sixth Extinction: An Unnatural History.* New York: Henry Holt, 2014.

Kolko, Gabriel. *The Triumph of Conservatism: A Reinterpretation of American History, 1900–1916.* New York: Free Press, 1977 (1963).

Kraft, Michael E., and Sheldon Kamieniecki, eds. *Business and Environmental Policy: Corporate Interests in the American Political System.* Cambridge: MIT Press, 2007.

Krasner, Stephen. *Defending the National Interest: Raw Materials Investments and U.S. Foreign Policy.* Princeton: Princeton University Press, 1978.

Kroenig, Matthew. *Exporting the Bomb: Technology Transfer and the Spread of Nuclear Weapons.* Ithaca: Cornell University Press, 2010.

Kryza, Frank T. *The Power of Light: The Epic Story of Man's Quest to Harness the Sun.* New York: McGraw-Hill, 2003.

Kurczy, Stephen. "International Energy Agency Says 'Peak Oil' Has Hit." *The Christian Science Monitor*, November 11, 2010. Web.

Kurman, Krishan. *Visions of Empire.* Princeton: Princeton University Press, 2017.

Lafer, Gordon. *The One Percent Solution: How Corporations Are Remaking America One State at a Time.* Ithaca: Cornell University Press, 2017.

Laird, Frank N. *Solar Energy, Technology Policy, and Institutional Values.* New York: Cambridge University Press, 2001.

Layzer, Judith A. "Deep Freeze: How Business Has Shaped the Global Warming Debate in Congress." In *Business and Environmental Policy*, ed. Michael E. Kraft and Sheldon Kamieniecki. Cambridge: MIT Press, 2007.

———. *Open for Business: Conservatives' Opposition to Environmental Regulation.* Cambridge: MIT Press, 2012.

Lester, Richard K., and David M. Hart. *Unlocking Energy Innovation: How America Can Build a Low-Cost, Low-Carbon Energy System.* Cambridge: MIT Press, 2012.

Levi, Michael A. *The Canadian Oil Sands: Energy Security vs. Climate Change.* New York: Council on Foreign Relations, 2009.

Lindsey, Brink, and Steven Teles. *The Captured Economy: How the Powerful Enrich Themselves, Slow Down Growth, and Increase Inequality.* New York: Oxford University Press, 2017.

Lochbaum, David. *The NRC and Nuclear Power Plant Safety in 2010: A Brighter Spotlight Needed.* Cambridge, MA: Union of Concerned Scientists, 2011.

Lodgaard, Sverre. *Nuclear Disarmament and Non-Proliferation: Towards a Nuclear-Weapon-Free World?* New York: Routledge, 2010.

Logan, John R., and Harvey L. Molotch. *Urban Fortunes: The Political Economy of Place.* Berkeley: University of California Press, 1987 (2007).

Lowi, Theodore J. *The End of Liberalism: The Second Republic of the United States.* New York: Norton, 1979.

Lowrance, William O. "Nuclear Futures for Sale: To Brazil from West Germany, 1975." *International Security* 1, no. 2 (1976): 147–166.

Lucas, Nigel. *Western European Energy Policies: A Comparative Study of the Influence of Institutional Structures on Technical Change.* Oxford: Clarendon, 1985.

Luger, Stan. *Corporate Power, American Democracy, and the Automobile Industry.* New York: Cambridge University Press, 2000.

MacAvoy, Paul W. *The Natural Gas Market: Sixty Years of Regulation and Deregulation.* New Haven: Yale University Press, 2001.

Madrigal, Alexis. *Powering the Dream: The History and Promise of Green Technology.* Cambridge: Da Capo Press, 2011.

Magat, Richard. *The Ford Foundation at Work: Philanthropic Choices, Methods, and Styles.* New York: Plenum, 1979.

Magnusson, Lars. *Mercantilism: The Shaping of an Economic Language.* New York: Routledge, 2015.

Manley, John F. "Neo-pluralism: A Class Analysis of Pluralism I and Pluralism II." *American Political Science Review* 77, no. 2 (1983): 368–383.

Marks, Steven G. *The Information Nexus: Global Capitalism from the Renaissance to the Present.* New York: Cambridge University Press, 2016.

Martin, Richard. *Coal Wars: The Future of Energy and the Fate of the Planet.* New York: St. Martin's Press, 2015.

Martinez, J. Michael. "The Carter Administration and the Evolution of American Nuclear Nonproliferation Policy, 1977–1981." *Journal of Policy History* 14, no. 3 (2002): 261–292.

Maslin, Mark. *Global Warming: A Very Short Introduction*. New York: Oxford University Press, 2009.

Mazower, Mark. *Governing the World: The History of an Idea*. New York: Penguin, 2012.

McConnell, Grant. *Private Power and American Democracy*. New York: Knopf, 1966.

McShane, Clay. *Technology and Reform: Street Railways and the Growth of Milwaukee, 1887–1900*. Madison: State Historical Society of Wisconsin, 1974.

———. *Down the Asphalt Path: The Automobile and the American City*. New York: Columbia University Press, 1994.

Miliband, Ralph. *The State in Capitalist Society*. New York: Basic Books, 1969.

Miller, Arthur Selwyn. *The Modern Corporate State: Private Governments and the American Constitution*. Westport: Greenwood, 1976.

Miller, Jerry. *Stockpile: The Story Behind 10,000 Strategic Nuclear Weapons*. Annapolis: Naval Institute Press, 2010.

Miller, Roger. "Selling Mrs. Consumer: Advertising and the Creation of Suburban Socio-Spatial Relations, 1910–1930." *Antipode* 23, no. 3 (1991): 263–306.

Mills, C. Wright. *The Power Elite*. New York: Oxford University Press, 1956.

Mintz, Beth, and Michael Schwartz. *The Power Structure of American Business*. Chicago: University of Chicago Press, 1985.

Molotch, Harvey. "The City as a Growth Machine: Towards of Political Economy of Place." *American Journal of Sociology* 82, no. 2 (1976): 309–322.

———. "Capital and Neighborhood in the United States." *Urban Affairs Quarterly* 14, no. 3 (1979): 289–312.

Mom, Gijs. *The Electric Vehicle: Technology and Expectations in the Automobile Age*. Baltimore: Johns Hopkins University Press, 2004.

Moore, Jason W. "The Modern World-System as Environmental History? Ecology and the Rise of Capitalism." *Theory and Society* 32, no. 3 (2003): 307–377.

Moroney, John R. *Power Struggle: World Energy in the Twenty-First Century*. Westport: Praeger, 2008.

Morriss, Roger. *The Foundations of British Maritime Ascendancy: Resources, Logistics and the State, 1755–1815*. New York: Cambridge University Press, 2011.

Muller, Peter O. *Contemporary Suburban America*. Englewood Cliffs: Prentice-Hall, 1981.

Nau, Henry. *National Politics and International Technology: Nuclear Reactor Development in Western Europe*. Baltimore: Johns Hopkins University Press, 1974.

Nelkin, Dorothy, and Michael Pollak. *The Atom Besieged: Antinuclear Movements in France and Germany*. Cambridge: MIT Press, 1981.

Nersesian, Roy L. *Energy for the 21st Century*. Armonk: M. E. Sharpe, 2007.

Newman, Peter, and Jeff Kenworthy. "Greening Urban Transportation." In *State of the World: Our Urban Future*, ed. Linda Starke. New York: W.W. Norton, 2007.

Newman, Peter, and Jeffrey Kenworthy. *Sustainability and Cities: Overcoming Automobile Dependence*. Washington, DC: Island Press, 1999.

Newman, Peter, Timothy Beatley, and Heather Boyer. *Resilient Cities: Responding to Peak Oil and Climate Change*. Washington, DC: Island Press, 2009.

Nexon, Daniel H., and Thomas Wright. "What's at Stake in the American Empire Debate." *American Political Science Review* 101, no. 2 (2007): 253–271.

Njølstad, Olav. *Nuclear Proliferation and International Order: Challenges to the Non-Proliferation Treaty*. New York: Routledge, 2010.

Nordhaus, William. *A Question of Balance*. Cambridge: MIT Press, 2008.

Nordlinger, Eric A. *On the Autonomy of the Democratic State*. Cambridge: Harvard University Press, 1981.

Nuclear Energy Policy Study Group. *Nuclear Power Issues and Choices*. New York: Ford Foundation/MITRE, 1977.

O'Connor, James. *The Fiscal Crisis of the State*. New York: Transaction, 2002.

Olien, Diana Davids, and Roger M. Olien. *Oil in Texas: The Gusher Age, 1895–1945*. Austin: University of Texas Press, 2002.

Olien, Roger M., and Diana Davids Olien. *Oil and Ideology: The Cultural Creation of the American Petroleum Industry*. Chapel Hill: University of North Carolina Press, 2000.

Olliff, Martin T. *Getting Out of the Mud: The Alabama Good Roads Movement and Highway Administration, 1898–1928*. Tuscaloosa: The University of Alabama Press, 2017.

Olney, Martha L. "Credit as a Production-Smoothing Device: The Case of Automobiles, 1913–1938." *Journal of Economic History* 49, no. 2 (1989): 377–391.

———. *Buy Now, Pay Later: Advertising, Credit, and Consumer Durables in the 1920s*. Chapel Hill: University of North Carolina Press, 1991.

Oreskes, Naomi, and Erik M. Conway. *The Collapse of Western Civilization: A View from the Future*. New York: Columbia University Press, 2014.

Ormrod, David. *The Rise of Commercial Empires: England and the Netherlands in the Age of Mercantilism, 1650–1770*. New York: Cambridge University Press, 2008.

O'Sullivan, Meghan L. "Trump Can Harness the Energy Boom." *New York Times*, September 15, 2017, A27.

———. *Windfall: How the New Energy Abundance Upends Global Politics and Strengthens American Power*. New York: Simon & Schuster, 2017.

Painter, David S. *Oil and the American Century: The Political Economy of U.S. Foreign Oil Policy, 1941–1954*. Baltimore: Johns Hopkins University Press, 1986.

Panel on the Impact of the Peaceful Uses of Atomic Energy. *Peaceful Uses of Atomic Energy*, vols. 1–2. Washington, DC: Government Printing Office, 1956.

Parish, Theodore A., Vyacheslav V. Khromov, and Igor Carron, eds. *Safety Issues Associated with Plutonium Involvement in the Nuclear Fuel Cycle.* New York: Springer, 1999.

Parra, Francisco. *Oil Politics: A Modern History of Petroleum.* New York: I. B. Tauris, 2004.

Parmar, Inderjeet. "American Foundations and the Development of International Knowledge Networks." *Global Networks* 2, no. 1 (2002): 13–30.

———. *Foundations of the American Century: The Ford, Carnegie, and Rockefeller Foundations in the Rise of American Power.* New York: Columbia University Press, 2011.

Parr, Adrian. *The Wrath of Capital: Neoliberalism and Climate Change Politics.* New York: Columbia University Press, 2013.

Paterson, Matthew. *Automobile Politics.* New York: Cambridge University Press, 2007.

Pauly, Robert J., Jr. *U.S. Foreign Policy and the Persian Gulf: Safeguarding American Interests through Selective Multilateralism.* Burlington: Ashgate, 2005.

Paxson, Frederic L. "The American Highway Movement, 1916–1935." *American Historical Review* 51, no. 2 (1946): 239–241.

Pfau, Richard. *No Sacrifice Too Great: The Life of Lewis L. Strauss.* Charlottesville: University Press of Virginia, 1984.

Philip, George. *The Political Economy of International Oil.* Edinburgh: Edinburgh University Press, 1994.

Pierson, Paul. "Increasing Returns, Path Dependence, and the Study of Politics." *American Political Science Review* 94, no. 2 (2000): 251–267.

Pieterse, Jan Nederveen. *Globalization or Empire?* New York: Routledge, 2004.

Piketty, Thomas. *Capital in the Twenty-First Century,* trans. Arthur Goldhammer. Cambridge: Belknap Press, 2014.

Plumer, Brad. "Why Hurricane Irma Could Hurt a Lot." *New York Times,* September 8, 2017, A17.

Podobnik, Bruce. *Global Energy Shifts: Fostering Sustainability in a Turbulent Age.* Philadelphia: Temple University Press, 2006.

Poulantzas, Nico. *Political Power and Social Classes.* London: New Left Books, 1973.

Powell, James Lawrence. *The Inquisition of Climate Science.* New York: Columbia University Press, 2011.

Power, Max S. *America's Nuclear Wastelands: Politics, Accountability, and Cleanup.* Pullman: Washington State University Press, 2008.

Proceedings of the World Symposium on Applied Solar Energy, Phoenix, AZ, Nov. 1–5, 1955. San Francisco: Jorgenson & Co., 1956.

Qiyu, Xu. *Fragile Rise: Grand Strategy and the Fate of Imperial Germany, 1871–1914*, trans. Joshua Hill. Cambridge: MIT Press, 2017.

Report of the Committee on Recent Economic Changes, of the President's Conference on Unemployment. *Recent Economic Changes in the United States*, vols. 1–2. New York: McGraw-Hill, 1929.

Report of the President's Conference on Unemployment. Washington, DC: Government Printing Office, 1921.

Rich, Andrew. *Think Tanks, Public Policy, and the Politics of Expertise*. New York: Cambridge University Press, 2004.

Roberts, Paul. *The End of Oil: On the Edge of a Perilous New World*. New York: Houghton Mifflin, 2004.

Roelofs, Joan. *Foundations and Public Policy: The Mask of Pluralism*. Albany: State University of New York Press, 2003.

Rogers, Douglas. *The Depths of Russia: Oil, Power, and Culture after Socialism*. Ithaca: Cornell University Press, 2015.

Rome, Adam. *The Bulldozer in the Countryside: Suburban Sprawl and the Rise of American Environmentalism*. Cambridge: Cambridge University Press, 2001.

Romm, Joseph, J. *The Hype about Hydrogen: Fact and Fiction in the Race to Save the Climate*. Washington, DC: Island Press, 2004.

Rose, Andreas. *Between Empire and Continent: British Foreign Policy before the First World War*, trans. Rona Johnston. New York: Berghahn, 2017.

Ross, Michael L. *The Oil Curse: How Petroleum Wealth Shapes the Development of Nations*. Princeton: Princeton University Press, 2012.

Rutledge, Ian. *Addicted to Oil: America's Relentless Drive for Energy Security*. New York: I. B. Tauris, 2005.

Saccarelli, Emanuele, and Latha Varadarajan. *Imperialism Past and Present*. New York: Oxford University Press, 2015.

Sanders, M. Elizabeth. *The Regulation of Natural Gas: Policy and Politics, 1938–1978*. Philadelphia: Temple University Press, 1981.

Schultz, Stanley K. *Constructing Urban Culture: American Cities and City Planning, 1800–1920*. Philadelphia: Temple University Press, 1989.

Shaffer, Brenda. *Energy Politics*. Philadelphia: University of Pennsylvania Press, 2009.

Shaffer, Ed. *The United States and the Control of World Oil*. New York: St. Martin's Press, 1983.

Shindo, Charles J. *1927 and the Rise of Modern America*. Lawrence: University Press of Kansas, 2010.

Simmons, Matthew R. *Twilight in the Desert: The Coming Saudi Oil Shock and the World Economy*. New York: Wiley, 2005.

Skocpol, Theda. *States and Social Revolutions*. Cambridge: Cambridge University Press, 1979.

———. "Bringing the State Back In: Strategies of Analysis in Current Research." In *Bringing the State Back In*, ed. Peter Evans, Dietrich Rueschemeyer, and Theda Skocpol. Cambridge: Cambridge University Press, 1985.

———. "A Brief Response [to G. William Domhoff]." *Politics and Society* 15, no. 3 (1986/87): 331–332.

———. *Protecting Soldiers and Mothers: The Political Origins of Social Policy in the United States.* Cambridge: Harvard University Press, 1992.

Skocpol, Theda, Marshall Ganz, and Ziad Munson. "A Nation of Organizers: The Institutional Origins of Civic Voluntarism in the United States." *American Political Science Review* 94, no. 3 (2000): 527–546.

Skowronek, Stephen. *Building a New American State: The Expansion of National Administrative Capacities, 1877–1920.* Cambridge: Cambridge University Press, 1982.

Smil, Vaclav. *Global Catastrophes and Trends: The Next Fifty Years.* Cambridge: MIT Press, 2008.

St. Clair, David J. *The Motorization of American Cities.* New York: Praeger, 1986.

Stilgoe, John. *Borderland: Origins of the American Suburb, 1820–1939.* New Haven: Yale University Press, 1988.

Stewart, Richard Burleson, and Jane Bloom Stewart. *Fuel Cycle to Nowhere: U.S. Law and Policy on Nuclear Waste.* Nashville: Vanderbilt University Press, 2011.

Stoff, Michael B. *Oil, War, and American Security: The Search for a National Policy on Foreign Oil, 1941–1947.* New Haven: Yale University Press, 1980.

Stokes, Doug, and Sam Raphael. *Global Energy Security and American Hegemony.* Baltimore: Johns Hopkins University Press, 2010.

Strum, Harvey. "Eisenhower's Solar Energy Policy." *The Public Historian* 6, no. 2 (1984): 37–50.

———. "The Association for Applied Solar Energy/Solar Energy Society, 1954–1970." *Technology and Culture* 26, no. 3 (1985): 571–578.

Strum, Harvey, and Fred Strum. "American Solar Energy Policy, 1952–1982." *Environmental Review* 7 (Summer 1983): 135–153.

Tabuchi, Hiroko. "U.S. Climate Change Policy: Made in California." *New York Times,* September 27, 2017, A1.

Taylor, Dorceta E. *The Environment and the People in American Cities: 1600s–1900s.* Durham: Duke University Press, 2009.

Temby, Owen. "Trouble in Smogville: The Politics of Toronto's Air Pollution during the 1950s." *Journal of Urban History* 39, no. 4 (2013): 669–689.

Temby, Owen, and Joshua MacFadyen. "Urban Elites, Energy, and Smoke Policy in Montreal during the Interwar Period." *Urban History Review* 45, no. 1 (2016): 37–49.

Temby, Owen, and Peter Stoett, eds. *Towards Continental Environmental Policy?: North American Transnational Networks and Governance.* Albany: State University of New York Press, 2017.

Temby, Owen, and Ryan O'Connor. "Property, Technology, and Environmental Policy: The Politics of Acid Rain in Ontario, 1978–1985." *Journal of Policy History* 27, no. 4 (2015): 636–669.

Tilly, Charles. *Coercion, Capital, and European States, AD 990–1992.* Cambridge: Blackwell, 1992.

Todd, Emmanuel. *After the Empire: The Breakdown of the American Order*, trans. C. Jon Delogu. New York: Columbia University Press, 2003.

Tooze, Adam. *The Wages of Destruction: The Making and Breaking of the Nazi Economy*. New York: Viking, 2007.

Touraine, Alain. *Anti-nuclear Protest: The Opposition to Nuclear Energy in France*. New York: Cambridge University Press, 1983.

Truman, David B. *The Governmental Process: Political Interests and Public Opinion*. New York: Knopf, 1951.

Turner, Henry Ashby, Jr. *General Motors and the Nazis: The Struggle for Control of Opel, Europe's Biggest Carmaker*. New Haven: Yale University Press, 2005.

Twentieth Century Fund Task Force on the International Oil Crisis. *Paying for Energy*. New York: McGraw-Hill, 1975.

Twentieth Century Fund Task Force on United States Energy Policy. *Providing for Energy*. New York: McGraw-Hill, 1977.

Useem, Michael. *The Inner Circle: Large Corporations and the Rise of Business Political Activity in the U.S. and U.K.* Oxford: Oxford University Press, 1984.

"Using the E.P.A. to Prop Up Big Coal." *New York Times*, September 18, 2017, A22.

Van Til, Jon. *Living with Energy Shortfall*. Boulder: Westview, 1982.

Vandenbosch, Robert, and Susanne E. Vandenbosch. *Nuclear Waste Stalemate: Political and Scientific Controversies*. Salt Lake City: University of Utah Press, 2007.

Vietor, Richard H. *Environmental Politics and the Coal Coalition*. College Station: Texas A&M University Press, 1980.

———. *Energy Policy in America since 1945*. New York: Cambridge University Press, 1984.

Wald, Matthew L. "Atomic Goal: 800 Years of Power from Waste." *New York Times*, September 25, 2013, B1.

Walker, Samuel. *The Road to Yucca Mountain: The Development of Radioactive Waste Policy in the United States*. Los Angeles: University of California Press, 2009.

Wallerstein, Immanuel Maurice. *The Modern World-System*, vols. 1–2. New York: Academic Press, 1974/1980.

Weale, Albert. *The New Politics of Pollution*. New York: Manchester University Press, 1992.

Weinstein, James. *The Corporate Ideal in the Liberal State: 1900–1918*. Boston: Beacon Press, 1968.

Weiss, Marc. *The Rise of the Community Builders: The American Real Estate Industry and Urban Land Planning*. New York: Columbia University Press, 1987.

Wells, Christopher W. *Car Country: An Environmental History*. Seattle: University of Washington Press, 2014.

Wetherly, Paul. *Marxism and the State: An Analytical Approach.* New York: Palgrave, 2005.

Wetherly, Paul, Clyde W. Barrow, and Peter Burnham, eds. *Class, Power and the State in Capitalist Society: Essays on Ralph Miliband.* New York: Palgrave Macmillan, 2008.

Wilber, Tom. *Under the Surface: Fracking, Fortunes, and the Fate of the Marcellus Shale.* Ithaca: Cornell University Press, 2012.

Williams, Frederick. "The Nuclear Non-Proliferation Act of 1978." *International Security* 3, no. 2 (1978): 45–50.

Williams, William Appleman. *The Roots of the Modern American Empire.* New York: Random House, 1969.

Wills, John. *Conservation Fallout: Nuclear Protest at Diablo Canyon.* Reno: University of Nevada Press, 2006.

Wilson, Joan Hoff. *American Business and Foreign Policy, 1920–1933.* Lexington: University Press of Kentucky, 1971.

Winters, Jeffrey A. *Oligarchy.* New York: Cambridge University Press, 2011.

Winters, Jeffrey A., and Benjamin I. Page. "Oligarchy in the United States." *Perspectives on Politics* 7, no. 4 (2009): 731–751.

Wonder, Edward F. *Nuclear Fuel and American Foreign Policy: Multilateralization for Uranium Enrichment.* Boulder: Westview, 1977.

Wood, Ellen Meiksins. *The Origin of Capitalism.* New York: Monthly Review Press, 1999.

———. *Empire of Capital.* New York: Verso, 2003.

Yago, Glenn. *The Decline of Transit: Urban Transportation in German and U.S. Cities, 1900–1970.* New York: Cambridge University Press, 1984.

Yergin, Daniel. *The Prize: The Epic Quest for Oil, Money, and Power.* New York: Simon & Schuster, 1991.

———. *The Quest: Energy, Security, and the Remaking of the Modern World.* New York: Penguin, 2011.

Yetiv, Steve A. *Crude Awakenings: Global Oil Security and American Foreign Policy.* Ithaca: Cornell University Press, 2004.

———. *Explaining Foreign Policy: U.S. Decision-Making in the Gulf Wars.* Baltimore: Johns Hopkins University Press, 2011.

Zedalis, Rex J. *The Legal Dimensions of Oil and Gas in Iraq: Current Reality and Future Prospects.* New York: Cambridge University Press, 2009.

Zimmerman, Julian H. *The FHA Story in Summary, 1934–1959.* Washington, DC: U.S. Federal Housing Administration, 1959.

Index